CREATION V. EVOLUTION

WHAT THEY WON'T TELL YOU IN BIOLOGY CLASS

What Christians Should Know About Biblical Creation

Second Edition

Daniel A. Biddle, Ph.D. (editor)

Copyright © 2016 by Genesis Apologetics, Inc.
E-mail: staff@genesisapologetics.com

 GENESIS apologetics

http://www.genesisapologetics.com: A 501(c)(3) ministry equipping youth pastors, parents, and students with Biblical answers for evolutionary teaching in public schools.

CREATION V. EVOLUTION:
What They Won't Tell You in Biology Class
What Christians Should Know About Biblical Creation
Second Edition
by Daniel A. Biddle, Ph.D. (editor)

Printed in the United States of America

ISBN-13: 978-1522861737

ISBN-10: 1522861734

All rights reserved solely by the author. The author guarantees all contents are original and do not infringe upon the legal rights of any other person or work. No part of this book may be reproduced in any form without the permission of the author. The views expressed in this book are not necessarily those of the publisher.

Unless otherwise indicated, Bible quotations are taken from the HOLY BIBLE, NEW INTERNATIONAL VERSION®. Copyright © 1973, 1978, 1984 International Bible Society. Used by permission of Zondervan. All rights reserved.

The "NIV" and "New International Version" trademarks are registered in the United States Patent and Trademark Office by the International Bible Society. Use of either trademark requires the permission of the International Bible Society.

Dedication

To my wife, Jenny, who supports me in this work. To my children Makaela, Alyssa, Matthew, and Amanda, and to your children and your children's children for a hundred generations—this book is for all of you. To Dave Bisbee and Mark Johnston, who planted the seeds and the passion for this work.

We would like to acknowledge Answers in Genesis (*www.answersingenesis.com*), the Institute for Creation Research (*www.ICR.org*), and Creation Ministries International (*www.creation.com*). Much of the content herein has been drawn from (and is meant to be in alignment with) these Biblical Creation ministries.

Guard what has been entrusted to you, avoiding worldly and empty chatter and the opposing arguments of what is falsely called "knowledge"—which some have professed and thus gone astray from the faith. Grace be with you.
—1 Tim. 6:20–21

"This is the Lord's doing; it is marvelous in our eyes."
— Psalm 118:23

Contents

About the Authors 9
Preface 13
Introduction 18
Chapter 1: Dealing Effectively with Evolution Teaching: Tips for Parents, Teachers, and Students 27
Chapter 2: Can We Trust the Bible? 40
Chapter 3: Did Noah's Flood Really Happen? 57
Chapter 4: The Age of the Earth, Dating Methods, and Evolution 88
Chapter 5: Do Fossils Show Evolution? 109
Chapter 6: Natural Selection and Evolution: Do Darwin's Finches Prove Evolution? 122
Chapter 7: Did Hippos Evolve into Whales? 132
Chapter 8: A Brief History of Human Evolution in Textbooks 146
Chapter 9: Typical Ape-to-Human Progression in Public School Textbooks 182
Chapter 10: What about the Different "Races" of People? 207
Chapter 11: Are Humans and Chimps 98% Similar? 218
Chapter 12: How Modern Genetics Supports a Recent Creation 241
Chapter 13: Vestigial Structures in Humans and Animals 246
Conclusion 262
Helpful Resources 266
Endnotes 267

About the Authors

David V. Bassett, M.S. earned his Bachelor of Science in Geology at the University of Texas in El Paso and a Master's of Science in Geological Science from Columbia Pacific University, maintaining a 4.0 post-graduate academic record. He is a high school science teacher with over 28 years' experience in Christian education and has been the Science Department Head of Ovilla Christian School in Ovilla, TX since March 1996. Since then, he has been at the Creation Evidence Museum, located on the bank of the Paluxy River in Glen Rose, Texas, where he has served as the Assistant to the Director, Dr. Carl E. Baugh. Mr. Bassett is a voting member of the Creation Research Society and is the current president of the Metroplex Institute of Origin Science for the Dallas-Ft. Worth area.

Dr. Jerry Bergman has five Master's degrees in the science, health, psychology, and biology fields, a Ph.D. in human biology from Columbia Pacific University, and a Ph.D. in measurement and evaluation from Wayne State University. Jerry has taught biology, genetics, chemistry, biochemistry, anthropology, geology, and microbiology at Northwest State Community College in Archbold Ohio for over 30 years. He is currently an Adjunct Associate Professor at the University of Toledo Medical School. He has over 1,000 publications in 12 languages and 32 books and monographs, including *Vestigial Organs Are Fully Functional*; *Slaughter of the Dissidents: The Shocking Truth About Killing the Careers of Darwin Doubters; The Dark Side of Darwin*; *Hitler and the Nazis Darwinian Worldview: How the Nazis Eugenic Crusade for a Superior Race Caused the Greatest Holocaust in World History* and *The Darwin Effect. Its influence on Nazism, Eugenics, Racism, Communism, Capitalism & Sexism*. Professor Bergman has also taught at the Medical College of Ohio as a research associate in the Department of Experimental Pathology, at the University of

Toledo, and at Bowling Green State University. Jerry is also a member of MENSA, a Fellow of the American Scientific Association, a member of The National Association for the Advancement of Science, and member of many other professional associations. He is listed in Who's Who in America, Who's Who in the Midwest and in Who's Who in Science and Religion.

Dr. Daniel A. Biddle is president of Genesis Apologetics, Inc. a 501(c)(3) organization dedicated to equipping youth pastors, parents, and students with Biblical answers for evolutionary teaching in public schools. Daniel has trained thousands of students in Biblical creation and evolution and is the author of several Creation-related publications. Daniel has a Ph.D. in Organizational Psychology from Alliant University in San Francisco, California, an M.A. in Organizational Psychology from Alliant, and a B.S. in Organizational Behavior from the University of San Francisco. Daniel has worked as an expert consultant and/or witness in over 100 state and federal cases in the areas of research methodologies and statistical analysis. Daniel's ministry experience includes over two decades of Church service and completing graduate work at Western Seminary.

David A. Bisbee is the Vice President of Genesis Apologetics, Inc., a non-profit 501(c)(3) organization that equips Christian students attending public schools and their parents with faith-building materials that reaffirm a Biblical creation worldview. Genesis Apologetics is committed to providing Christian families with Biblically- and scientifically-based answers to the evolutionary theory that students are taught in and public schools. Mr. Bisbee's professional experience includes over 25 years in the field of energy efficiency. For the last 14 years, he has been in charge of a research program which tests energy efficiency technologies in real-world environments. Mr. Bisbee has presented the results of these projects through numerous published reports and educational seminars throughout the

United States. Dave's ministry experience includes over 10 years teaching Sunday school classes and creation science presentations.

Roger Patterson is a writer and editor with Answers in Genesis, one of the largest Creation Ministries in the U.S. Roger earned his B.S. Ed. degree in biology and chemistry from Montana State University-Billings. Before joining Answers in Genesis, he taught high school students for eight years in Wyoming's public school system and assisted the Wyoming Department of Education in developing assessments and standards for use in its schools. For many years, he taught from an evolutionary perspective in his classroom until God opened his eyes to the truth of Scripture.

Dr. Jonathan D. Sarfati has a B.Sc. (Hons.) in Chemistry and a Ph.D. in Spectroscopy (Physical Chemistry). Dr. Sarfati is a research scientist and editorial consultant for Creation Ministries International (CMI) in Brisbane. In this capacity, he is co-editor of Creation magazine, and also writes and reviews articles for *Journal of Creation*, CMI's in-depth, peer-reviewed publication, as well as contributing to CMI's website, *http://www.creation.com*. Dr. Sarfati has authored or co-authored several notable books, including *Refuting Evolution* (now over 500,000 copies in print), *The Creation Answers Book*, *Refuting Evolution 2*, *Refuting Compromise*, *15 Reasons to Take Genesis as History*, *By Design: Evidence for Nature's Intelligent Designer—the God of the Bible*, and *The Greatest Hoax on Earth? Refuting Dawkins on Evolution*.

Roger Sigler, M.A. is a licensed professional geoscientist in the State of Texas. His diverse background in geology spans oil and gas exploration, core analysis, geothermal systems, groundwater problems, and environmental abatement projects. His latest employment is in core, geological, and drilling fluid analyses at Intertek's Westport Technology Center. He is also a part-time geology instructor at Wharton County Junior College. He has taught creation science since 1989, and helped form the Greater Houston Creation Association where he was president from 1997-2001. He acquired a Master's degree in Geology from the Institute for Creation Research in 1998. He has been published in the 1998 and 2003 *Proceedings of the International Conference on Creationism* and co-authored a poster session on catastrophic debris flows at the 2011 Geological Society of America. He is a member of the Geological Society of America, Houston Geological Society, American Association of Petroleum Geologists, and Creation Research Society. He is married, has two children, and attends Christ Covenant Church in Houston, Texas.

Dr. Jeffrey Tomkins has a Ph.D. in Genetics from Clemson University, a M.S. from the University of Idaho, and a B.S. from Washington State University. He was on the Faculty in the Department of Genetics and Biochemistry, Clemson University, for a decade, where he published 57 secular research papers in peer-reviewed scientific journals and seven book chapters on genetics, genomics, proteomics, and physiology. For the past several years, Dr. Tomkins has been a Research Scientist at the Institute for Creation Research and an independent investigator publishing ten peer-reviewed creation science journal papers, numerous semi-technical articles, and two books including *The Design and Complexity of the Cell*.

Cornelius Van Wingerden, M.S. taught high school science and math for 21 years. He retired from teaching high school in 2011. Van holds a B.S. in Geology from San Diego State University, an M.S. in Geology from the ICR Graduate School, Santee, California, and a M.A. in Science Education from California State University, Bakersfield. While at ICR, he studied large debris flows found in the Kingston Peak Formation, Death Valley Region.

Preface
Daniel A. Biddle, Ph.D.

This book is essential for any high school or college-aged Christian attending public school—especially before taking biology and earth science classes. Most biology and earth science classes in today's public schools teach evolutionary theory as fact, and only rarely mention creation possibilities outside of this theory, such as Biblical Creation.

Did you know that **44%** of young adults who abandon their Christian faith started developing their doubts in high school?[1] When these "ex-Christians" were asked, "What makes you question the Bible the most," **40%** gave responses that had to do with Biblical Creation, including Noah's Flood, the age of the Earth, and the Genesis account. This book, written by leading Creation Scientists, provides solid answers to these critical questions that will help Christian high school and college students solidify their faith to withstand the evolution-based teaching that is so prevalent in today's schools.

The evolutionary teaching included in most public school biology and earth science classes starkly contrasts the Biblical Creation account. In some cases, when not taught *both* creation and evolution perspectives, young Christians lose their faith, or end up with a watered-down faith that robs them of the abundant life that Christ longs to provide.

Today, Christians hold different beliefs about origins. Sometimes these differences can lead to wide and tense divisions within the Church. This book was not written to widen the existing divide. While one's position on origins is critical when it comes to holding to the authority of Scripture, love and acceptance between brothers and sisters in the faith are also important. Indeed, without maintaining relationships with each other, these dialogues regarding origins cannot even take place.

With this said, this book is written from a "Young Earth" origins position for three reasons. First, I believe that this is the most obvious and plain interpretation of Scripture. That is, God conveyed his Word to us in a way that the six-day creation account would be understood as written, such as in Genesis 1 and Exodus 20:11. Secondly, after reviewing the creation evidence, I believe the science stacks heavily in the "young" direction. Finally, with biblical teachers being held to a higher level of accountability (James 3:1), I find it assuring to convey the creation account given in the Bible using the *original and obvious* language the Lord provided.

This "Genesis is real history" view is not rare among Christian circles. The vast majority of Private Christian schools hold to a historical view of Genesis and include young-earth teaching throughout their earth and life science classes. This is also true for most home school families, who often use the same textbooks. Research shows that these "younger" origin perspectives also span outside of these conservative Christian circles. For example, according to a recent Gallup poll, when over 1,000 Americans[2] were surveyed about human beginnings and creation, 46% responded by affirming they believe that God spontaneously created humans less than 10,000 years ago. This percentage has remained almost constant, averaging about 45% from 1982 to today. Alternative views included "theistic evolution" (the belief that humans evolved under God's guidance) with 32% of the responses, and secular evolution at 15%.[3] Looking at this more broadly, "some 78% of Americans today believe that God had a hand in the development of humans in some way, just slightly less than the percentage who felt this way 30 years ago."

I am saddened by so many people going through life not knowing about their Creator or His Creation in ways that He intended for us all to know through His Word. So many people live and die without knowing and experiencing three important truths: (1) God created *one human race in general* (Genesis 1), (2) each of us are created *specifically* by God ("For you created my inmost being; you knit me together in my mother's womb," Psalm 139:13), and (3) we are each created with *intention and purpose for this life* ("And we know that in all things God works for the good of those who love him, who have been called according to his purpose," Romans 8:28).

Personally, I find it very reassuring to see *and* experience a union between God's Word and His Creation. It's amazing to just take walks in the mountains and see how massive rock and sediment layers were curled up and buckled by Noah's *cataclysmic* Flood when the continental plates were shifted as God destroyed the "old world" (2 Peter 3:6). Clearly, an earth-shattering process occurred when God "blotted out *every living thing* that was upon the face of the land, from man to animals to creeping things and to birds of the sky, and they were blotted out from the earth" (Genesis 7:23). At times, God even gives hints about the process that was involved in such a re-creation of the face of the world:

> He established the earth upon its foundations, so that it will not totter forever and ever. You covered it with the deep as with a garment; the waters were standing above the mountains. At Your rebuke they fled. At the sound of Your thunder they hurried away. *The mountains rose; the valleys sank down to the place which You established for them.* You set a boundary that they may not pass over, So that they will not return to cover the earth. (Psalms 104:5–9, NASB)

The topics included in this book were selected by reviewing the evolutionary topics covered in most high school and college biology and earth science textbooks, then surveying Christian students on the topics that seemed to be most convincing. There are many other important topics that could be included in a book like this, but we let the students choose (by survey) which ones were most important to them. What follows are mostly scientific reasons why the most convincing evolutionary arguments have not convinced us, and thus why we believe the Bible had it right all along.

Overview of the Book

The Introduction of the book provides a discussion regarding the importance of the perspectives that we bring to understanding our origins, including the assumptions required and faith required for both the evolutionary and creationist positions. It also discusses the importance of the topics covered by this book, and how they can shape our worldviews which can permeate virtually every part of our lives.

Chapter 1 provides some reasons why creation-evolution training matters. We also give some practical tips for dealing with this topic that should be helpful for parents, students, and teachers.

Chapter 2 answers the question "Can We Trust the Bible?" by looking at the "big picture" of the Bible (i.e., how it was assembled) while also focusing on one particular chapter of the Bible (Isaiah 53) because of its significance to Christians. It also contains evidence that became available to test the Bible's reliability after the Dead Sea Scrolls were discovered.

Chapter 3 covers Noah's Flood and provides compelling evidence from around the world that the Flood really did happen—exactly as described in the Bible. The evidence reviewed includes a review of the major fossil deposits around the world, coal deposits, Earth's sedimentary rocks, how the Flood was involved in shaping the mountains and landscapes, and some specifics regarding the feasibility of Noah's Ark, such as its dimensions and how all of the various animals could have fit.

Chapter 4 reviews some of the challenges and inaccuracies of the common methods that are used to date the age of the Earth in an effort to prove evolution. Additional evidences which provide clues to a younger creation are also reviewed, including coal deposits, diamonds, soft tissues that are supposedly millions of years old, and the ocean. This chapter is important because mainstream biology textbooks will even admit that an "ancient world" is essential for supporting evolutionary theory: "Evolution takes a long time. If life has evolved, then Earth must be very old…Geologists now use radioactivity to establish the age of certain rocks and fossils. This kind of data could have shown that the Earth is young. If that had happened, *Darwin's ideas would have been refuted and abandoned.* Instead, radioactive dating indicates that Earth is about 4.5 billion years old—plenty of time for evolution and natural selection to take place"[4] (emphasis added).

Chapter 5 investigates the fossil record, including "ancestral," "transitional," and "divergent" forms that are necessary for the theory of evolution and "gradualism" to hold up. Chapter 6 reviews fundamental evolution teachings, such as natural selection and evolution. This chapter answers difficult questions such as "Do Darwin's Finches Prove Evolution?" Chapter 7 takes a careful look into one of the "poster children" of evolution theory: Whale evolution. Chapters 8 through 13 discuss the topic of human evolution as represented in school textbooks, starting first with a historical review (Chapter 8), the current human evolution "icons" that are typically included in textbooks (Chapter 9), the "race groups" (Chapter 10), the chimp-human DNA similarity issue (Chapter 11), how modern genetics reveal the recent explosion of human variability (Chapter 12), and vestigial structures (Chapter 13).

Introduction
Roger Patterson

Have you ever heard the phrase "the facts speak for themselves"? Well, stop and think about it for a moment. Is it true? The answer is no. Sure, there might be some facts that when put together can seem to have only one explanation, but that is not always the case.

Every fact must be *interpreted* to really have any meaning. Think about a fossil, for instance. We could make a list of observations, facts, about the fossil. We could record its mass, measure various dimensions, describe the type of minerals it is made of, etc. Those are observations—data everyone can agree on. We could measure its density using different methods and ask somebody to repeat our tests so that they could verify our results.

But what about questions like: "How old is the fossil?" or "How did the creature die?" The fossil doesn't have a tag attached to it with answers to those questions. The fossil—the fact—cannot speak for itself to tell us those answers. In order to come to conclusions, the facts must be interpreted. Because people interpret evidence, they will naturally be biased in the way they think. No matter what anyone tells you, they do have some bias. The basic set of biases you have is called your worldview. We use our worldview like a set of glasses to help us see the world clearly.

As we think about scientific study, we really need to think about it in two categories. First, there is operational or observational science. This is the type of scientific study that the scientific method helps us do. We observe, test, and repeat experiments to try to obtain a consistent result. We can create lots of great technologies by applying observational science. For instance, since chemical reactions are predictable, we know that when certain chemicals mix together, we will get a certain reaction. This has allowed us to make airbags, medicines, fuels, and all kinds of useful things.

Second, there is historical science, also referred to as origins or forensic science. This is when we take the things we know about the present (from observational science) and try to figure out the past. For example, if I find a fossil fish in a layer of rocks, I can make all kinds of observations, but to answer how the fish got in the rock layer, how it died, or how long ago that happened, I have to interpret those observations. I put the pieces together with other things I know and try to understand the history of this fish.

Which type of science do you think is more accurate and reliable, observational or historical? Well, determining the age of the fish fossil (historical science) requires a lot more interpretation and relies on more assumptions than measuring the bones or doing a chemical analysis to see what minerals are in the rock that surround it (observational science). We must be much more careful with the conclusions of historical science because worldview influences historical science much more than observational science.

What We Believe Really Matters

If I told you that I know a man who walked on water, would you believe me? The way you answer that question is going to reveal some of your bias. Someone might reply that they know the density of a person is greater than the density of water, so the person would sink if they tried to walk on water. We would call this person an empiricist—they demand experimental evidence to believe something—at least, that's what they say about themselves. Another might respond that it is against the laws of nature—this person might be a materialist or a naturalist, insisting that miracles can't happen.

But what about Jesus? Didn't He walk on water? Sure He did. Did I see Him? No. Was it normal? No. But I believe He walked on water because I look at the world from a Christian worldview, or a biblical worldview. Similarly, I believe God created the entire universe just as the Bible describes, not from a big bang billions of years ago. I believe

He created the different kinds of plants and animals and that they did not evolve over millions of years. I have faith that all of these things are true, but it is not a blind faith. My faith is based on something bigger than myself. It is "the substance of things hoped for, the evidence of things not seen" (Hebrews 11:1).

Many will say that this viewpoint makes my thinking unscientific. I disagree. That is only true if I accept that scientists must deny the existence of miracles and rely entirely on a materialistic or naturalistic worldview. In other words, the materialist who believes that the universe only consists of matter and energy has *faith* that is the case! After all, he can't always detect spiritual truths with his broken ways of thinking (2 Corinthians 4:4). The empiricist has to exercise faith that his senses are reliable because there is no way to test his senses without using his senses. These people are putting their faith in themselves and their own thinking. They have faith that the universe created itself from nothing; I have faith that God created the universe from nothing.

Everyone puts their faith in something. Rather than a blind faith, I choose to put my faith in Jesus Christ, the Creator and Sustainer of the universe (Hebrews 1:1–4). Knowing that He created everything and having a written record of the history of the universe in the Bible, I have a great starting point to begin thinking about the world around me. When I think about science, I am trying to understand how God made things and how He designed them to work and live together with other organisms.

The God of Science

God must exist for science to even be possible! When a scientist performs an experiment, he expects nature to behave according to the laws it has shown in the past. When was the last time you put a teapot on the stove and expected it to freeze? Why does the world follow these laws? Because all known laws arise from lawgivers, the only rational answer is that there was a

Lawgiver—the God of the Bible—who created the universe to follow certain patterns we call laws. In fact, He tells us that we should expect nature to behave in a uniform way; for example, in Genesis 8:22. But that doesn't mean that He can't intervene at times in miraculous ways, as we see described in the Bible.

Logic is another necessity for scientific study. But what is logic? You can't smell it, take its temperature, or see what color it is. It is immaterial (not made of matter) and is true everywhere in the universe. How can a materialistic worldview account for something that is not made of matter? It can't. Logic is only rational if God exists and has created the universe and our human minds in a special way. Similar to chemical or physical laws, the laws of logic upon which every thought rests also require a Lawgiver. The Bible tells us that God thinks, and He has created mankind in His image. We are able to use our God-given reason to understand the world around us.

So, if God did not exist, there would be no consistent laws of nature and no logic. We wouldn't be able to understand the world around us. Science is impossible without the Creator God of the Bible. Now, there are a lot of fancy philosophical arguments that people try to use to get away from the truth that God exists, but these people are using the very brains that God gave them to try to tell you He doesn't exist. The Apostle Paul helps us to understand why this is so in Romans 1:18–32 and 1 Corinthians 1:18–31. If the universe came from a random event like the big bang and everything formed thereafter by random chance, why would we expect to find order, laws of logic, and laws of nature? Why would we expect to find anything at all? We wouldn't. So to say that God cannot be a part of our science and history is not rational.

Absolute Authority

How do you know what is true? Do people get to vote on truth? Can truth change over time? These are important things to consider as we study science and try to understand things in the present and the past. As we consider claims made by textbooks, teachers, or video documentaries, many of the ideas are going to be contrary to Scripture. Many of the arguments may appear to be convincing and there may be lots of evidence used to support the claims, but what if these ideas are different than the Bible's claims? Which authority, God's Word or man's words, are you going to trust? There are only two choices! We can either look to a human authority—man determines truth—or a biblical standard—God determines truth.

For example, scientists who embrace evolutionary interpretations of genetics claim that there was never a single couple at the beginning of the human race. Rather, they claim there was a larger population of original humans. If we accept that, then we have to reject God's description of specially creating Adam and Eve as the first pair that gave rise to every human on the Earth (Genesis 1–4). We even must then reject Jesus' references to the first couple, for example in Mark 10:6! Likewise, you would have to reject that there was ever a Tower of Babel from which all of the different people groups emerged. If you start from the wrong starting point you always come to the wrong conclusions.

The Bible contains a true, eyewitness testimony (God Himself) of the creation of the world. If we build our thinking about science and history and every other subject from God's Word, we have a true foundation to build upon. If we build our thinking on man's ideas apart from the Bible, we are starting from a subjective position invented by God-rejecting sinners rather than a true position. You must decide who you are going to trust.

Two Revelations

God has revealed Himself to man in two ways—*general* and *special* revelation. God has created a universe for us to study and learn about Him. Psalm 19 tells us that the heavens declare the glory of God. Romans 1 tells us that mankind can know certain things about God by looking at the creation. The design that is obvious in nature points to the Designer. All of this is referred to as God's general revelation given to everyone through all of time.

God has given man the task of studying His creation and using that knowledge to rule over the Earth and its creatures (Genesis 1:26–28). But this general revelation is limited. For example, what could you learn about God from a virus killing a dog or a tiger killing a deer to eat it? What about all of the terrible diseases in the world? What do they teach us about God?

To answer these questions rightly, we must look to special revelation—the Bible. God has revealed many wonderful truths in the Bible that we would not know otherwise. Many people doubt that God is good because of all of the evil in the world. But the Bible tells us that the world was not always like this—it is broken. God created the world in a perfect state about 6,000+ years ago. He created all of the animals and man to be vegetarians (Genesis 1:29–31). Adam's disobedience and sin broke the world (the Fall of man) and brought a curse from God (Genesis 3) that will someday be lifted (Romans 8:20–22). The Father sent His Son to redeem man from his sin, and one day, the Son will come again and the world will be restored to its original perfection—no more disease or death, forever.

The Bible is not a textbook that tells us about the structure of atoms or the way the digestive system works. But without the special revelation given to us as a starting point, we cannot rightly understand the general revelation we see in the world around us. Where the Bible does speak to scientific issues, we know we can trust it.

Table 1 provides several examples that demonstrate this. Scientists through the centuries have often erred in matters of science. But not the Holy Bible, which has been shown to be scientifically accurate. While the Bible is not primarily a science text, many scientific matters are mentioned in passing; and when mentioned, with careful study they can be confirmed to be accurate![5]

Table 1. The Bible and Science Agree

Formerly Believed	Currently Believed	The Bible Always Said
Only between 1000 and 1200 stars in the whole universe.	Trillions upon trillions of stars; they cannot be counted by man!	Jeremiah 33:22a "As the host of heaven **cannot be numbered**..."
The Earth is flat.	The Earth is round.	Isaiah 40:22a "It is he that sits upon the *circle* of the earth..."
Light does not move, it is just there.	Light moves and has physical properties; "light waves" or photons.	Job 38:19a "Where is the way where *light dwells*? ..."
The Steady State Theory, the stars are just out there.	Each star is unique, and two of the star constellations have gravitational binding.	Job 38:31 "Can you bind the sweet influences of **Pleiades**, or loose the bands of **Orion**?"
Bad blood should be bled out, to make a person well.	Blood is vital to life, sometimes a transfusion is needed to add blood.	Leviticus 17:11a "For the *life of the flesh is in the blood*:..."
Air has no weight, it is just there.	Oxygen, nitrogen, carbon-dioxide have atomic weights that can be measured.	Job 28:25a "To make the *weight for the winds*..."
Winds blow straight across the Earth.	Air currents move in large circular patterns.	Ecclesiastes 1:6b "... and *the wind returns again according to his circuits.*"
The Earth is carried on someone's back.	The Earth floats free in space.	Job 26:7b "... and **hangs the earth upon nothing**."
People just get sick; hand washing is not important.	Many diseases spread by contact; wash your hands in running water.	Leviticus 15:13b "... and wash his clothes, and *bathe his flesh in running water*..."
The stars are all similar to each other.	Each and every star is actually unique.	I Corinthians 15:41b "...for *one star differs from another star* in glory."
Something from nothing for no reason – "The Big Bang" model (poof! look a universe!)	Every action has an equal and opposite reaction; that is real science. Cause and effect; input is needed to make output.	Genesis 1:1 "In the beginning God created the heaven and the earth."

Apologetics—Giving a Defense of the Faith

If you are a Christian, you are going to face challenges to your faith from many different angles. The key to withstanding these challenges is found from the writings of the Apostle Peter, a man who knew trials:

> But even if you should suffer for righteousness' sake, you are blessed. 'And do not be afraid of their threats, nor be troubled.' But sanctify the Lord God in your hearts, and always be ready to give a defense to everyone who asks you a reason for the hope that is in you, with meekness and fear; having a good conscience, that when they defame you as evildoers, those who revile your good conduct in Christ may be ashamed. For it is better, if it is the will of God, to suffer for doing good than for doing evil. (1 Peter 3:14–17, NKJV)

We get the term apologetics from this verse. The Greek word *apologia* is translated as "reason" or "defense" in this passage. It doesn't mean that we are to apologize, but that we provide an explanation for why we believe what we believe. Just as evangelism is sharing the good news of forgiveness in sins through Jesus, apologetics is sharing the reasons the Bible can be trusted, by giving biblical explanations for scientific models (e.g., how Noah's Flood can explain the rock layers and fossils or how radiometric dating can't be trusted).

So you can see that apologetics and evangelism are very tightly connected. Explaining why we think and believe the Bible is true in its descriptions of historical and scientific ideas should always be connected to why we believe it is true with respect to spiritual things. If the Bible's history can't be trusted, why should we trust what it says about spiritual matters? Since we know God is a God of truth, we can trust the historical, scientific, and spiritual truths He has revealed to us in the Bible.

The key to apologetics is to set apart Christ as Lord in your heart, fully trusting in Jesus for your salvation and as the Creator and revealer of truth. You will never know the answer to every question you are asked, but you can trust that there are reasonable answers from the Bible or from a biblical understanding of the world. There are many people who can help you find answers, other Christians who can support you and encourage you with fellowship and prayer. Getting support from your family and church is another important aspect of standing firm in your faith.

You will likely encounter other Christians who believe they can accept the big bang or evolution and still trust the Bible. That is simply not possible, since those theories directly contradict the Bible. However, responding to such people in gentleness and respect is essential. Many Christians have not considered the contradiction in the order of events between the Bible and evolutionary ideas, the problem of death before sin, the meaning of a historical Adam, and the global effects of Noah's Flood. Point them to the Bible as the ultimate authority by which we must judge every other idea. Show them how well the facts fit the Scriptures in a way that makes them want to understand.

When we have the opportunity to challenge claims that are contrary to Scripture, we must make sure that we are asking or responding in a gentle and respectful way. We can trust that the Holy Spirit will help us respond in love and truth, always relying on God's Word as our absolute authority. In the end, the study of science and defending our faith must share the hope of eternal life in the Lord Jesus Christ. In other words, debunking evolution or showing the errors in the big bang theory can be helpful, but there is no hope of salvation from sin in scientific theories. We should always practice the skill of telling people about who Jesus is and what He has done to provide salvation to all who believe.

Chapter 1: Dealing Effectively with Evolution Teaching: Tips for Parents, Teachers, and Students
Daniel A. Biddle

To Parents: Does Evolution Teaching Impact Christian Students?

The answer is a resounding "yes." Many studies conducted over the last 10 years (e.g., Gallup, Barna, and Lifeway) show that between 50% and 69% of young adults leave the Christian faith after high school. The book, *Already Gone: Why your Kids will Quit Church and What you can do to Stop it*[6] provides a complete review on this topic. While the personal stories behind each departure varies, some of these youth leave because of **intellectual doubt** in the Christian faith—doubt stemming from the three years of evolution teaching they received in public schools.

We have collectively trained thousands of students on Creation- and Evolution-related topics and have watched many students (including our own) progress through public school and develop their beliefs about origins, worldviews, and their identity as it relates to these topics. While it's difficult to categorize the experiences of young students as they wade through the variety of origin-related ideas, we propose the five outcomes below as a starting place (these start at the "worst" outcome and move to the "best"):

1. **Lose their Faith**: Evolution teaching talks them out of their Christian faith.
2. **Apathy**: They lose the benefit of knowing they are created by God with purpose and intent, and made to enjoy and honor the incredible world that God created.
3. **Integration**: They become theistic evolutionists. Their "god" is one who creates through "experimental cruelty" in a "hands off" fashion.
4. **Defense**: They hold strong personally, but don't help others out of the cloud of dissolution.

5. **Evangelism**: They are so strong in their faith that they challenge evolution teaching and help convince others of the truth.

We hear stories from parents about their children returning home after the first year of college "no longer Christians"—with many citing evolution teaching as the reason. So how can parents move their children higher on the list above? Our recommendation is that Creation training should start in elementary school and continue through high school, preferably at a 2-to-1 ratio (e.g., 100 instruction hours compared to the 50 hours of evolution instruction they are likely to receive).

Tips for Students

Christian students in public school can have some amazing ministry opportunities. These opportunities can be maximized by following these tips:

1. Realize that your teacher and school are not "the enemy." Evolution is required curriculum in most states and many outstanding Christians are teachers in these schools!
2. Prepare for each specific evolution topic before it's covered in class. Our website is a great place to start: *www.genesisapologetics.com.*
3. Don't argue with your teacher, regardless of their position on evolution.
4. Ask good questions during class. Remember, while your teacher may believe in evolution, many of your fellow students may be undecided and it may be your question that helps them lean the right way.
5. Ask good follow-up questions. Sometimes good questions need to have even better follow-up questions prepared.
6. Talk with your fellow students after class.

7. Help arrange a Creation-Evolution seminar and invite your fellow classmates to attend.

25 Great Creation-Evolution Questions

Below are several examples[7] of good questions that can be asked during biology class. They should be presented "in love and respect"—these are not for starting or ending arguments; but rather for opening dialogue.

1. When it comes to evolution theory, how do we *know* it's true?
2. Has evolution ever been observed (i.e., "macro" evolution where one "kind" turns into another)?
3. What assumptions are being made when someone asserts that evolution is true?
4. Are you aware of any **observable** evidence for evolution that doesn't require faith?
5. Are there any examples showing when non-life started life? (life from non-life in contradiction to the law of biogenesis)
6. How did life originate?
7. How did the DNA code originate?
8. Living things look like they were designed, so how do evolutionists know that they were not designed?
9. How did sex originate and evolve? When, where, why, and how did life learn to reproduce itself?
10. Where are the millions of transitional fossils that should exist if evolution theory is true? Why don't we see a reasonably smooth continuum among all living creatures, or in the fossil record, or both? For example, Darwin said, "… as by evolution theory, innumerable transitional forms must have existed, why do we not find them embedded in countless numbers in the crust of the earth?" (Origin of Species, 1859) and "Why is not every

geological formation and every stratum full of such intermediate links? Geology assuredly does not reveal any such finely graduated organic chain; and this is the most obvious and serious objection which can be urged against the theory?" (Origin of Species, 1872). In addition, Colin Patterson, Senior Paleontologist at the British Museum of Natural History (home of the world's largest fossil collection over 7 million specimens), stated: "If I knew of any, (evolutionary transitions) fossil or living, I would have included them in my book!"[8] Other evolutionists have noted the same challenge: "The known fossil record fails to document a single example of phyletic evolution accomplishing a major morphologic transition, and hence offers no evidence that the gradualistic model can be valid."[9]

11. If museums and fossil databases contain over 1,000 fossilized bats and 100,000 fossilized turtles, why haven't they found any fossils that have been classified as "pre-bats" or "pre-turtles"? Why are they always found in complete form?[10] After finding so many specimens in complete, shouldn't *some* predecessors would have been found by now?

12. How do "living fossils" remain unchanged over supposed hundreds of millions of years, if evolution has changed worms into humans in the same time frame?

13. How did blind chemistry create mind/intelligence, meaning, altruism and morality?

14. What is the mechanism for getting new complexity such as new vital organs? How, for example, could a caterpillar evolve into a butterfly?

15. How could organs as complicated as the eye or the ear or the brain of even a tiny bird ever come about by chance or natural processes? How could a bacterial motor evolve?

16. Where did the space for the universe come from?
17. Where did matter come from?
18. Where did the laws of the universe come from (gravity, inertia, etc.)?
19. How did matter get so perfectly organized?
20. Creationists and evolutionists agree that micro-evolution (i.e., change within a species over time) occurs and is scientifically verifiable. What evidence is there for "macro-evolution" (i.e., large unobserved changes)?
21. How can the existence and nature of *laws* be accounted for (e.g., laws of morality, nature, and logic)? Laws of morality make sense in the Christian worldview where God created human beings in His own image (according to a natural reading of Genesis) and therefore has the right to set the rules for our behavior.
22. If we are simply chemical accidents, why should we feel compelled to behave in a particular fashion?
23. If laws of morality are just what bring the most happiness to the most people, then why would it be wrong to kill just one innocent person if it happened to make everyone else a lot happier?
24. If laws of morality are just the adopted social custom, then why was what Hitler did wrong? (Laws of nature make sense in the Christian worldview; God upholds the entire universe by His power. God is beyond time, and has promised to uphold the future as He has the past [Genesis 8:22].)
25. How does the material brain have access to these immaterial laws?

Four Power Questions to Ask Evolutionists

Mike Riddle, President of the Creation Training Initiative, has a powerful presentation titled, "Four Power Questions to ask an Evolutionist." We provide a summary of these questions below.[11]

Question 1: *What caused the universe to come into existence and where did the original energy or matter come from?*

This question focuses at the *foundation* of evolution theory. Without a cause and without matter, how can the universe exist today? There are only three possible responses to this question: (1) The universe created itself; (2) The universe has always existed; or (3) The universe had to be created. Riddle points out the limitations of the first two options, and leaves the third as the only viable choice:

- Response 1: The universe created itself. For something to create itself it would have to both exist (to have the power to act) and not exist (to be created) at the same time. This is a contradiction—an illogical position to take. Based on all known scientific understanding and logic we know that from nothing, nothing comes. Therefore, this is not a legitimate response. A person arguing this way has violated the law of non-contradiction and is ignoring good science. This now leaves two possible choices.
- Response 2: The universe has always existed (no beginning). To analyze this response, we need to understand some basics about the second law of thermodynamics. The second law is concerned with heat—the flow of thermal energy. Everything in the universe is losing its available energy to do work. To illustrate this concept, consider an example called "No Refills." Imagine that you have just been given a new car for free! All expenses for the lifetime of the car are

paid. Sounds like a good deal. However, there is one catch. You are only allowed to have one tank of gas and never allowed to refill the tank. Once you have driven the car and used up all the gas, the car can no longer be used for transportation. In other words, the gas (energy source) has been used up and cannot be reused to propel the car. This is what the second law of thermodynamics deals with. Usable energy is constantly becoming less usable for doing work. Unless the car obtains new fuel from an outside source, it will cease to function after it exhausts its first tank of gas. Likewise, the universe is constantly converting useful energy into less usable forms. As one example, stars are fueled by hydrogen gas that is used up as it is converted into heavier elements. But the problem is this: for any given region of space, there is only a finite amount of available energy. There is just only so much hydrogen available per cubic meter. This means that unless the universe obtains new useable energy from an outside source, it will cease to function in a finite amount of time. Stars will no longer be possible, once the hydrogen is gone. The fact that the universe still contains useable energy indicates that it is not infinitely old—it had a beginning. However, there is no "outside source" available. The universe is everything according to the secular worldview. Like the car, the universe would cease to function after its first "tank of gas" is exhausted. But if the universe were infinitely old, it should have used up that energy a long time ago. Putting it another way, if stars have eternally been processing hydrogen into heavier elements, then there would be no hydrogen left! But there is. The fact that the universe still contains useable energy indicates that it is not infinitely old—it had a beginning.

- Response 3: The universe had to be created. Since the universe could not create itself and it had to have a beginning, the only logical solution is that the universe had to be created! This leaves us with the original question to the evolutionist, "Where did the matter come from to create the universe?" Any reply not recognizing that the universe was created ignores the laws of science and logic.

Question 2: *How could non-living chemicals give rise to living cells when the probability of a simple protein arising by chance are statistically impossible?*

The theory of evolution holds that the earth formed about 4.6 billion years ago by natural processes. Then, over a long period of time, chemicals bonded together in a "primordial soup" to form molecules, which then joined together to make a living cell. Given that proteins, molecules, and living cells are extraordinarily complex, is this even possible?

In an attempt to answer this question, chemical Scientists Dr. Walter Bradley and Dr. Charles Thaxton[12] calculated the probability of *amino acids* "naturally" forming into a protein to be: 4.9×10^{-191}. This is well beyond the laws of probability, which has a theoretical maxium of 1×10^{-50}, and a protein is *not even close* to becoming a complete living cell. Dr. Fred Hoyle and Dr. Chandra Wickramasinghe[13] calculated that the probability of getting a *cell* by natural processes to be: $1 \times 10^{-40,000}$. Indeed, it takes an all-powerful God to create life: "For by Him all things were created that are in heaven and that are on earth, visible and invisible, whether thrones or dominions or principalities or powers. All things were created hthrough Him and for Him" (Colossians 1:16).

Question 3: *The Fossil Record—where are the transitionary fossils that show gradual change?* If evolution really happened, the fossil record would include millions of transitions from one creature to the next—but these are missing! Further, as explained in this book and others, the fossils that evolutionists claim are in fact "transitions" are woefully lacking.

For example, Luther Sunderland, a creationist and aerospace engineer wrote a letter to Dr. Colin Patterson,

Director of the British Museum of Natural History, concerning transitional fossils. Dr. Patterson, a well known and highly respected evolutionist, had just finished writing a book about evolution. Even though he believes in evolution, Dr. Patterson didn't include any pictures of transitional fossils. When Sunderland wrote Dr. Patterson to inquire about this, his answer was amazing:

> I wrote to Dr. Patterson and asked him why he didn't put a single picture of an intermediate form or a connecting link in his book on evolution. Dr. Patterson now, who has seven million fossils in his museum, said the following when he answered my letter: 'I fully agree with your comments on the lack of direct illustration of evolutionary transitions in my book. **If I knew of any, fossils or living, I certainly would have included it.... I will lay it on the line. There is not one such fossil for which one might make a watertight argument.**'[14]

Question #4: *Where did the dinosaurs come from?* Secular scientists have been struggling with this question for decades. The standard story is that dinosaurs evolved about 220 million years ago and died off about 65 million years ago. But where did they come from? Evolutionists still struggle with the origin of the dinosaurs. For example, the popular *Illustrated Encyclopedia of Dinosaurs*[15] states: "The question of the origins of dinosaurs in one that has puzzled paleontologists for many years." The *Natural History Museum Book of Dinosaurs*[16] states: "Where did the dinosaurs come from? That apparently simple question has been the subject of intense debate amongst scientists for over 150 years."

By contrast, the Bible has a straight-forward explanation: God created dinosaurs on the Sixth Day of Creation (Genesis 1), and the vast majority of them were wiped out by Noah's Flood (Genesis 6–9). The fossil record is full of dinosaurs that suddenly died in watery graves around the world.

The Bible has answers for who created life (God), what was created (all things), how life was created (by His power), when it was created (in the beginning), and how long it took to create (six days). There is such a reward in life for those who trust Him at His Word: "The fear of the Lord is the beginning of knowledge, but fools despise wisdom and instruction" (Proverbs 1:7).

What can Christian Teachers Say Regarding Creation & Evolution in Public School?

Can teachers share their faith in school? After school? Can they say they disagree with evolution theory before they cover that section in the textbook? We provide some answers to these questions in this section. First, however, please know that there are no "pat" answers that can be supplied for these questions because each school district, state, and circumstance is different. For answers to specific questions, we recommend contacting Liberty Counsel (*http://www.lc.org*) or the Pacific Justice Institute (*http://www.pacificjustice.org*). With this, we provide the following insights and recommendations regarding this topic:

- Some studies show that teachers exercise discretion in how they cover evolution theory in U.S. public schools. For example, a study reviewed in the New York Times[17] found that only 28% of public school biology teachers consistently follow the NRC recommendations to "describe straightforwardly the evidence for evolution and explain the ways in which it is a unifying theme in all of biology." The study also found that "13% explicitly advocate creationism, and spend at least an hour of class time presenting it in a positive light" and 60% avoid the creation-evolution controversy by endorsing neither evolution nor creation.

- In many classrooms, certain sections of the text may be skipped and other areas emphasized. We have seen teachers skip evolution entirely, and other teachers emphasize evolution by teaching it well beyond the required curriculum using extra-curricular exercises and videos.
- The amount of leeway a Christian teacher has regarding creation-evolution topics varies by state and district. Basically, a teacher signs a contract to be an agent of the state (or county or district) and must teach what they are told to teach in most areas, especially where local control of schools has been replaced by state curricula. A Christian who has signed a contract to teach the prescribed curriculum should not do something dishonest or contrary to what they are hired to do, provided the instructions given to them otherwise comply with the Constitution.
- In general, teachers can present a balanced treatment of the concept of origins in science class (or other classes, as appropriate to the subject matter or material to be covered). If discussion would take an inordinate amount of class time, or derail scheduled discussion, students that have questions regarding origins can be encouraged to research the matter for themselves, ask their parents, or discuss after class so that instruction can continue.
- On an **indiviual basis** (i.e., teacher-student relationships) where teachers are not acting in their official capacity or during the school day, teachers are free to share their personal opinions, beliefs, and perspectives on a variety of topics, including God, evolution, and Biblical creation. This privilege is protected by First Amendment rights shared by teachers and students alike. Teachers can even lead after-school Bible clubs, for that matter, in the same schools in which they teach, during contracted hours.

- Teachers can generally emphasize that (macro) evolution is a **theory**. Teachers do not have to affirm macro-evolution ("molecules-to-man") as a "fact," but they are generally required to teach the subject as represented in the textbook. Teaching students only one side of the evidence does not promote critical thinking and scientific rigor. Students should be made aware of both the strengths and weaknesses of evolution theory—just as they should be with other theories. Much of the criticism around evolution comes from secular scientists (e.g., evolution-based articles by the late Steve Gould are critical of the traditional Darwinian interpretation of the fossil record). As such, teachers should supplement the molecules-to-man evolutionary theory, particularly if they use classroom-approved texts or resources.
- Some schools have an academic freedom or critical thinking provision in a school policy or union contract. While a teacher may be able to present viewpoints of origins side-by-side, the teacher should not actively promote a religious Christian view while teaching creation; however, teachers are encouraged to overview creation within the science curriculum. A teacher can overview religion in whatever topic is taught, so long as it is relevant. In teaching about origins, one can overview different theories of creation.
- One can discuss evolution and some of the counter arguments from a creation or abrupt appearance perspective. For example, while there might be evidence of minor change or adjustment over time (e.g., micro-evolution or "adaptation"), there is no evidence of major change (e.g., one "kind" evolving into another). Likewise, there is no evidence of flora (plant) and fauna (animal) transfer. One can overview the various theories and then say: "Now there are a lot of different theories about evolution and abrupt appearance. Whatever theory one holds, all theories have one thing in common: faith."

It takes a major leap in faith to assume that evolution demonstrates how animals and plants originated. The theory of abrupt appearance or creation also requires faith. While there is evidence to support creation, nobody was there at the beginning. Nobody was there for evolution and nobody was there for creation. Whichever theory of origins one ultimately accepts, neither can be considered a proven fact because they are not observable, testable, and repeatable today. Evolution is believed by faith, and creation is believed by faith. Students should be informed that evolution is one faith-based theory, just like creation is a faith-based theory. Rather than elevating evolution and tearing down creation, one can show that both are on the same level—i.e., both are theories or beliefs, not established fact. Indeed, if one discusses the evidence for and against evolution, it becomes obvious that one must have more faith to believe in evolution than in creation.

In the context of evolution, academic freedom provides enough leeway in which teachers may juxtapose facts about evolution, with other facts which may lead to an alternative viewpoint of origins. Teachers should always teach with the goal of broadening students' intellectual horizons, but should do so mindful of the sensitivities required by their position in light of current court understandings of the Establishment Clause, and if they do receive a direct order to cease or refrain from doing something touching the area of faith, contact Liberty Counsel (*http://www.lc.org*) or the Pacific Justice Institute (*http://www.pacificjustice.org/*) before proceeding further.

Chapter 2: Can We Trust the Bible?
Daniel A. Biddle, Ph.D.

Recent research has revealed a serious epidemic with today's Christian youth. So many are caught up in an unfortunate pattern that goes something like this:[18]

1. They grow up in a Christian home and attend church regularly, but they don't receive solid biblical teaching or training regarding various worldviews;
2. Their faith is challenged by evolutionary teaching when they attend public high school or college;
3. Their questions and doubts go unanswered because of their complacency, lack of interest, or the failure of parents and/or church leadership to equip them with biblical grounding and a solid awareness of various worldviews; and
4. They fall away from their faith, and their generational Christian line is lost.

Many teens today are in Step 1 above, some are in Steps 2–3, and some are recovering from Step 4. Fortunately, some have not entered the cycle above because of their biblical grounding. Whatever your current position, we encourage you to *slowly and steadily* take in the words of this Chapter—written about the most important book in history, the Bible.

Overview

So many people ask: Who wrote the Bible? How was the Bible put together? How do we know the stories in the Bible actually happened? How do we know that it has been accurately translated over the years? These are all fair questions. To start answering some of these questions, we will begin by looking at the big picture, then follow with closer look.

The big picture begins with the Bible's 66 books (39 books in the Old Testament and 27 books in the New

Testament) which were written by over 40 different authors from various walks of life, including scholars, kings, priests, shepherds, farmers, physicians, tent-makers, fishermen, and philosophers. The first books of the Bible were compiled around 1450 B.C. and the last books before A.D. 90—a timespan of about 1,500 years. It was written in three languages: Hebrew, Aramaic, and Greek. The most important characteristic of the Bible—and one that makes it different than any other book ever published—is that it is inspired by God (2 Timothy 3:16–17 and 2 Peter 1:19–21).

Despite such a diverse background, the Bible is unlike any other book written in history in its historical accuracy, agreement with demonstrable science and archaeology, and consistency—both internally and externally. The Bible has been translated into over 2,000 languages, and ranks highest among the most widely printed and studied books in the world.

Let's take a closer look into how the Bible was put together. The first 39 books of the Bible (the Old Testament) were solidified and used authoritatively in its complete form by the Hebrews well before Christ. The books of the New Testament were written between about A.D. 30 and A.D. 90 and were formally "canonized" into the set of 27 books we have today sometime before the year A.D. 375 The word "canon" comes from the Greek word "kanon," which means *measuring rod*. This word was used by those who officially verified an assembled set of 27 books because they stood up to the measuring tests of "divine inspiration and authority."

What led to this final "canonization" process? Theology and history books have thousands of pages on this topic. So we'll consider just a few highlights between the time the New Testament was *inspired* by God through original manuscripts men wrote and *assembled* into the "final canon":[19]

- Paul regarded Luke's writings to be as authoritative as the Old Testament (1 Timothy 5:18; see also Deuteronomy 25:4 and Luke 10:7).

- Peter recognized Paul's writings as Scripture (2 Peter 3:15–16).
- Some of the books of the New Testament were being circulated among the churches (Colossians 4:16; 1 Thessalonians 5:27).
- Clement of Rome mentioned at least eight New Testament books (A.D. 95).
- The writings of Ignatius of Antioch acknowledged about seven New Testament books (A.D. 115).
- The writings of Polycarp, a disciple of John the Apostle, acknowledged 15 of the books (A.D. 108). Later, Irenaeus mentioned 21 New Testament books (A.D. 185).
- Hippolytus of Rome recognized 22 of them (A.D. 170–235).

Before the final set of 27 books was formally recognized, an earlier "canon" was compiled in A.D. 170. This Canon, called the Muratorian Canon, included all of the New Testament books except Hebrews, James, and 3 John. These three books were already God-inspired even though the members of the Muratorian Canon may not have recognized them as so. In A.D. 363, the Council of Laodicea stated that only the Old Testament and the 27 books of the New Testament were to be read in the churches. The Council of Hippo (A.D. 393) and the Council of Carthage (A.D. 397) also affirmed the same 27 books as authoritative.

We owe these ancient councilmen. They sifted through false gospels and other writings that early deceivers claimed were God-inspired so that later generations of Christians could trust, study, know, teach and believe in the Scriptures. Some of the features they recognized in the canon were:

- Did the text describe mythological or pointless miracles, or genuine miracles which always accompanied and authorized a message—the Gospel.
- Did the people who lived through the events that the text describes reject those texts as being false, or accept them as having occurred as described?
- Did the text contain any logical or biblical contradictions? If so, it must not have come from the same Divine co-author, who is not a God of confusion, but of order—and who is passionate about clearly revealing who He is to as many as will listen; and
- Was the text written by an apostle or one authorized by an apostle?

After this "canonization" period, a definitive version of the Bible was recorded in Greek, called the *Codex Vaticanus* in about A.D. 350 The classic King James version, as well as the New King James, relied on the very important *Textus Receptus* copies of Scripture. The Codex is one of the oldest extant manuscripts of the Greek Bible (Old and New Testament), and has been kept in the Vatican Library since the 15th century. Another ancient Bible is the *Aleppo Codex*, which is a medieval bound manuscript of the Hebrew Bible written around A.D. 930. The first English translation of the Bible was made in A.D. 1382 by John Wycliffe and was the first book ever mass-produced on the printing press in A.D. 1454 by Johannes Gutenberg.[20]

Given this brief history of the Bible, let's put the Bible through some tests that historians use when analyzing the historical accuracy and reliability of ancient manuscripts. First, let's evaluate whether *what we have today matches what was written originally*. In the Bible's case, this was about 2,000 years ago and earlier. Second: *Do the recorded events describe true events?* Let's see how the Bible holds up to each of these important questions.

Does the Bible We Have Today Match the Original?

One of the primary ways to answer this important question is to look at the *time gap* between the original writing (called the *autograph*) and the copies that still exist today. As a general rule, the closer the copy is to the original, the greater the accuracy and reliability. Ancient manuscripts like the Bible were written on fragile material such as papyrus, which is a thin paper-like material made from papyrus plants. Because papyrus eventually decays or gets worn out, ancient writers would continually make new copies using this material and others.[21]

Dating these ancient texts is done by a variety of methods, such as analyzing the material on which it was written, letter size and form, punctuation, text divisions, ornamentation, the color of the ink, and the texture and color of the parchment.[22] Table 2 shows the results of this "test of time" for the Biblical New Testament compared to several other historical documents.

Table 2. How the New Testament Compares to Other Ancient Writings[23]

Author/Work	Date Written	Earliest Copies	Time Gap	Num. Copies
Homer (Iliad)	800 B.C.	400 B.C.	400 yrs.	643
Herodotus (History)	480–425 B.C.	A.D. 900	1,350 yrs.	8
Thucydides (History)	460–400 B.C.	A.D. 900	1,300 yrs.	8
Plato	400 B.C.	A.D. 900	1,300 yrs.	7
Demosthenes	300 B.C.	A.D. 1100	1,400 yrs.	200
Caesar (Gallic Wars)	100–44 B.C.	A.D. 900	1,000 yrs.	10
Tacitus (Annals)	A.D 100.	A.D. 1100	1,000 yrs.	20
Pliny (Natural)	A.D. 61–113	A.D. 850	750 yrs.	7
Secundus (History)				
New Testament (Fragment)	A.D. 50–100	A.D. 114	50 yrs.	5,366
New Testament (Books)		A.D. 200	100 yrs.	
New Testament (Most Content)		A.D. 250	150 yrs.	
New Testament (Complete)		A.D. 325	225 yrs.	

Table 2 reveals two important facts. First, the New Testament has many more original copies compared to several other famous pieces of literature (5,366 compared to only hundreds for other famous texts). Second, it reveals that the time span between the original and these copies is closer than almost any other work compared!

Answering the important question, *"Is the Bible we have today what was written down originally?"* requires evaluating the *number of manuscript copies* that were made of the original. Generally speaking, the greater number of copies of the original available, the easier it is to reproduce the original. Taking the 5,366 copies of the New Testament and adding the copies from other languages (such as Latin, Ethiopic, and Slavic) results in more than 25,000 total manuscripts (hand-written copies) that pre-date the printing press in the 15th century! By comparison, the runner-up historical text (Homer's Iliad) has only 643.[24]

With this, the New Testament clearly passes both the *time gap* and the *number of manuscript copies* tests. And if the New Testament doesn't pass this test, one must certainly disregard most other historical texts as inaccurate and/or unreliable!

There is more.

Have you ever had a computer crash, resulting in a total loss of all your data? I have—it's definitely not fun! One of the most difficult challenges about computer crashes is losing the *original copies* of your important homework assignments or work reports. However, when I've experienced these situations, I'm usually able to completely reconstruct all of my important "final versions" through my *email files* because I sent copies of the final versions to friends and/or clients. This is the same situation with the original bible documents and the letter exchanges between the Church Fathers—we can completely reconstruct over 99% of the original Bible (New Testament) from just their letters!

Even if all of the copies of the Bible from A.D. 300 to today were destroyed, the complete New Testament (except for only 11 verses)[25] could be reconstructed using only quotations by the Early Church Fathers in the first few hundred years after Christ! This is because the Church Fathers frequently quoted large sections of Scripture in their letters to each other. In addition, if these Church Fathers quoted from the entire New Testament, then the New Testament had to have been widely circulating before this time—long enough to be regarded as reliable by the early church. This shows that the entire New Testament was already assembled and considered reliable within 50 years from the disciples.[26]

Is What Was Written in the Bible True?

Three of the four Gospels, books that include the narrative of Jesus' life, were written by *direct eye witnesses* of the events in Jesus' life: Matthew, Mark, and John. Luke, when writing the story of Jesus' life for Theophilus, a high-ranking official at the time,[27] wrote: "Many have undertaken to draw up an account of the things that have been fulfilled among us, *just as they were handed down to us by those who from the first were eyewitnesses and servants of the word*" (Luke 1:1–2, emphasis added). Luke continues to state that he carefully vetted his account of Jesus' life and ministry: "With this in mind, since I myself have carefully investigated everything from the beginning, I too decided to write an orderly account for you, most excellent Theophilus, so that you may know the certainty of the things you have been taught" (Luke 1:3–4). Additional examples of this careful research and transcription include:

- 1 John 1:3: "We proclaim to you what we have seen and heard, so that you also may have fellowship with us. And our fellowship is with the Father and with his Son, Jesus Christ."
- 2 Peter 1:16: "For we did not follow cleverly devised stories when we told you about the coming of our Lord Jesus Christ in power, but we were eyewitnesses of his majesty."
- John 20:30–31: "Jesus performed many other signs in the presence of his disciples, which are not recorded in this book. But these are written that you may believe that Jesus is the Messiah, the Son of God, and that by believing you may have life in his name."

In addition, several of the writers of the New Testament did their writing and speaking among people who were present at the events of Jesus life. For example, in Acts 2:22, Peter stated while under interrogation, "Fellow Israelites, listen to this: Jesus of Nazareth was a man accredited by God to you by miracles, wonders and signs, which *God did among you through him, as you yourselves know*" (emphasis added). Paul used this reference to his audience's common knowledge of Christ when he defended himself against Festus: "What I am saying is true and reasonable. *The king is familiar with these things*, and I can speak freely to him. I am convinced that none of this has escaped his notice, because it was not done in a corner" (Acts 26:25–26, emphasis added).

Furthermore, most of the writings of the New Testament were written during a time when the community knew about Jesus, Jesus' followers, or knew of people who did. "For what I received I passed on to you as of first importance: that Christ died for our sins according to the Scriptures, that he was buried, that he was raised on the third day according to the Scriptures, and that he appeared to Cephas, and then to the Twelve. After that, he appeared to more than five hundred of the brothers and sisters at the same time, most of whom are still living, though some have fallen asleep" (1 Corinthians 15:3–6, emphasis added).

Finally, consider the fact that 11 of the 12 disciples died terrible deaths—being killed for their unchanging testimony of who Christ was, and of His resurrection. They were so sure that Christ was who He claimed to be that they signed their testimony with their own blood!

Isaiah 53 and the Dead Sea Scrolls

In 1947, shepherds chasing a lost sheep in the caves above the Qumran Valley northwest of the Dead Sea made one of the most significant archaeological discoveries of our time— the Dead Sea Scrolls. The scrolls were found in numerous clay jars, and numbered over 900, 200 of which include numerous sections and fragments of every book in the Old Testament except the book of Esther. Though few of its scholars dare admit it, they even contain fragments of several New Testament books.[28]

One of the most significant scrolls is called the "Great Isaiah Scroll," which includes the same Book of Isaiah that we have today in modern bibles, but dates to 125 B.C.[29] The Great Isaiah Scroll is significant for two reasons. First, it was written before the Lord Jesus Christ was yet born and it includes a chapter (Chapter 53) which includes specific and clear prophecies about the torture, death, burial, and resurrection of Christ. Second, its discovery now allows us to test three versions of the Bible representing different time periods: Pre-Christ Dead Sea Scroll, A.D. 930, and today. We can even compare how the English translation of this important text survived or changed through the years!

Table 3 provides a word-by-word comparison of these three versions so you can see for yourself how reliable the translation process has been through the millennia:

Table 3. Comparison of Isaiah 53 between the Dead Sea Scrolls, the Aleppo Codex, and the Modern Bible [30]

Verse	Dead Sea "Great Isaiah" Scroll (125 B.C.)	Aleppo Codex (A.D. 930)	Modern Translation (NIV)
1	Who has believed our report and the arm of YHWH [(1)] to whom has it been revealed?	Who would have believed our report? And to whom hath the arm of the LORD been revealed?	Who has believed our message and to whom has the arm of the LORD been revealed?
2	And he shall come up like a suckling before us and as a root from dry ground there is no form to him and no beauty to him and in his being seen and there is no appearance that we should desire him.	For he shot up right forth as a sapling, and as a root out of a dry ground; he had no form nor comeliness that we should look upon him, nor beauty that we should delight in him.	He grew up before him like a tender shoot, and like a root out of dry ground. He had no beauty or majesty to attract us to him, nothing in his appearance that we should desire him.
3	He is despised and rejected of men, a man of sorrows and knowing grief and as though hiding faces from him he was despised and we did not esteem him.	He was despised, and forsaken of men, a man of pains, and acquainted with disease, and as one from whom men hide their face: he was despised, and we esteemed him not.	He was despised and rejected by men, a man of sorrows, and familiar with suffering. Like one from whom men hide their faces he was despised, and we esteemed him not.
4	Surely our griefs he is bearing and our sorrows he carried them and we esteemed him beaten and struck by God and afflicted.	Surely our diseases he did bear, and our pains he carried; whereas we did esteem him stricken, smitten of God, and afflicted.	Surely he took up our infirmities and carried our sorrows, yet we considered him stricken by God, smitten by him, and afflicted.
5	and he is wounded for our transgressions, and crushed for our iniquities, the correction of our peace was upon him and by his wounds he has healed us.[(2)]	But he was wounded because of our transgressions, he was crushed because of our iniquities: the chastisement of our welfare was upon him, and with his stripes we were healed.	But he was pierced for our transgressions, he was crushed for our iniquities; the punishment that brought us peace was upon him, and by his wounds we are healed.
6	All of us like sheep have wandered each man to his own way we have turned and YHWH has caused to light on him the iniquity of all of us.	All we like sheep did go astray, we turned every one to his own way; and the LORD hath made to light on him the iniquity of us all.	We all, like sheep, have gone astray, each of us has turned to his own way; and the LORD has laid on him the iniquity of us all.
7	He was oppressed and he was afflicted and he did not open his mouth, as a lamb to the slaughter he is brought and as a ewe before her shearers is made dumb he did not open his mouth.	He was oppressed, though he humbled himself and opened not his mouth; as a lamb that is led to the slaughter, and as a sheep that before her shearers is dumb; yea, he opened not his mouth.	He was oppressed and afflicted, yet he did not open his mouth; he was led like a lamb to the slaughter, and as a sheep before her shearers is silent, so he did not open his mouth.

50

8	From prison and from judgment he was taken and his generation who shall discuss it because he was cut off from the land of the living. Because from the transgressions of his people a wound was to him	By oppression and judgment he was taken away, and with his generation who did reason? for he was cut off out of the land of the living, for the transgression of my people to whom the stroke was due.	By oppression and judgment he was taken away. And who can speak of his descendants? For he was cut off from the land of the living; for the transgression of my people he was stricken.
9	And they gave wicked ones to be his grave and [(3)] rich ones in his death although he worked no violence neither deceit in his mouth.	And they made his grave with the wicked, and with the rich his tomb; although he had done no violence, neither was any deceit in his mouth.	He was assigned a grave with the wicked, and with the rich in his death, though he had done no violence, nor was any deceit in his mouth.
10	And YHWH was pleased to crush him and He has caused him grief. If you will appoint his soul a sin offering he will see his seed and he will lengthen his days and the pleasure of YHWH in his hand will advance.	Yet it pleased the LORD to crush him by disease; to see if his soul would offer itself in restitution, that he might see his seed, prolong his days, and that the purpose of the LORD might prosper by his hand:	Yet it was the LORD's will to crush him and cause him to suffer, and though the LORD makes his life a guilt offering, he will see his offspring and prolong his days, and the will of the LORD will prosper in his hand.
11	Of the toil of his soul he shall see {+light+} and he shall be satisfied and by his knowledge shall he make righteous even my righteous servant for many and their iniquities he will bear.	Of the travail of his soul he shall see to the full, even My servant, who by his knowledge did justify the Righteous One to the many, and their iniquities he did bear.	After the suffering of his soul, he will see the light [of life] and be satisfied; by his knowledge my righteous servant will justify many, and he will bear their iniquities.
12	Therefore I will apportion to him among the great ones and with the mighty ones he shall divide the spoil because he laid bare to death his soul and with the transgressors he was numbered, and he, the sins of many, he bore, and for their transgressions he entreated.	Therefore will I divide him a portion among the great, and he shall divide the spoil with the mighty; because he bared his soul unto death, and was numbered with the transgressors; yet he bore the sin of many, and made intercession for the transgressors.	Therefore I will give him a portion among the great, and he will divide the spoils with the strong, because he poured out his life unto death, and was numbered with the transgressors. For he bore the sin of many, and made intercession for the transgressors.

Notes: (1) The tetragrammaton (YHWH) is one of the names of the God of Israel used in the Hebrew Bible. (2) There is a scribal thumb print over lines 10 to 12 in the Dead Sea "Isaiah" Scroll (lines 10–12 include verses 5–7 in modern Bibles). However, while this obscures some letters, all letters are "reconstructible with certainty" (see: *http://www.ao.net/~fmoeller/qum-44.htm*); (3) a scribbled word probably accusative sign "eth."

Reading the three columns in Table 3 shows an incredibly high degree of similarity. In fact, regarding this

51

specific Chapter in Isaiah, renowned Christian philosopher and apologist Norman Geisler writes:

> Of the 166 words in Isaiah 53, there are only 17 letters in question. Ten of these letters are simply a matter of spelling, which does not affect the sense. Four more letters are minor stylistic changes, such as conjunctions. The remaining three letters comprise the word "light" which is added in verse 11, and does not affect the meaning greatly. Furthermore, this word is supported by the Septuagint and IQ Is [first cave of Qumran, Isaiah scroll]. Thus, in one chapter of 166 words, there is only one word (three letters) in question after a thousand years of transmission—and this word does not significantly change the meaning of the passage.[31]

How is this possible? How can these three different documents being translated and transcribed over a 2,000 year timeframe with such *exact* similarity? One explanation is simply that God watched over the process. Practically speaking, he used many incredible scribes to do it. For example, the Talmudists (Hebrew scribes and scholars between A.D. 100 and A.D. 500) had an incredibly rigorous system for transcribing biblical scrolls. Samuel Davidson describes some of the disciplines of the Talmudists in regard to the Scriptures:[32]

> A synagogue roll must be written on the skins of clean animals, prepared for the particular use of the synagogue by a Jew. These must be fastened together with strings taken from clean animals. Every skin must contain a certain number of columns, equal throughout the entire codex. The length of each column must not extend over less than 48 or more than 60 lines; And the breadth must consist of thirty letters. The whole copy

must be first-lined; And if three words be written without a line, it is worthless. The ink should be black, neither red, green, nor any other color, and be prepared according to a definite recipe. An authentic copy must be the exemplar, from which the transcriber ought not in the least deviate. No word or letter, not even a yod, must be written from memory, the scribe not having looked at the codex before him... Between every consonant the space of a hair or thread must intervene; Between every new parashah, or section, the breadth of nine consonants; Between every book, three lines. The fifth book of Moses must terminate exactly with a line; But the rest need not do so. Besides this, the copyist must sit in full Jewish dress, wash his whole body, not begin to write the name of God with a pen newly dipped in ink, and should a king address him while writing that name, he must take no notice of him.

Why is Isaiah 53 so important to Christians? Because Isaiah 53 includes at least 12 highly specific prophecies regarding the life, death, and resurrection of Christ. The details in this chapter would not be nearly as important if they were written after Christ's birth, but the fact that we can confirm that the chapter was in fact written before Christ proves beyond reasonable doubt both the accuracy and Divine authorship of the Bible. Consider these 13 prophecies, written by Isaiah about 700 years before Christ was even born, alongside references of their New Testament fulfilments:

1. He would not be widely believed (John 1:10–12).
2. He would not have the look of Majesty (Luke 2:7).
3. He would be despised and suffer (Matthew 26:67–68; 27:39–43).

4. He would be concerned about health needs (Matthew 8:17) and would die for our sins (1 Peter 2:24).
5. His pain/punishment would be for us (Matthew 28:20; Romans 4:25).
6. All of us have sinned (Romans 3:10–18).
7. He would not respond to charges (Matthew 26:63).
8. He was to be oppressed and killed (Matthew 26:65–68).
9. He was associated with criminals during life and at death (Matthew 27:38; 27:57–60).
10. He would be buried in a rich man's tomb (Isaiah 53:9).
11. He would be crushed, suffer and die, yet live (Luke 23:44–48; Luke 24:36–44).
12. He would bear our sins (1 Peter 2:24).
13. He would have a portion with the great (Philippians 2:8–11).

The very fact that it has now been confirmed that this was written before Christ is amazing. How could anyone fulfill each of these prophecies, many of which happened after Christ's death and were clearly out of His control (i.e., if he wasn't God)? Finally, consider these prophecies about Christ that were all penned before He was born, and their fulfilments:[33]

Table 4. Forty-three (43) Prophecies Fulfilled by Jesus

Prophecies About Jesus	Old Testament Scripture	New Testament Fulfillment
Messiah would be born in Bethlehem.	Micah 5:2	Matthew 2:1; Luke 2:4–6
Messiah would be born of a virgin.	Isaiah 7:14	Matthew 1:22–23; Luke 1:26–31
Messiah would come from the line of Abraham.	Gen. 12:3; Gen. 22:18	Matthew 1:1; Romans 9:5
Messiah would be a descendant of Isaac.	Gen. 17:19; Gen. 21:12	Luke 3:34
Messiah would be a descendant of Jacob.	Numbers 24:17	Matthew 1:2
Messiah would come from the tribe of Judah.	Genesis 49:10	Luke 3:33; Hebrews 7:14
Messiah would be heir to King David's throne.	2 Sam. 7:12-13; Isa. 9:7	Luke 1:32–33; Romans 1:3
Messiah's throne will be anointed and eternal.	Ps. 45:6-7; Daniel 2:44	Luke 1:33; Hebrews 1:8–12
Messiah would be called Immanuel.	Isaiah 7:14	Matthew 1:23
Messiah would spend a season in Egypt.	Hosea 11:1	Matthew 2:14–15
Children would be massacred at Messiah's birthplace.	Jeremiah 31:15	Matthew 2:16–18
A messenger would prepare the way for Messiah.	Isaiah 40:3-5	Luke 3:3–6
Messiah would be rejected by his own people.	Psalm 69:8; Isaiah 53:3	John 1:11; John 7:5
Messiah would be a prophet.	Deuteronomy	Acts 3:20–22
Messiah would be preceded	Malachi 4:5-6	Matthew 11:13–14
Messiah would be declared the Son of God.	Psalm 2:7	Matthew 3:16–17
Messiah would be called a	Isaiah 11:1	Matthew 2:23
Messiah would bring light to	Isaiah 9:1-2	Matthew 4:13–16
Messiah would speak in parables.	Ps.78:2-4; Is. 6:90	Matthew 13:10-15,34–35
Messiah would be sent to heal the brokenhearted.	Isaiah 61:1-2	Luke 4:18–19
Messiah would be a priest after Melchizedek order.	Psalm 110:4	Hebrews 5:5–6
Messiah would be called King.	Ps. 2:6; Zechariah 9:9	Matthew 27:37; Mark 11:7–11
Messiah would be praised by little children.	Psalm 8:2	Matthew 21:16
Messiah would be betrayed.	Ps. 41:9; Zech.11:12-13	Luke 22:47; Mt:14–16
Messiah's betrayal money used to buy a potter's field.	Zechariah 11:12-13	Matthew 27:9–10
Messiah would be falsely accused.	Psalm 35:11	Mark 14:57–58

Messiah would be silent before his accusers.	Isaiah 53:7	Mark 15:4–5
Messiah would be spat upon and struck.	Isaiah 50:6	Matthew 26:67
Messiah would be hated without cause.	Ps. 35:19; Psalm 69:4	John 15:24–25
Messiah would be crucified with criminals.	Isaiah 53:12	Matthew 27:38; Mark 15:27–28
Messiah would be given vinegar to drink.	Psalm 69:21	Matthew 27:34; John 19:28–30
Messiah's hands and feet would be pierced.	Ps. 22:16; Zech. 12:10	John 20:25–27
Messiah would be mocked and ridiculed.	Psalm 22:7-8	Luke 23:35
Soldiers would gamble for Messiah's garments.	Psalm 22:18	Luke 23:34; Matthew 27:35-36
Messiah's bones would not be broken.	Exodus 12:46;	John 19:33-36
Messiah would be forsaken by God.	Psalm 22:1	Matthew 27:46
Messiah would pray for his enemies.	Psalm 109:4	Luke 23:34
Soldiers would pierce Messiah's side.	Zechariah 12:10	John 19:34
Messiah would be buried with the rich.	Isaiah 53:9	Matthew 27:57-60
Messiah would resurrect from the dead.	Ps.16:10; Ps. 49:15	Matthew 28:2-7; Acts 2:22–32
Messiah would ascend to heaven.	Psalm 24:7–10	Mark 16:19; Luke 24:51
Messiah would be seated at God's right hand.	Ps. 68:18; Ps. 110:1	Mark 16:19; Matthew 22:44
Messiah would be a sacrifice for sin.	Isaiah 53:5–12	Romans 5:6-8

Chapter 3: Did Noah's Flood Really Happen?
Van Wingerden, M.S. & Daniel A. Biddle, Ph.D.

Because the Bible is very specific about Noah's Flood—including the approximate date, the people involved, the nature of the Flood, and the complete worldwide obliteration of all land-dwelling animals—there are only two logical positions to have on the topic: (1) it happened as described in the Bible, or (2) it didn't happen at all. There are no "middle choices." What are the implications for each of these two positions?

If it happened as described in the Bible, we can extract certain lessons that can even apply to our lives today. These include: (1) there is a God who hates sin and judged the entire world for it, (2) the Bible is inspired by God (because the event was foretold and required supernatural power to complete), and (3) God gave the world a massive "do-over" opportunity. There are more, but these are some of the basics that have substantial implications in our lives today. If it didn't happen as described in the Bible, these truths are on unstable ground and the billions of fossils around the world are in need of some other explanation. In this Chapter, we hope to share with the reader some of the key evidence that we have found regarding Noah's Flood that have led us to the first choice: It really happened as described by the Bible.

Overview

Geology text books, especially at the college level, describe many advancing and retreating oceans occurring over millions of years that deposited the sedimentary rocks found on the North American continent. Tens of thousands of feet of sediment are deposited on the continent along with millions of fossils found in the layers. The rock layers found in Grand Canyon of Arizona are given as evidence for the many advancing and retreating oceans. The fossils found in these layers are also used to show the many changing environments taking place during the millions of years while animals were evolving.

This Chapter will refute this conventional theory and present an alternate explanation: the worldwide, catastrophic Flood that happened in the time of Noah. The data, sedimentary structures and fossils, found in the rocks will show that the rock layers deposited in the Grand Canyon and the North American continent did not take millions of years. When you read this chapter, ask yourself what makes more sense while thinking what the truth is.

There is plenty of evidence from various sources in support of a worldwide flood in the past. The scientific evidence actually shows that some kind of flood was destructive and utterly catastrophic. It rearranged the entire Earth's surface. Much of the geography or landscape we see today is a result of that flood. It deposited most of the fossils and sediments we observe today. The flood also involved slamming landmasses that shoved great mountains upward. All over the world we can see evidence of this in common roadside geology (see Figure 1 as an example).

Figure 1. Example of Landmasses that "Buckled" During Noah's Flood

The flood we know from science matched *Noah's Flood,* and was a worldwide, catastrophic event that will never occur again.[34] It completely wiped out all living land animals except those on board Noah's Ark. There is much observable evidence for Noah's Flood in the rock record, historical accounts, and the Bible. In this chapter, we will investigate some of these.

The Fossil Record

Most people are fascinated with fossils; especially big fossils like dinosaurs, or small ones like birds, reptiles and fish that are well preserved and not broken apart. But many people are unaware that finding a whole fossil intact with all its bones in place is rare. Many fossils are found in what scientists call fossil graveyards. These fossil graveyards contain a mixture of many different kinds of fossils that have been *transported by large volumes of water* (see Figure 2).

Figure 2. Fossil Graveyard Example

The bones are typically fragments that have been broken apart during the transportation process as enormous mounds of mud and sediment were shifted during the Flood. By studying some of these fossil graveyards, we can gather clues that will demonstrate that the Flood was in fact catastrophic and worldwide, as stated in Genesis 7:20–23:

> The waters rose and covered the mountains to a depth of more than fifteen cubits [at least 22 feet]. *Every living thing* that moved on land perished—birds, livestock, wild animals, *all the creatures* that swarm over the earth, and *all mankind*. Everything on dry land that had the breath of life in its nostrils died. *Every living thing* on the face of the earth was wiped out; people and animals and the creatures that move along the ground and the birds were wiped from the earth. *Only Noah was left*, and those with him in the ark. (emphasis added)

If this passage in Genesis is true, we would expect to find *billions of dead things buried in rock layers laid down by water all over the Earth.*[35] And this is exactly what we find! In fact, such evidence exists *all over the world*. Next, we will discuss several example locations where mass Flood graves have been found.

Chilean Desert

There are at least 75 fossilized whales in the Chilean desert. One must ask: "How did they get there?" Even more amazing, the graveyard is located on top of a hill close to one half mile (a little less than a kilometer) from the Pacific Ocean. The whales "have been found in a roadside strip the length of two football fields—about 262 yards long and 22 yards wide."[36] Twenty of the whales were even found perfectly intact. Most scientists agree that the whales died at the same time, and for the same reason. But how did they die? A catastrophic flood such as Noah's Flood can certainly provide a possible explanation. Since they were deposited atop many miles of sedimentary rock layers that the Flood likely formed, this Chilean fossil graveyard might represent a pod of whales that got cut off from waters flowing off the newly rising South American continent probably during the latter months of the year-long Flood event.

Thousands of Buried Centrosaurs in Hilda, Canada

At least 14 dinosaur "bonebeds" rest in a region in Canada called Hilda. They contain thousands of buried Centrosaurs *found in the same stratigraphic column* (a term used in geology to describe the vertical location of rocks in a particular area). The authors who completed the most extensive study of the area described the sediment in which these dinosaurs are buried as "mudstone rich in organic matter deposited on the tract of land separating two ancient rivers."[37] They also concluded that each of the 14 bonebeds were actually parts of a single, massive "mega-bonebed" that occupied 2.3 square kilometers! Stop and think about this for a minute. How did thousands of dinosaurs—of the same species—get herded up and simultaneously buried in mud? These authors even concluded that the massive bonebed was formed when a herd of Centrosaurs *drowned during a flood*. These bonebeds are also found with aquatic vertebrates such as fish, turtles, and crocodiles, showing that water was definitely involved in their transport and burial. In addition, almost no teeth marks indicated any scavenging after these animals died (probably because most of them died at the same time!).

Massive Dinosaur Graveyard Found in China

An online article on Discovery.com describes the dinosaur graveyard in China as the largest in the world, writing, "Researchers say they can't understand why so many animals gathered in what is today the city of Zhucheng to die." Thousands of dinosaur bones have been found stacked on top of each other in "incredible density" right before they "suddenly vanished from the face of the Earth."[38] Most of the bones are found within a single 980-foot-long ravine in the Chinese countryside, about 415 miles southeast of Beijing. Clearly, processes were going on in the past so violent that we can only imagine them.

10,000+ Duck-billed Dinosaurs Buried Alive in Montana

In his article titled, "The Extinction of the Dinosaurs," Creation researcher Michael J. Oard describes some of the numerous dinosaur graveyards that are found all over the world.[39] He believes this is solid evidence of Noah's worldwide Flood. Oard reported that one of the largest bonebeds in the world is located in north-central Montana:

> Based on outcrops, an extrapolated estimate was made for 10,000 duckbill dinosaurs entombed in a thin layer measuring 2 km east-west and 0.5 km north-south. The bones are disarticulated and disassociated, and are orientated east-west. However, a few bones were standing upright, indicating some type of debris flow. Moreover, there are no young juveniles or babies in this bone-bed, and the bones are all from one species of dinosaur.

Two other scientists, Horner and Gorman, also described the bonebed: "How could any mud slide, no matter how catastrophic, have the force to take a two- or three-ton animal that had just died and smash it around so much that its femur—still embedded in the flesh of its thigh—split lengthwise?"[40] Oard concluded that a cataclysmic event is the best explanation for the arrangement of the bones.

Karoo Basin in South Africa

One of the most remarkable fossil graveyards is found in South Africa in a location known as the Karoo Basin. It was once estimated to contain 800 billion fossil remains. That number was shown to be an overestimation, but the fossils may still be in the billions.[41] Regardless, the fossil bed covers an area over 200,000 square miles, making it one of the largest fossil deposits on Earth.[42] The fossil debris contains many species of plants, insects, fish, reptiles and amphibians. Quite a mixture—everything stirred together as some catastrophic soup! The rock layers containing these fossils were most likely deposited towards the end of the Flood in the same kind of rock layers containing the petrified logs that make up the famous Painted Desert Formation of the Southwestern United States.

Redwall Limestone in the Grand Canyon

Another remarkable fossil graveyard bed and mass kill is located in a seven-foot layer of what was once lime mud now hardened within the Redwall Limestone. The layer contains perhaps billions of cigar-shaped (orthocone) nautiloids.[43] Nautiloids are extinct today, but those with coiled shells resembled the chambered nautilus, a squid-like animal inside a shell. This single extensive bed covers an area of 11,583 square miles, about the size of the state of Maryland, and extends from the Grand Canyon in Arizona all the way to Las Vegas, Nevada, and overlaps into southern Utah. During the Flood, a widespread underwater mud flow wiped out these ocean-dwelling swimmers and deposited the mass kill towards the western edge of North America. Even today, underwater avalanches can cause fast-flowing wedges of muddy debris that cut through the ocean floor, but we have never observed them at the size of Maryland! Because of the slender conical shape of the nautiloid, they act like wind vanes. When the nautiloids exit the tumbling debris flow, some of the shells align with the direction of the current (i.e., the retreating Flood waters). A geologist can use this data to calculate direction of the torrential debris flow.

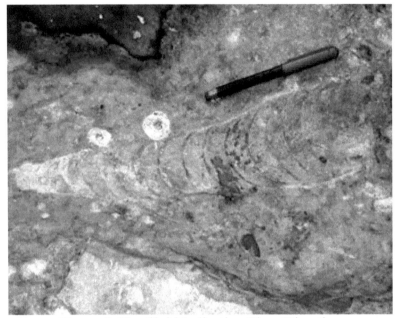

Figure 3. Nautiloid Indicating Flow Direction

Burgess Shale in the Canadian Rockies

The Burgess Shale in the Canadian Rockies at an elevation of 6,700 feet contains a remarkable collection of ancient fossilized life. Not only are the hard body parts such as bones, teeth, and shells preserved, but soft body tissue such as muscles, gills, and digestive systems are also fossilized (many "with soft parts intact, often with food still in their guts"[44]— making it obvious that they were immediately buried). It is rare to find soft body parts fossilized. It is important to understand that an animal or plant becomes a fossil only if it is buried rapidly. Scavengers would eat the animal if it were not completely buried immediately after it dies.

Another researcher remarks with the same findings: "The Burgess Shale is, therefore, an enormous fossil graveyard, produced by countless animals living on the sea floor being catastrophically swept away in landslide-generated turbidity currents, and then buried almost instantly in the resultant massive turbidite layers, to be exquisitely preserved and fossilized."[45]

Ordovician Soom Shale in South Africa

This massive fossil area is 30 feet thick, spans hundreds of miles, and contains thousands of exceptionally-preserved fossils.[46] The eurypterids even show "walking appendages that are normally lost to early decay after death" and "some of the fibrous muscular masses that operated these appendages."[47] Snelling continues: "The evidence is clearly consistent with catastrophic burial of countless thousands of these organisms over thousands of square kilometers, which implies that the shale itself had to be catastrophically deposited and covered under more sediments before burrowing organisms could destroy the laminations."[48]

Other Major Fossil Deposits

Still not convinced? Need more proof? The world contains many other fossil graveyards that include numerous types of animal and plant life. Ambitious readers are encouraged to explore these other fossil grounds, including:

- Green River Formation of Wyoming (alligators, fish, birds, turtles, clams, insects, a horse, lizards, lemur-like primates, squirrel-like mammals, ferns, and palm leaves).
- Montceau-les-Mines, France (hundreds of thousands of marine creatures were buried with amphibians, spiders, scorpions, millipedes, insects, and reptiles).[49]
- Mazon Creek area near Chicago (more than 400 species represented by over 100,000 fossils).

- Devonian Thunder Bay Limestone formation in Michigan (spans hundreds of miles and is over 12 feet thick in many places. Includes millions of fossils buried in the Flood).
- Carboniferous Francis Creek Shale in Illinois (fossil graveyard containing specimens representing more than 400 species).
- The Triassic Mont San Giorgio Basin in Italy and Switzerland ("Over 300 feet deep and about four miles in diameter, containing thousands of well-preserved fossils of fish and reptiles, including fossilized fish contain embryos inside their abdomens, and a fossilized Tanystropheus, a 4.5-meter giraffe-necked saurian, which also contains the remains of unborn young"[50]).
- Triassic Cow Brand Formation in Virginia (contains a mixture of fossilized terrestrial, freshwater, and marine plants, insects, and reptiles that were buried together in a massive graveyard).[51]
- The Cretaceous Santana Formation in Brazil (thousands of marine and land fossils, including sharks, crocodiles, and pterosaurs).
- Siwalki Hills north of Delhi, India (ranges 2,000 to 3,000 feet high and includes thousands of fossils).
- The Morrison Formation (one million square miles in 13 U.S. states and three Canadian provinces, including dinosaur bones fossilized together with fish, turtles, crocodiles, and mammals).
- Geiseltal in Germany (contains "a complete mixture of plants and insects from all climatic zones and all recognized regions of the geography of plants or animals"[52]).

Not too many fossils are being formed today. Only a worldwide catastrophic flood could produce the many fossil-bearing sediments and fossil graveyards we observe around the world today. Much of this evidence—particularly the fossils of the smaller, more delicate animals and soft tissue—stands in great contrast to Darwin's assertion that "No organism wholly soft can be preserved."[53] The only way to preserve countless millions of intricate fossils all over the world is to bury them quickly in mud and sediment! Even clams, which open after they die, are found around the world in fossil graveyards in the closed position, indicating they were buried rapidly.[54]

Coal Deposits

Evolutionists claim that coal deposits have been formed over millions of years. If this is true, David Cloud asks this compelling question: "How can they sometimes contain perfectly-preserved fossils, including two-ton dinosaurs, which would have to have been covered almost instantly? For example, in 1878, miners working in the Mons coalfield in Belgium discovered 39 iguanodon dinosaur skeletons, many of them complete, at a depth of 322 meters. They were 10 meters long and weighed two tons each. 'For their bodies to be rapidly buried would require rates of deposition thousands or even millions of times greater than the average 0.2 millimeters per year proposed by uniformitarians.'"[55]

During my college days, I had the opportunity to study several coal mines in western Kentucky. I was surprised to find evidence showing their rapid accumulation. This contradicts the swamp model which states it takes tens of millions of years of slow accumulation and burial of plant material before it will turn to coal. Between the layers of coal deposits, we found layers of sandstone, limestone and clays, all containing marine fossils and plant material. Sedimentary structures in these layers indicated they were deposited in fast-moving waters. One coal bed was even cut or channeled by a deposit of sandstone.

Figure 4. Sandstone Channel Cutting Coal Beds in Western Kentucky

Because these coal beds associate with the upper and lower strata (a layer of sedimentary rock or soil), they were also deposited rapidly during a catastrophic event. This challenges the slow and gradual swamp model. Not only that, coal deposits do not have the deep-penetrating roots that swamp and peat soils have. The Flood formed coal beds as water action sorted plant debris.

Polystrate Fossils

In many coal and sediment deposits, fossilized trees are found standing in an upright position. These are called polystrate fossils because they are encased within and cross several layers of sedimentary rock.

Figure 5. Polystrate Fossil Tree[56]

If the sandstone or clay was deposited very slowly, the trees would rot and not be preserved. The sediments had to rapidly bury the trees in order for them to stay upright and fossilize. Other kinds of fossils are buried and encased or extend into multiple layers of sediment. Dr John Morris notes, "I've seen hundreds of individual fossils whose body width exceeds the width of the banded layers in which they are encased."[57] It would be impossible for a dead fish or animal to stay in an upright position and be perfectly fossilized, with all parts intact, if the sediments accumulated slowly.

One such example is the "Kamikaze" ichthyosaur described by Tas Walker and Carl Wieland.[58] This ichthyosaur (an extinct dolphin-like marine reptile) was found "buried in a vertical, nose-down position at 90 degrees to the rock layers." Walker and Wieland continue: "Unlike most fossils, the head was preserved in three dimensions, and had not been flattened by the weight of sediment above it...The skull was enclosed vertically within three geological layers, which have been dated according to long-age beliefs, by reference to the fossils they contain. Curiously, the layers span an 'age' of about one million years, and that presents something of a problem for long-age geologists."

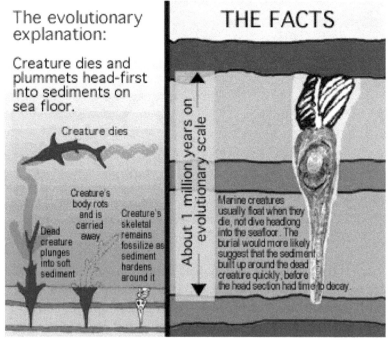

Figure 6. Ichthyosaur Head Spanning Three Layers (supposedly deposited over one million years)[59]

You don't have to be a fossil expert to see the problems with this situation. Just how can a complete ichthyosaur head be buried in a vertical position *slowly* over a million years? It is much more likely that this animal was killed and buried rapidly during Noah's Flood, and that all these layers formed at nearly the same time. There have also been several fossils recovered that were *in the process of giving birth*.[60]

The Earth's Sedimentary Rocks

The most common type of rock found on the Earth's surface is sedimentary rock deposited by water. We learn in the study of earth science that sedimentary rocks are made of broken pieces of preexisting rock. The clasts or pieces range from very small, such as those in mud, to large cobbles and even house-sized boulders. "Strata" is a term applied to layers of all types of sedimentary rocks. Many people don't realize that the sediments or strata were laid down and spread out over vast amounts of land surface. Some cover nearly the entire continent of North America. These are called blanket sandstones. Also the Earth's strata occur in six thick packages called megasequences. Each megasequence shares the same kind of material, clast patterns, and fossils which enables scientists to trace the sequence for long distances.

The Tapeats Sandstone is one of the lowest blanket sandstones. It was deposited at the start of the Flood in areas of North America. Evidence within the Tapeats strata, such as ripple beds and well-developed cross-beds, is consistent with rapid deposition. Cross-beds and ripples form when water currents are fast and strong.

Figure 7. Well Developed Cross-beds in Sandstone Indicates Rapidly Moving Waters

Additionally, large boulders are found at the base of the Tapeats Sandstone. This also shows that currents were strong and violent, ripping up and pulverizing the underlying bed rocks.

Another layer named the Redwall Limestone is found in the Grand Canyon and extends under other local names across America as far as Tennessee and Pennsylvania. The same kinds of sediments and fossils are even found across the Atlantic Ocean in England. Geologist Andrew Snelling states, "Every continent contains layers of sedimentary rocks that span vast areas. Many of these layers can even be traced across continents."[61] Only a world-covering flood could deposit such vast amounts of sediment as a single layer!

The Bible states that at the beginning of the Flood, "... all the fountains of the great deep burst open ..." (Genesis 7:11). Geologists have found deposits of large boulders and megabreccia beds—composed of very large angular fragments of rock laid down in a mud flow—that outcrop on the edges of most continents. The Kingston Peak Formation located in the Mojave Desert of California is a leading example of this type of deposit. These megabreccia beds are also found in Utah and Idaho, and extend into Canada as well. They show where the edge of the North American continent probably was at the start of the Flood.

Figure 8. Megabreccia. These deposits were most likely laid down at the start of the Flood when the ancient continent broke apart.

Mountain Building

Many people I run into know that fossil deposits are found in the highest mountains on Earth. They consider, "How could fossils that once lived on the ocean floor be found in the world's tallest mountains?" Most elevated mountains of the world contain strata with marine and plant fossils. For example, whale fossils are found high in the Andes Mountains with other marine fossils such as clams and giant oysters.[62] The peak of Mount Everest contains fossil ammonites.

Figure 9. The Pyramidal Summit of Mt. Everest is Composed of Fossil Bearing Limestones

Other examples of fossils at high elevation include the Burgess Shale mentioned above, and the Matterhorn, which sits at 14,690 feet in the Swiss Alps. It is composed of sedimentary layers which contain marine fossils such as clams, oysters, and fish! Much of the sedimentary layers in these mountains are folded, tilted, and "cracked" (faulted) due to the tectonic forces that raised them. If these mountain ranges are tens of millions of years old then they shouldn't be as elevated. They should be worn down as hills or eroded away completely based on the current rate of erosion. In fact, subsequent research has verified what John Morris wrote in *The Young Earth: The Real History of the Earth, Past, Present, and Future* about how modern erosion rates would have erased all continents in 50 million years or so, since erosion occurs faster than uplift.

I've talked to many people who don't understand that most mountains were formed very recently in so-called geologic time. Geologic time is referred to as "deep time," and it starts at about 4.5 billion years ago. Of course, even as a geologist I am unconvinced of deep time, instead preferring the biblical time scale. If we searched the internet or textbooks for "mountain building" we would find that, on average, the tallest mountains started uplifting around 60 million years ago. So, assuming for argument the conventional age of the Earth as 4.5 billion years old and accepting geologic "deep time," let's compare geologic time to a twenty-four hour day. The 60 million year-old mountain building events would only take about the last eighteen minutes of a twenty-four hour day to appear. So, mountain building is a recent geologic event within the evolutionary time frame.

Now some scientists think, based on the fossils, that today's highest mountains are a lot younger than the 60 million years stated above.[63] Pliocene fossils, deposited about 5 million years ago using the conventional geologic time frame, are found in the Himalayas and Andes Mountains. So, compared to the twenty-four hour day above, these mountains appeared in the last two minutes of the day!

Bristlecone Pines

Consider the Bristlecone Pines, believed to be some of the oldest living organisms on the Earth. These hardy, twisted pines grow in arid regions of Western North America at altitudes between 5,600 and 11,200 feet. Researchers can estimate the ages of these trees by counting the "growth rings," which typically grow at a rate of one per year, but can grow more than one ring during wet years. One such Bristlecone Pine, called the "Methuselah" pine (named after the biblical character Methuselah, who lived to be 969 years old[64]) has an estimated age of 4,845 years. Just this year, an even older tree was found with an estimated age of 5,063.[65]

Figure 10. Bristlecone Pines on the tops of White Mountains, California

Is this just a coincidence that these trees are found on high elevated mountains? Or, could the Bristlecone pines have rooted at the end of the Flood on dry land and then have been uplifted during the mountain building process at that time? The fact that the Earth's oldest trees are found on the mountain tops fits well with recent mountain building episodes towards the end of the catastrophic Flood of Noah. The truth is that it makes more sense that the mountains rose *rapidly* at the end of the Flood—after the many ocean-dwelling animals were buried and fossilized (mostly clams) and seeds were sprouted. As mentioned earlier, given the current rate of mountain uplift and erosion, uplift had to be faster than erosion or the mountains would be worn away.

One must also ask the question: "Why are there no trees alive today that significantly exceed typical Flood date estimates (around 2350 B.C.)?" This is especially convincing given that several tree species have the ability to live longer than 6,000 years, but no such trees are found! In addition to the Bristlecone Pines discussed above, the giant sequoias in California can also live longer, but the oldest living sequoias can only be traced back about 3,200 years.[66] The answer is that these trees began their lives after the Flood.

Landscapes Formed by Catastrophic Processes

When the Flood waters drained from the Earth, many landscapes were formed that can't be explained by isolated local floods or slower processes supposedly occurring over thousands and even millions of years. These landscapes are referred to as erosional remnants or left-overs. They are not forming today. The list is long so we will discuss only some of the more obvious surface features. There are many elevated areas around the world that have very conspicuous flat-topped surfaces. The Colorado Plateau, for example, is made of several plateaus that range in elevation between 5,000 feet to 11,000 feet above sea level and covers an area of 130,000 square miles.

Figure 11. Western Edge of the Colorado Plateau East of Las Vegas, Nevada (notice peneplained surfaces on the plateau)

Most people are familiar with the plateaus, mesas, and buttes found in such places as Grand Canyon and Canyonlands National Park. Large volumes of receding Flood waters washed away thousands of feet of sediment, leaving relatively flat-lying surfaces forming these plateaus, mesas and buttes.

Figure 12. Canyonlands in Eastern Utah

These flat surfaces are called peneplains or planation surfaces and are only formed by strong currents of water spread over large areas. Peneplains are found worldwide and are not forming today.[67] The Beartooth Mountains of Montana and western Wyoming contain a remarkable peneplained surface at the summit that rises 12,000 feet above sea level.

Figure 13. Beartooth Mountains

These flat-topped surfaces are best explained by large-scale sheet erosion due to the retreating Flood waters that occurred as mountains were building.

In western North America, the many dry lake basins were filled with water and formed a network of connected lakes in the recent past. Ancient Lake Manley filled the Death Valley basin and connected with lakes found in the Mojave Desert to the south. The Great Salt Lake in Utah which covers an area of 1,700 square miles and average depth of sixteen feet looks large, but is actually much smaller than the lake that once occupied that territory. If ancient Lake Bonneville was around today, it would have swallowed the Great Salt Lake and surrounding areas. Lake Bonneville was eleven times larger than Great Salt Lake and one thousand feet deep. The shorelines of the ancient lake are found 984 feet above the present lake level.

Figure 14. Great Salt Lake with Wasatch Mountains in the Background (when Lake Bonneville was around the lake level was about 1000 feet higher as recorded in the shore lines in the mountains)

What happened to the lake's water? Apparently, the natural dam that once held Lake Bonneville broke. It must have been terrible to witness the ancient catastrophe, as the lake discharged its huge volume of water towards the north, running over southeastern Idaho through the Snake River basin and out to the Pacific Ocean. It left an array of carved canyons in its wake.

Most river beds today are considered underfit because the current river or stream is too small to have eroded the valley in which it flows. Wide river channels or river valleys attest to the large amounts of water the river carried in the past. If we looked at the Snake River valley we would see that the current river does not fit the valley. The valley was formed rapidly by the catastrophic release of ancient Lake Bonneville. Many areas in Utah and Nevada show that large volumes of water drained from the land in the past. The Virgin River in Utah starts near Zion National Park, follows the Virgin River Gorge, and empties into Lake Mead, Nevada. This is what we see in the modern landscape on Earth: evidence that in the past large volumes of water drained from the land. A world-encompassing flood could have filled ancient large lakes that later drained, producing the erosional remnant landscapes we see in western North America and worldwide.

Noah's Ark

If there was a worldwide Flood, then all life on Earth would have been blotted out. But today the planet teems with millions of plants and animals. Where did they come from? The Bible states that Noah built an Ark, Genesis 6:15. On board were his wife, his three sons with their wives, as well as animals of every kind. Some question the size of this boat, how many animals were on the boat, and how the animals repopulated Earth after the waters drained. These are good questions when asked by someone who genuinely wants answers. Let us answer each in turn.

The Bible gives us the dimensions of the Ark: 300 x 50 x 30 cubits. In ancient times, a cubit was measured by the length from a man's elbow to the tip of his fingers. Using the long or royal cubit definition, this translates to Ark dimensions of about 510 x 85 x 51 feet. Using a more conservative cubit of about 17.5 inches, the Ark would have been approximately 437.5 x 72.92 x 43.75 feet. This translates to a total volume of about 1,396,000 cubic feet. The inside dimensions of a 40-foot school bus gives about 2,080 cubic feet of space. Therefore, 671 school buses without their wheels and axels could fit inside of Noah's Ark. If each bus carried 50 students, then 33,550 kids could easily fit in the Ark. Wow! And there would even be enough room left over for food and other supplies. The Ark had plenty of room!

Figure 15. Life-size Replica of Noah's Ark (Built by John Huibers in Dordrecht, Netherlands)

Figure 16. Life-size Replica of Noah's Ark (Notice the giraffe on the front of the ship)

Another interesting fact about the Ark is that God knew *exactly what He was doing* when He gave Noah the specific dimensions for building the Ark. In fact, in 1993 Dr. Seon Won Hong[68] conducted a scientific study to investigate the seaworthiness of the Ark at the renowned ship research center KRISO (now called MOERI) in South Korea.[69] After evaluating the seaworthiness of over 10 various ship dimensions, the study showed that the Ark dimensions given in the Bible were ideal for handling everything a highly turbulent sea could throw at it.

In fact, this study showed that the Ark could handle 100-foot waves.

An earlier study conducted in the 17th Century by Peter Jansen of Holland showed that the length-to-width ratio of the Ark (about 6-to-1) was ideal for such a massive, non-powered sea vessel (some oil tankers are 7-to-1). He also demonstrated using replica models of the Ark that it was almost impossible to capsize.[70]

How Many Animals Were aboard the Ark?

Noah only took air-breathing, land-dwelling, animals with nostrils onto the Ark. Some marine creatures like fish and amphibians could survive the Flood. Some seeds would sprout and root various plants and trees, and Genesis 6:21 tells us that Noah brought plants and seeds onto the Ark as well. How many animals were there? There are many estimates as to this number. First, it is important to understand that not every species (under most current definitions of this term) had to be on the Ark—only pairs of each animal *kind*. Equating "kind" with the standard "genus" names overestimates the number at 8,000 kinds.[71] A basic kind of animal for example would be a dog or cat. There are many different kinds of dogs today but Noah only had to take two dogs, a male and a female (e.g., wolves, coyotes, and domestic dogs can inter-breed and represent the same "kind").

Taking two of each "kind" means that no more than 16,000 animals had to be on the Ark to reproduce the animal life we see today. What about those few animals that grew to great sizes, like sauropod dinosaurs? Rather than bringing large animals that may have passed their reproductive primes, it is likely that Noah brought younger adolescent animals on the Ark. All the animals, a large measure of which were probably bird kinds, averaged about the size of a sheep.[72] Reflecting on our school bus comparison, a lot of small animals could fit on the Ark with room to spare.

After the Flood, dry land appeared[73] and the animals left the Ark to repopulate the Earth. The climate and geographical conditions must have changed drastically. So, the basic kinds of animals would have to adapt to different environments. This is what scientists see today. The same kind of animal can adapt to a different environment by changing certain characteristics. For example, some birds can change the size and shape of their beak in order to eat certain nuts or insects. The bird hasn't changed into a different kind of animal such as a reptile, and it hasn't even generated a non-bird body feature. It is still a bird with a different size and shape beak. This process has generated from the original "kinds" that left the Ark—the many different animal and plant varieties we see today.

The drastic climate changes that occurred after the Flood also led to humans living shorter lives,[74] the ice age,[75] and many of the dinosaurs that survived the Flood via the Ark to go extinct faster than many other animals (e.g., due to the scarce food supply and increased competition for habitat).[76]

Was the Flood Local or Global?

In an effort to try to align scripture with secular views of geology, some people represent that the Flood a local event limited to the area where Noah lived (i.e. the Mesopotamian Valley region). However, following the exercise of going through Genesis chapters 6 through 9 and underlining all of the sentences and words that indicate a global Flood usually leads to *hundreds* of words being underlined. The Scripture is exceedingly clear that the Flood was global, and not local. In addition, there are eight clear reasons for believing the Genesis Flood was a global, catastrophic event:

1. **Massive geologic layers:** The Genesis Flood laid down millions of cubic feet of sediment (i.e., mud) all over the globe which hardened into rock. These layers contain the vast majority of the fossil record and are often similar in composition. Some of these massive layers,

such as the Kaibab Upwarp in the Grand Canyon, are bent into steep curves, proving they were laid down rapidly and then bent before hardening into rock.
2. **Fossil record:** The fossil record is world-wide and shows evidence of rapid burial. Specific examples include clam and oyster shells on mountain tops that were fossilized in the closed position, fish buried in the process of eating other fish, and even fish that were buried while giving birth.
3. **The Flood covered the highest mountains**: Scripture says that the "waters rose and increased greatly on the earth, and the ark floated on the surface of the water. They rose greatly on the earth, and *all the high mountains under the entire heavens were covered.* The waters rose and covered the mountains to a depth of more than fifteen cubits." (Genesis 7:18-20, emphasis added). Since water seeks its own level, it would be impossible for the water to cover the highest mountains and still be only a local event.
4. **Purpose of the Flood**: Due to widespread problems caused by sin, God decided to wipe out all of mankind, the land dwelling animals and birds (except for those who were on the Ark). God said the earth "was corrupt and filled with violence" (Genesis 6:11-12), and that He was going to "bring floodwaters to destroy every creature on the face of the earth that has the breath of life in it" (Genesis 6:17). He also specifically mentioned people multiple times: "I will wipe from the face of the earth the human race I have created" (Genesis 6:7). Since it is highly improbable that all of the people on earth lived in the Mesopotamian Valley region, a local flood would not have accomplished God's purpose.
5. **Use of the words "all" and "every" and "everything" in Genesis chapters 6-9**: The words "all," "every" and "everything" are used 66 times in the Genesis Flood account. Many of these verses describe the creatures and people that perished during the flood. It is very

clear by the context of these passages that God meant He was going to destroy all living creatures that live on land (except for those on the Ark). For example: "Every living thing that moved on land perished—birds, livestock, wild animals, all the creatures that swarm over the earth, and all mankind. Everything on dry land that had the breath of life in its nostrils died. Every living thing on the face of the earth was wiped out; people and animals and the creatures that move along the ground and the birds were wiped from the earth. Only Noah was left, and those with him in the ark" (Genesis 7:21-23, emphasis added).

6. **The Ark**: It took Noah and his family over 100 years to build the Ark. If the Flood was just a local event, why would God tell Noah to build a ship over 400 feet long (Genesis 6:15) and then bring on board all of the different kinds of animals including birds to be saved? (Genesis 6:19-21). If the flood was only a local event, there would be no need for an ark—Noah and the animals that God wanted to save would have had plenty of time to travel to a safer area.

7. **God's Covenant**: in Genesis 9:11, God made a promise, "Never again will all life be destroyed by the waters of a flood; never again will there be a flood to destroy the earth." This promise doesn't make any sense if the flood was local.

8. **Jesus believed in a global flood**: In Luke 17:26-27, Jesus is discussing his worldwide return and rapture and said: "Just as it was in the days of Noah, so also will it be in the days of the Son of Man. People were eating, drinking, marrying and being given in marriage up to the day Noah entered the ark. Then the flood came and *destroyed them all*."

Conclusion

Only a catastrophic, worldwide flood could deposit thousands of feet of sedimentary rock layers that almost covered whole continents. Within these sediments, billions of dead animals were buried and fossilized, just as we would expect from the Bible's Flood account. Late Flood upheavals lifted some of these sedimentary rocks with their fossils to the highest peaks in the world for all to see. Continents, fossils, and mountains are what we would expect to see if there really was a worldwide Flood as described in Genesis.

Chapter 4: The Age of the Earth, Dating Methods, and Evolution
Roger Sigler, M.S.

    This section is important because an "ancient Earth" is foundational to evolutionary theory. As one high school biology textbook states: "Evolution takes a long time. If life has evolved, then Earth must be very old…Geologists now use radioactivity to establish the age of certain rocks and fossils. This kind of data could have shown that the Earth is young. If that had happened, *Darwin's ideas would have been refuted and abandoned*. Instead, radioactive dating indicates that Earth is about 4.5 billion years old—plenty of time for evolution and natural selection to take place"[77] (emphasis added).

    Thus, biology and earth science textbooks today will admit that "billions" (for the Earth) and "millions" (for life on Earth) of years are necessary for evolutionary theory to hold up. These books use these "ancient" dating ideas to assert that fossils are proof of biological evolution. What we will find out in this section, however, is that the age of God's Creation is younger than these textbooks state, and that the dating methods used to establish the "old Earth" are flawed in many respects.

Overview

    Fossil remains are found in sedimentary rock layers. Layers of sediment are formed when various size particles (e.g., dirt, rocks, and vegetation) accumulate in places such as deserts, rivers, lakes, and the ocean. Most texts teach that it takes a long time for these sediments to build up, with older layers buried beneath younger layers. Fossils found in lower layers are deemed to be older than those in the upper layers, older on the bottom younger on the top. This is called relative age dating. To help establish the relative ages of rock layers and their fossils, evolutionary scientists use *index fossils*.

    Index fossils are distinct fossils, usually an extinct organism, used to establish and correlate the relative ages of rock layers. Index fossils have a short stratigraphic or vertical range, which means they are found in only a few layers, though in many widespread places. Evolutionists assume that the creature evolved somehow, lived for a certain time period, and then died out. Textbooks are correct when they state that relative dating provides no information whatsoever about a fossil's absolute age. Nevertheless, most textbook writers and the scientists they cite all grew up with a belief in uniformitarian geologic processes. The principle of uniformity is a philosophy and an assumption that the slow geologic processes going on today is how the deposits of the past happened, or that the present is the key to the past. This assumption works well enough only for recent deposits such as the Quaternary and certain formations in the Tertiary periods (see Figure 17). However, if you really want to learn, keen observations in the field testify that the rock layers were laid down catastrophically.

What you are not being told is that many sedimentary deposits from most of the periods in the Paleozoic and Mesozoic eras are primarily marine, very extensive, and bear great evidence of very fast or catastrophic depositional processes. Fossils in pristine condition require that the animal or plant was buried rapidly; therefore, index fossils, rather than indicating a living environment over time, are nothing more than things buried quickly and suffocated under huge amounts of sediments transported by the ocean. Another thing is that these widespread oceanic deposits occur hundreds and even thousands of miles inland from the ocean. Furthermore, these marine sediments sit above granitic crust, composed primarily of granite and related rocks. Granite, by its very nature, floats so as to be a foundation for land, not the ocean.

At the present time the ages shown on the geologic time scale are based on radiometric age dating. In many textbooks, radiometric ages are considered absolute ages. However, as you will soon learn, it is far from absolute as far as dating goes, though is useful for other things. By reading this section you will learn the truth and know more about the evidences for a young Earth than most adults. You will discover why the land, sea, and air are young; how dinosaur bones and other fresh fossils are young; and why diamonds belched from the bowels of the Earth were made fast and are young, even though all of these things originated as living things on the Earth's surface! So let's get started.

The Age of the Earth

The alleged age of the Earth is based on an interpretation of its radioactivity. The planet itself is given an age of 4.5 billion years and the various rock layers are given names with assigned ages (Figure 17). In many textbooks, radiometric ages are considered absolute ages. In reality, the ages are far from absolute. To understand exactly why, we must first learn the basics of radioactive elements, and of the techniques used when treating these systems of elements as clocks.

The ages of the geologic periods shown in Figure 17 are based primarily on radioactive isotopes. Many elements on the periodic table have radioactive forms. Stable atoms have a set number of protons, neutrons, and orbital electrons. Isotopes are atoms of the same elements with the same number of protons but different numbers of neutrons, so these atoms are radioactive. This means its nucleus is not stable and will change or transmutate into another element over time by emitting particles and/or radiation.

EON	ERA	PERIOD	EPOCH	Alleged Age Years	Young Earth Evidences
Phanerozoic (This is where most fossils occur)	Cenozoic	Quaternary	Holocene	10,000	
			Pleistocene	2,600,000	Soft Frog with bloody bone marrow
		Tertiary	Pliocene	5,300,000	
			Miocene	23,000,000	⇐ Salamander muscle
			Oligocene	30,900,000	⇐ Young coal, Penguin feathers, Lizard skin
			Eocene	55,800,000	
			Paleocene	65,500,000	
	Mesozoic	Cretaceous		145,500,000	⇐ Young Diamonds, Young Coal
		Jurassic		201,600,000	Dinosaur DNA, blood, blood vessels and protein
		Triassic		251,000,000	
	Paleozoic	Permian		299,000,000	
		Pennsylvanian		318,000,000	⇐ Young Coal
		Mississippian		359,000,000	
		Devonian		416,000,000	
		Silurian		444,000,000	
		Ordovician		488,000,000	
		Cambrian		542,000,000	
Precambrian	Proterozoic Eon				⇐ Helium in zircon crystals
				2,500,000,000	
	Archean Eon			3,850,000,000	

Figure 17. Uniformitarian Geologic Time Scale (with problems noted). The time scale is placed vertically because older sedimentary deposits are buried beneath younger sedimentary deposits. The assumption of slow geologic processes and radiometric age dating has drastically inflated the age of the Earth and its strata.

A basic way to measure the rate of radioactive decay is called the half-life. This is the length of time needed for 50% of a quantity of radioactive material to decay. Unstable radioactive isotopes called parent elements decay (or give birth to) stable elements called daughter elements. Each radioactive element has its own specific half-life (see Table 5).

Table 5: Radiometric Isotopes and Half Lives

Examples of Radioactive Isotopes that Change into Stable Elements		
Radioactive Parent Element	Stable Daughter Element	Half-Life
Carbon-14 (^{14}C)	Nitrogen-14 (^{14}N)	5,730 Years
Potassium-40 (^{40}K)	Argon-40 (^{40}Ar)	1.3 Billion Years
Uranium-238 (^{238}U)	Lead-206 (^{206}Pb)	4.5 Billion Years
Rubidium-87 (^{87}Rb)	Strontium-87 (^{87}Sr)	48.6 Billion Years

Note: Carbon 14 is not used to date minerals or rocks, but is used for organic remains that contain carbon, such as wood, bone, or shells.

To find the age of a rock, geologists review the ratio between radioactive parent and stable daughter products in the rock or in particular minerals of the rock. Igneous rocks—those that have formed from molten magma or lava—are the primary rock types analyzed to determine radiometric ages. For example, let's assume that when an igneous rock solidified, a certain mineral in it contained 1000 atoms of radioactive potassium (^{40}K) and zero atoms of argon (^{40}Ar). After one half-life of 1.3 billion years, the rock would contain 500 ^{40}K and 500 ^{40}Ar atoms, since 50% has decayed. This is a 500:500 or 500 parent/500 daughter ratio, which reduces to 1:1 or 1/1 ratio. If this was the case, then the rock would be declared to be 1.3 billion years old. If the ratio is greater than 1/1, then not even one half-life has expired, so the rock would be younger. But if the ratio is less than 1/1, then the rock is considered older than the half-life for that system.

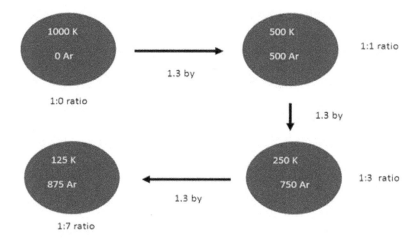

Figure 18. Decay of Radioactive potassium-40 to argon-40. Decay of Radioactive potassium-40 to argon-40. "BY" means "billions of years," K is potassium, Ar is argon. After three half-lives of this system, totaling 3.9 billion years, only 125 of the original set of 1000 radioactive potassium-40 atoms remain, assuming that the system has decayed evenly for all that time.

Dating a rock requires four basic assumptions:

1. Laboratory measurements that have no human error or misjudgments;
2. The rock began with zero daughter element atoms;
3. The rock maintained a "closed system;" (defined below) and
4. The decay rate remained constant.

Let's describe each of these. Measuring the radioactive parent and stable daughter elements to obtain the ratio between them must be accurate, and it usually is. But keep in mind that most laboratory technicians in dating labs have been trained in a belief of an old Earth, which may set preconceived ideas about the time periods they expect. They all memorized the typical geologic time scale, and thus may not have an open mind to the idea that the accurately measured isotope ratios may have come from processes other than radioisotope decay.

Next, this technician assumes that all the radioactive parent isotopes began decaying right when the mineral crystallized from a melt. He also assumes none of the stable daughter element was present at this time. How can anyone claim to know the mineral really began with 100% radioactive parent and 0% daughter elements? What if some stable daughter element was already present when the rock formed?

A closed system means that no extra parent or daughter elements have been added or removed throughout the history of the rock. Have you ever seen an atom? Of course not. It is really microscopic, but we must think about this assumption on an atomic level. For example, decay byproducts like argon and helium are both gases. Neither gas tends to attach to any other atom, meaning they are rarely involved in chemical reactions. Instead of reacting with atoms in rock crystals, they build up in rock systems and can move in and out of the rocks. In fact, a leading expert in isotope geology states that most minerals do not even form in closed systems. He emphasizes that for a radioactive-determined date to be true, the mineral must be in a closed system.[78] Is there any such thing as a closed system when speaking of rocks?

The constant-decay rate assumption involves the decay rate remaining the same throughout the history of the rock. Lab experiments have shown that most changes in temperature, pressure, and the chemical environment have very little effect on decay rates. These experiments have led researchers to have great confidence that this is a reasonable assumption, but it may not hold true. Is the following quote an overstatement of known science? "Radioactive transmutations must have gone on at the present rates under all the conditions that have existed on Earth in the geologic past."[79] Some scientists have found incredible evidence in zircon minerals showing that radioactive decay rates were much higher in the past.

Some of these assumptions are analogous to walking into a room where "...there is a burning candle sitting on the table. How long has that candle been burning? This can be calculated if the candle's *burn rate* and *original length* is known. However, if the original length is not known, or if it cannot be verified that the burning rate has been constant, it is impossible to tell for sure how long the candle was burning. A similar problem occurs with radiometric dating of rocks. Since the initial physical state of the rock is unknowable, the age can only be estimated according to certain assumptions."[80]

Helium and Accelerated Decay Rate

The amount of radiometric decay that has happened in igneous rocks like granite containing the mineral zircon is most often calculated by measuring the amount of radioactive uranium-238 and the amount of stable lead-206 within a given crystal. Decaying uranium-238 forms eight helium atoms on its way to becoming Lead-206. The helium atoms are temporarily trapped within the zircon crystal, which is considered about as closed a system as possible in the world of minerals. However, helium atoms are small, very lightweight, fast-moving, and do not form chemical bonds that would lock them with other atoms. They can therefore leak out of solids and into the atmosphere by passing through microscopic cracks in minerals, or by diffusing right through the solid walls of the mineral itself; that is, through the spaces in the crystal's net-like atomic arrangement. Think of a crystalline atomic lattice as a cage made of chain-link fencing. Dogs remain trapped in the cage, but squirrels can pass through the spaces. Helium atoms are like the small animals. They can squeeze through the spaces of the atomic lattice. Have you ever wondered why those helium balloons given at parties do not stay afloat for very long? It's because the helium atoms leak through the rubber.

In the 1970s, Los Alamos National Laboratories collected core samples of the Jemez granodiorite. It is considered a Precambrian granitic rock and bears an assigned age of 1.5 billion years based on uranium-238 – lead-206 dating. The rate of helium that leaks out or diffuses through the granodiorite was then measured at an internationally renowned laboratory. By dividing the amount of helium left in the rock with the measured diffusion rate of helium through the zircon crystals and other nearby minerals (e.g., mica), it is possible to measure how long ago the radioactive decay happened—as long as we make the required assumptions. This is the same concept as measuring the age of a helium balloon by knowing the amount of helium left in it and dividing by the rate at which the helium left the balloon. Amazingly, the radiometric decay that generated the helium within these zircon crystals had to have happened within the last 6000 +/-2000 years. There is no known mechanism which could have forced the helium to remain within these rocks for a longer period of time.

So here is the great mystery: One clock is based on the decay of one parent isotope uranium-238 into two daughter products, lead-206 and helium. The other clock is based on the rate that the helium produced from the decay diffuses through the mineral zircon. Since helium is therefore tightly coupled to the U-238 to Pb-206 decay process, nobody expected to find much helium in the rock believed to be 1.5 billion years old. However, the high concentrations of helium in the zircons show that the helium production time period must have been short and the nuclear decay process must therefore have been greatly accelerated. This would also explain why there just simply is not enough radioactively produced helium in the atmosphere to account for billions of years of decay.

Helium in the Atmosphere

Some of the helium produced from the U-238 – Pb-206 decay process enters the atmosphere from the Earth's crust. It quickly rises through the lower atmosphere like letting go of a helium-filled party balloon. The estimated rate is 2,000,000 atoms/cm^2/second. But forces such as gravity, escape velocity, and changes in temperature and density in the upper atmosphere significantly reduce the rate that helium atoms can escape into outer space. The amount of helium that escapes into outer space is estimated to be only 50,000 atoms/cm²/second. If the Earth's atmosphere had zero helium when it was formed, then today's measured amount of 1.1×10^{20} atoms/cm² would have been produced in just 2 million years.[81] This is about 500 times younger than the secular age of most granitic rocks, and more than 2,000 times younger than the evolutionary age of the Earth.

Brand New Rocks Give Old "Ages"

There is now a great abundance of evidence in the science literature about rocks giving ages much older than they really are. Warnings go back to the late 1960s and 1970s, but most of the scientific community is still not paying attention. Radiogenic argon and helium contents of recent basalt lava erupted on the deep ocean floor from the Kilauea volcano in Hawaii were measured. Researchers calculated up to 22,000,000 years for brand new rocks![82] The problem is common (see Table 6).

Table 6: Young Volcanic Rocks with Really Old Whole-Rock K-Ar Model Ages [83]

Lava Flow, Rock Type, and Location	Year Formed or Known Age	^{40}K-^{40}Ar "Age"
Kilauea Iki basalt, Hawaii	A.D. 1959	8,500,000 years
Volcanic bomb, Mt. Stromboli, Italy	A.D. 1963	2,400,000 years
Mt. Etna basalt, Sicily	A.D. 1964	700,000 years
Medicine Lake Highlands obsidian, Glass Mountains, California	<500 years	12,600,000 years
Hualalai basalt, Hawaii	A.D. 1800–1801	22,800,000 years
Mt. St. Helens dacite lava dome, Washington	A.D. 1986	350,000 years

The oldest real age of these recent volcanic rocks is <500 years. But most are even much younger than this; people witnessed the molten lava solidify into rock just decades ago. In fact, many of these were only about 10 years old or less when tested. And yet ^{40}K-^{40}Ar dating gives ages from 350,000 to >22,800,000 years.

Potassium-Argon (^{40}K-^{40}Ar) has been the most widespread method of radioactive age-dating for the Phanerozoic rocks, where most of the fossils are. The initial condition assumption is that there was no radiogenic argon (^{40}Ar) present when the igneous rock formed. But just like the helium problem, there is too much (^{40}Ar) present in recent lava flows, so the method gives excessively old ages for recently formed rocks. The argon amounts in these rocks indicate they are older than their known ages. Could the argon have come from a source other than radioactive potassium decay? If so, then geologists have been trusting a faulty method.

These wrong radioisotope ages violate the initial condition assumption of zero (0%) radioactive argon present when the rock formed. Furthermore, there was insufficient time since cooling for measurable amounts of ^{40}Ar to have accumulated in the rock, due to the slow radioactive decay of ^{40}K. Therefore, radiogenic Argon (^{40}Ar) was *already present* in the rocks as they formed.

Radiometric age dating should no longer be sold to the public as providing reliable absolute ages. Excess argon invalidates the initial condition assumption for potassium dating, and excess helium invalidates the closed-system assumption for uranium dating. The ages shown on the uniformitarian geologic time scale should be removed.

Coal Deposits Are Young

Carbon dating is used for organic materials such as wood, bone and other materials that contain carbon, not inorganic rocks. Radioactive carbon or carbon-14 (^{14}C) has been found in coal and other ancient materials deep in the geologic record. Given the short ^{14}C half-life of 5,730 years, organic materials purportedly older than 100,000 years (nearly 18 half-lives) should contain absolutely no detectable ^{14}C.[84]

Recall that the way scientists use radioisotope dating is by first measuring the ratio of radioactive parent versus stable versions of an element. Carbon dating works a bit differently, instead basing an age calculation on the ratio of radioactive carbon (^{14}C) to normal carbon (^{12}C). Carbon-14 decays to nitrogen, not carbon. Using a formula that compares that ratio, called the "percent modern carbon" or "pMC" in a sample to a standard modern pMC ratio, scientists calculate carbon ages for carbon-containing materials.

Astonishing discoveries over the past 30 years come from highly sensitive Accelerator Mass Spectrometer (AMS) methods used to test organic samples show measurable amounts of ^{14}C from every portion of the fossil-bearing rock layers all around North America (see Table 7).

Table 7: Carbon in Coal Deposits[85]

Coal Seam Name	Location	Geologic Interval of Deposition	^{14}C/C (pMC)
Bottom	Freestone County, TX	Eocene	0.30
Beulah	Mercer County, ND	Eocene	0.20
Pust	Richland County, MT	Eocene	0.27
Lower Sunnyside	Carbon County, UT	Cretaceous	0.35
Blind Canyon	Emery County, UT	Cretaceous	0.10
Green	Navajo County, AZ	Cretaceous	0.18
Kentucky #9	Union County,	Pennsylvanian	0.46

	KY		
Lykens Valley #2	Columbia County, PA	Pennsylvanian	0.13
Pittsburgh	Washington County, PA	Pennsylvanian	0.19
Illinois #6	Macoupin County, IL	Pennsylvanian	0.29

    The percentage of modern carbon (pMC) ranges (0.10–0.46) in the coal seams corresponds to radiocarbon ages roughly from 40,000 to 60,000 carbon years. But the conventional interval from the bottom of the Pennsylvanian layers to the top of the Eocene layers spans many millions of years, from 318,000,000 to 34,000,000 years. So which age are we supposed to believe, that coal is hundreds of millions, tens of millions, or only tens of thousands of years old? Maybe all are wrong.

    Furthermore, $^{14}C/C$ ratios have about the same average amount of pMC regardless of the supposed geologic ages assigned to them. For Pennsylvanian coal, the average is 0.27; for Cretaceous coal, the average is 0.21; and for Eocene coal, the average is 0.26. These all show about the same pMC. What might this consistency indicate? It looks like the plant debris that eventually became coal was uprooted or died at about the same time. There is no doubt that the tectonic upheaval that occurred during Noah's Flood did this when the fountains of the great deep ruptured according to Genesis 7:11. The dead plant debris then floated and sank at different weeks during the Flood and in some number of years afterwards as geologic processes of the Earth steadily stabilized. As a result of this cataclysmic Flood, continuous deposition of huge amounts of sediments compressed the plant debris into coal seams in various stratigraphic levels.

    Not only have scientists discovered young-looking, still radioactive carbon in coal, but also in fossils including wood, amber, dinosaur bones, and other Earth materials like the one we discuss next.

Diamonds Are Forever Young

Equally as remarkable as radioactive carbon in coal is the presence of ^{14}C in diamonds. Diamonds are almost purely carbon. These gorgeous crystals and the mineral inclusions trapped inside them when growing give evidence they formed at great depths. Based on the types of mineral inclusions, diamonds now sampled and mined at or near the Earth's surface originated under extreme temperatures and pressures deep within the Earth, at depths from around 200 km to over 1000 km.[86]

Recently, diamonds were discovered that contain isotopically light organic carbon. This means that the carbon originated by photosynthesis on the Earth's surface. The organic carbon from some living things (maybe algae?) that died ended up on the ocean floor, and was then subducted along with oceanic crust deep into the mantle. The authors of one technical study wrote that "subducted organic carbon can retain its isotopic signature even into the lower mantle."[87] They estimate that the diamonds formed at a depth of about 1000 km (600 miles) or so based on mineral inclusions within them (see Table 8).

Table 8: Carbon in Diamonds from Kimberlite Pipes[88]

Kimberlite Pipe	Location	Geologic Interval of Eruption	$^{14}C/C$ (pMC)
Kimberley-1	Kimberley, South Africa	Cretaceous	0.02
Orapa-A	Orapa mine, Botswana, Africa	Cretaceous	0.01
Orapa-F	Orapa mine, Botswana, Africa	Cretaceous	0.03
Letlhakane-1	Letlhakane mine, Botswana, Africa	Cretaceous	0.04
Letlhakane-3	Letlhakane mine, Botswana, Africa	Cretaceous	0.07

Then, mainly during the Cretaceous interval during the Flood, explosive eruptions all around the world brought the diamonds up from these great deep places back to the Earth's surface, where they are now found in unique igneous structures called kimberlite pipes. Even some jewelry television commercials assert the whole process takes about a billion years or so. But like coal, there should not be any detectable carbon-14, if diamonds are really that old.

And yet, diamonds from five different mines in Africa were studied (Table 8). The diamonds contain measurable radioactive carbon-14 with an average of 0.03–0.04 pMC, which equates to roughly 65,000 radiocarbon years.[89] These diamonds were supposed to have formed long before the Cretaceous eruption, supposedly 145,500,000 years ago. The 65,000-year time period is a tiny fraction of time compared to the imaginary inflated age of 145,500,000 years. Radioactive carbon in pre-Cretaceous diamonds clearly refutes the millions-of-years age assignment for Cretaceous materials as well as the supposed billion years to make diamonds.

Fresh Meat in Old Rocks

Recent discoveries of fresh tissues within fossils all around the world are quite surprising to paleontologists who assume that Earth's strata formed over millions of years of deposition. If the rock layers are really millions of years old, then fresh proteins, DNA, and cell tissue should no longer exist.

In the Yunnan Province, China, researchers discovered protein in sauropod dinosaur embryos found in fossil eggs supposedly 190,000,000 years old. These proteins don't even last one million years. The presence of apatite, the mineral component that vertebrate animals and man manufacture into bone, found interwoven with embryonic bone tissue proves that the protein originated from organic matter directly from the dinosaurs.[90]

Exceptionally preserved sauropod eggshells discovered in Upper Cretaceous deposits in Patagonia, Argentina, contain young-looking tissues of embryonic titanosaurid dinosaurs. Since these original dinosaur proteins decay very rapidly, the scientists involved in the study imagined that "virtually instantaneous mineralization of soft tissues" (mineralization occurs when the bone material is replaced by minerals from the soil) somehow preserved them for millions of years.[91] But repeated lab studies show that even mineralized proteins don't last longer than hundreds of thousands of years. Mineralization may have been rapid enough to retain fragments of original biomolecules in these specimens. Retaining is reasonable, but calling upon mineralization to preserve proteins for millions of years is unscientific. Their results demonstrate that organic compounds and other biological structures still look similar to those found in modern eggshells, showing that perhaps only thousands of years have elapsed since the dinosaur eggs were catastrophically buried by flood sediments.

In addition to these two examples, dozens of discoveries have been reported in several scientific journals, primarily from the 1990s to the present. Here are a few of the incredible fresh finds along with their conventional ages in millions of years (MY):

- Salamander muscle, 18MY
- Intact soft Frog with bloody bone marrow, 10MY
- Ichthyosaur skin, 190MY
- Hadrosaur blood vessels, 80MY
- Archaeopteryx feather proteins, 150MY
- Mosasaur blood protein fragments, >65MY
- Penguin feathers, 36MY
- Scorpion shell including shell protein, 240MY
- Psittacosaurus skin, 125MY
- DNA from Hadrosaur bone cell nuclei, 65MY
- Lizard tail skin proteins, 40MY
- Type I collagen proteins (and whole connective tissues including elastin and laminin) from Tyrannosaurus Rex and Hadrosaur dinosaurs[92]

Think about this list for a moment. The idea that a frog, still soft with still-bloody-red colored bone marrow is 10,000,000 years old is preposterous. First of all, just to preserve soft body parts requires rapid burial. But even when buried in sediments, can fresh meat such as a soft frog, skin, proteins, blood, muscle tissue, and DNA really last for millions of years? Almost all the relevant laboratory decay studies demonstrate otherwise. The truth is that proteins, even locked inside bone tissue have a maximum shelf life between 200,000 to 700,000 years in an optimal burial environment, and DNA molecules in bone are estimated to be undetectable after about 10,000 years.[93] Genuine, original body molecules and tissues show that fossils are maybe thousands, but not millions of years old. Can you find any of this scientific data in your biology textbook?

The Young Ocean

Evolutionists believe the ocean to be 3,000,000,000 years—that's 3 billion years—old. But the sodium (Na+) content of the ocean has been increasing. The processes which add and remove dissolved sodium to and from the seawater of the ocean have been well known for many decades (Table 9). Scientists can use this data to estimate maximum age ranges for oceans.

Table 9: Present Day Sodium Inputs and Outputs of Sodium to/from the Oceans[94]

Sodium (Na+) Added to the Ocean		Sodium (Na+) Removed from Ocean	
Process	Amount x 10^{10} kg/year	Process	Amount x 10^{10} kg/year
Rivers	19.2	Sea Spray	6.0
Ocean Sediments	11.5	Cation Exchange	3.5
Groundwater from Continents	9.6	Burial of Pore Water in Sea Floor Sediments	2.2
Glacial Activity	4.0	Alteration of Basalt	0.44
Sea Floor Vents	1.1	Zeolite formation	0.08
Atmosphere, Volcanism, Marine Coastal Erosion	0.3	Halite Deposition	<0.004
Total Input Rate	**45.7**	**Total Output Rate**	**12.2**

Only about 1/4 (12.2/45.7) of the present amount of sodium added to the ocean can be accounted for by known removal processes. This indicates that the sodium concentration of the ocean is not in equilibrium, but continues to increase. The increase in sodium is Input minus Output or 45.7 -12.2 = 33.5 x 10^{10} kg/year (Table 9). There is no way that this much added salt can be reconciled with a 3-billion-year-old ocean. The enormous imbalance shows that the ocean should contain *much more salt* if the ocean is really that old.

In 1990, the total amount of sodium in the ocean was estimated at 1.47×10^{19} Kg. The present-day increase of sodium to the oceans is 3.35×10^{11} kg/year (same as 33.5×10^{10} in above paragraph). If we begin with zero sodium–an ocean of pure fresh water–then the time to fill the ocean with sodium is $1.47 \times 10^{19} / 3.35 \times 10^{11}$ kg/year = 43,880,597 years or about 44 million years. This can be stretched to a maximum age of 62 million years when reduced input rates and maximum output rates are used.

But this does not mean the ocean is 44 to 62 million years old. The ocean must be much younger than this, since most ocean creatures need at least a little salt in their environment. Remember, the maximum age of 62 million years assumes that the ocean started as fresh water with 0% sodium and with no global catastrophic additions of sodium. Obviously, the original ocean contained a certain amount of sodium, making it far younger.

Just like sodium, rivers carry most of the sediments eroded from the continents into the ocean basins. The worldwide average depth of all the sediments on the seafloor is less than 1200 feet. More than 24,000,000,000 metric tons is dumped into the oceans each year. Only 1,000,000,000 tons of these deposits are dragged below the crust by tectonic plate subduction each year, which equates to 23,000,000,000 metric tons that accumulate on the seafloor. At this present rate, all these sediments would accumulate in only about 12,000,000 years into an empty ocean.[95]

Since the ocean is not likely to have begun as pure fresh water, the maximum age of 62,000,000 years based on salt content has been reduced to 12,000,000 years based on sediment input. But 12,000,000 years represents a maximum age limit because this assumes a completely empty ocean at the start and is based on present rates of deposition from the rivers.

In the Biblical Creation model, perhaps most of the sodium was added to the ocean by rapid geologic processes during creation, to support the marine life in the first place. God created the oceans on Day 3 to be inhabited on Day 5. Later,

Noah's Flood rapidly dumped who knows how much salt and sediment from its reworked continents into the ocean.

All the world's ocean floors look very young. They most likely resulted from catastrophic plate tectonic activity during the Flood.[96] When the floodwaters rapidly drained off emerging continents, the erosion and sedimentation rates into the oceans would have been exponentially greater than the present rate of accumulation. This is because the enormous ocean itself was receding off the continents at first. The volume of water and sediments carried back to the oceans was drastically higher during this receding process. In addition, perhaps more than a dozen "megafloods," like the one that carved the English Channel and another that carved Washington State's Snake River basin, catastrophically drained to quickly add more sediment during the post-Flood Ice Age. These events elevated sea level by 300 or so feet worldwide as tremendous ice sheets and glaciers melted over several centuries. Eventually it gave way to the lower amount of river sedimentation observed today. Thus, the best interpretation is that all the sediments on the ocean floor accumulated in just a few to several thousand years ago, since the Flood.

Summary of Young Earth Evidence

Why don't standard school textbooks include these solid scientific reasons and observations that refute conventional age assignments? Perhaps some scientists ignore the evidence for recent creation not because it's unscientific, but because they are simply unwilling to admit they are wrong, or unwilling to face the idea that there really hasn't been enough time for evolution to have occurred. There are other reasons, but they are all poor excuses for excluding these many solid reasons for a recent creation.

Interpretation of radiometric age dating by many in the scientific community has drastically inflated the age of the Earth. Old radioisotope ages assigned to newly formed rocks diminishes those techniques' reliability as "age" indicators. If it cannot be trusted for young rocks, then how can it be trusted for ones that are supposedly old? Two minerals, zircon and diamonds, are about as close to a closed system as we can imagine. And yet, zircon crystals contain too much helium and the atmosphere does not have enough to support the idea of an Earth that is billions or even millions of years old. Measurable amounts of carbon-14 in diamonds demonstrate that the Earth is only thousands of years old. Carbon-14 in coal of supposedly different ages indicates that the plant debris really lived in the same time period—what Biblical Creationists call the pre-Flood age. This is further demonstrated by the fact that the coals not only were sampled from different stratigraphic levels but also from widely separated locations. The consistency of the data and care with which they were acquired rule out contamination as an excuse for their young (relative to millions of years) carbon ages.

The carbon-14 ages of 40,000 to 65,000 years for coal seem to be very accurate and are much closer to the biblical age, but the Earth can even be younger than this. Fossils and fossil fuels demonstrate that the original Earth at the time of creation contained many more living things than today. The Flood and its aftereffects buried much of it. This large biomass—the total contribution of life to Earth's mass—is estimated to have been about 100 times greater than the total biosphere of living plants and animals today. This would have caused a much lower percent modern carbon (pMC) ratio of $^{14}C/C$, allowing us to reduce the calculated carbon ages to just several thousand years, which is more consistent with Scripture.[97]

This young age for the Earth matches quite well with the produced helium within the zircon crystals forming in about 6,000 years and the destruction of DNA within 10,000 years, which has even been found in dinosaur bones. These ages also match well with the recorded histories of mankind, the population growth rate of mankind which calculates to only a few thousand years, and the chronology in the Bible.

Chapter 5: Do Fossils Show Evolution?
David V. Bassett, M.S.

There is no more fundamentally important debate raging in the midst of the current global culture war of ideas than the controversy over origins. The creation-evolution issue is foundational to everyone's worldview and, as such, is a priority topic that must be regarded, wrestled with, and ultimately resolved. Since ultimate origins are "one-time only" happenings of the unobservable, non-repeatable past (referred to as "singularities"), they must *philosophically be accepted by faith*, based on what one believes about the beginning history of the Universe, of the Earth, of life, and of mankind. These faith-beliefs, in turn, result in predictions about the present-day world of which we are a part. Consequently, these expectations can be either confounded or confirmed by observable evidence and/or scientific experimentation. This line of reasoning can, and should, be applied to the fossil record of the Earth's surface rocks since these layers are present-day evidence of past geological processes and their fossil contents are present-day evidence of past biological organisms. The fossil record is thus where one should look to find scientific answers about the Earth's early history and its ancient life forms.

If the reader were to objectively examine the testimony of Earth's surface rocks and the fossil remains contained therein for insight regarding origins, they would find that the fossil record does not uphold *any* textbook claim that the fossils document evolutionary progression and random change through only natural means over hundreds of millions of years. It is this atheistic *religion of naturalism* (aka evolutionary humanism) which is being continuously—sometimes forcefully—promoted by our culture in an all-out attempt to secularize our society away from the belief that the cosmos has been created by a supernatural, eternal Being to whom we are morally responsible and inevitably accountable since we have been created—not evolved!—in His image. It is only this latter, Bible-based understanding (as revealed in the early chapters of the Book of Genesis) that is instead overwhelmingly confirmed by the fossil record's silent proclamation of detailed design, downward development and diversity, and the deluge-driven death of Noah's Flood!

In short, the fossils glaringly support the young-Earth Biblical history of the recent, special creation of our world followed by a single Earth-covering Flood on our planet less than 4,400 years ago. Thus, accepting the faith-claims of evolutionary naturalism or secular humanism as the proper perspective for interpreting the physical world (as relentlessly encouraged by today's public educational system and, unfortunately, also increasingly so by the private-school sector as well) is to be indoctrinated into a never-settled, anti-evidence religious system that is neither justified by thoughtful, consistent reasoning nor verified by solid, scientific evidence.

Introduction

Most scientific hypotheses describe experimentally repeatable occurrences which are directly observable in the present. Charles Darwin's concept of *"phyletic gradualism,"* the belief that all *phyla* (i.e., complex fundamental groups of living organisms) are biologically related to each other by means of *gradual*, upward evolution from a single-celled, ancestral form of the ancient past is, however, outside the scope of the scientific method of objective, observed, operational science.

By contrast, an explanatory framework, not a scientific hypothesis, deals with unique, irreversible, non-repeating, one-time-only events of the past—referred to as "ultimate origins" or "singularities." These fall in the realm of origin-science, also called forensic science. As first explained in the introduction to this book, origin-science hypotheses are open to both the individual opinion and worldview biases of the interpreter, and cannot be directly checked by the observation, theorization, and experimentation of the scientific method. Instead, their truth claims are evaluated by either comparing similarities between present and past causes or by considering circumstantial evidence through a pre-supposed, faith-based (biblical or naturalistic) worldview perspective.

Therefore, in the absence of direct observations made over supposed "deep time" (see introduction), Darwinists interpret the fossil record, or the remains of past life found within the rocks of the Earth's crust, as circumstantial evidence that biological species have originated solely by means of "natural selection" from a universal common ancestor. Do fossils really show the evolutionary "tree of life" preserved in stone? Thus, this Darwinian model shows that all life that has ever existed on Earth is one grand, biologically-related family would predict that this fossil record should show the following three features:

1. Ancestral Forms: Lowest rocks contain few relatively "simple" ancestral life forms (i.e., *the less-evolved root organisms*).
2. Intermediate Forms: Life forms gradually display new organs and other body designs in an uninterrupted, increasingly advanced chain (i.e., *the transitional trunk*).
3. Divergent Forms: Ever-increasing numbers of more and more genetically complex diverse organisms (i.e., *the more-evolved branches*) occupy the higher geological strata.

Upon closer inspection, however, the fossil record actually falsifies *all three* evolutionary model predictions. Instead, the fossil record biologically, paleontologically, and geologically supports *all* Biblical Creation criteria without exception. Each of these three will be evaluated next.

Strike One!—Evolutionary "Ancestral Forms" Never Existed

Rather than phyla coming about by natural selection somehow adding new genes and organs to pre-existent ancestors as Darwin's ideas predicted, the fossil record provides no hint in the lowest known fossil-bearing rocks (named "Precambrian" and "Cambrian") of single-celled organisms morphing into the multi-celled creatures. The "Cambrian Explosion" describes the sudden appearance of all the radically-different blueprint types of each animal all in one rock system. This gap—which has been confirmed within the fossil record globally—should not even exist locally if evolutionism is true.

Jonathan Wells, in his eye-opening book entitled *Icons of Evolution: Science or Myth?— Why Much of What We Teach about Evolution Is Wrong* wrote:

> …in Darwin's theory, there is no way phylum-level differences could have appeared right at the start. Yet that is what the fossil record shows… In other words, the highest levels of the biological hierarchy appeared right at the start. Darwin was aware of this, and considered it a major difficulty for his theory…Darwin was convinced, however, that the difficulty was only apparent…. Many paleontologists are now convinced that the major groups of animals really *did* appear abruptly in the early Cambrian. The fossil evidence is so strong, and the event so dramatic, that it has become known as "the Cambrian explosion," or "biology's big bang"[98] (emphasis added).

This sudden appearance of all the major, complex body-plans of biology in the lowest of the sedimentary rock layers without any clear-cut, "simpler" forms gradually leading up to them argues against evolution. This same evidence, however, can easily be interpreted as scientific support for the biblical teaching of an Earth-covering Flood rapidly burying the God-designed creatures of the pre-Flood ocean bottom at the very beginning of this catastrophe!

Strike Two!—Evolutionary "Transitional Forms" Never Existed

If all living things are indeed related to each other through a gradual development of pre-existing organisms as Charles Darwin said, and as is often illustrated by so-called branching "evolutionary tree" diagrams known as "phylogenetic charts," then we would expect to find countless intermediate species or transitional forms (i.e., one animal kind turning into another) between major biological groupings like phyla. Transitional *creatures*, supposedly exemplified by such headliners as ape-to-man "hominids," the coelacanth fish,[99] and Archaeopteryx (an extinct bird that evolutionists believe possesses some reptilian-like features causing it to be classified as an evolutionary transitional form[100]) are supposed to bridge classification boundaries by possessing transitional *features*.

However, even Archaeopteryx—promoted by evolutionists at one time as the prime example of an intermediate form or "missing link" candidate between reptiles and birds—would not qualify as a *transitional* fossil since its socketed teeth, long bony tail, and wing-claws are all *fully-formed* structures of its alleged fossil representatives, showing no signs of *partial* evolutionary development. Without true transitional structures, does the fossil record support or upsettingly contradict the Darwinian view of phyletic gradualism? Percival Davis and Dean H. Kenyon ask in their book, *Of Pandas and People* (1989):

> Does Darwin's theory match the story told by the fossils? To find out, we must first ask, what kind of story would it match? His theory posited that living things formed a continuous chain back to one or a few original cells. If the theory is true, the fossils should show a continuous chain of creatures, each taxon leading smoothly to the next. In other words, there should be a vast number of transitional forms connecting each

taxon with the one that follows. The differences separating major groups in taxonomy [such as invertebrates and the first fish] are so great that they must have been bridged by a huge number of transitional forms. As Darwin himself noted in *The Origin of Species* (1859), "The number of intermediate varieties, which formerly existed on earth [must] be truly enormous." *Yet this immense number of intermediates simply does not exist in the fossil record.* The fossils do not reveal a string of creatures leading up to fish, or to reptiles, or to birds. Darwin conceded this fact: "Why then is not every geological formation and every stratum full of such intermediate links? *Geology assuredly does not reveal any such finely graduated organic chain.*" Indeed, this is, in Darwin's own words, "the most obvious and gravest objection which can be urged against my theory"[101] (emphasis added).

    If evolutionary gradualism were true, then every organism's genetics would be evolving out of its inferior/past/ancestral code into a superior/future/descendant form. In short, *every life-form would be transitional* between what it once was and what it is evolving into. However, the fossil record does not match this idea. The origin of every distinct, self-bounded biological body plan is not connected by evolutionary intermediates with transitioning structures at all, either to the supposed "universal common ancestor" or to the plentiful variety within its own bounded phylum!
    Instead, all preserved and present phyla demonstrate *stasis*—the dominant fossil trend of maintaining anatomical sameness. They show essentially no change in appearance over time, though some show a decrease in size. In addition, 95% of the fossil record phyla are comprised of marine invertebrates, some of which are found throughout its entire vertical span of rocks. [102] Thus, the completeness of the fossil record is being

finally recognized after more than 150 years of fossil collecting and more than 200,000,000 fossils found. *Newsweek*'s 1980 admission of Darwin's elusive intermediate species being only imaginative is still embarrassingly accurate:

> The missing link between man and apes… is merely the most glamorous of a whole hierarchy of phantom creatures. *In the fossil record, missing links are the rule…* The more scientists have searched for the transitional forms between species, the more they have been frustrated.[103] (emphasis added)

In their journal disclosure, evolutionists Stephen Jay Gould and Niles Eldridge have honestly admitted the pseudo-scientific, philosophical origin of Darwin's view by their candid confession that *"Phyletic gradualism* [gradual evolution]… *was never 'seen' in the rocks* … It [gradualism] expressed the cultural and political biases of 19th century liberalism" (emphasis added).[104] Thus, the "onward and upward" notion of evolutionary progress involving innovation and integration was a product of various social prejudices, not science.

Darwin had every hope that future research would reveal numerous transitional forms in the fossil record.[105] Now, after 150+ years of digging and millions of additional fossils identified and catalogued, do we have enough evidence to conclude whether transitional forms exist? Remember, if evolution is true, it would take numerous "prior versions" to move between forms—e.g., from a mouse to a bat.

To investigate this issue, Dr. Carl Werner and his wife Debbie invested over 14 years of their lives investigating "the best museums and dig sites around the globe [and] photographing thousands of original fossils and the actual fossil layers where they were found."[106]

After visiting hundreds of museums and interviewing hundreds of paleontologists, scientists, and museum curators, Dr. Werner concluded: "Now, 150 years after Darwin wrote his book, this problem still persists. Overall, the fossil record is rich—200 million fossils in museums—but the predicted evolutionary ancestors are missing, seemingly contradicting evolution."[107] He continues with a series of examples:

- Museums have collected the fossil remains of 100,000 individual dinosaurs, but have not found a single direct ancestor for any dinosaur species.
- Approximately 200,000 fossil birds have been found, but ancestors of the oldest birds have yet to be discovered.
- The remains of 100,000 fossilized turtles have been collected by museums, yet the direct ancestors of turtles are missing.
- Nearly 1,000 flying reptiles (pterosaurs) have been collected, but no ancestors showing ground reptiles evolving into flying reptiles have been found.
- Over 1,000 fossil bats have been collected by museums, but no ancestors have been found showing a ground mammal slowly evolving into a flying mammal.
- Approximately 500,000 fossil fish have been collected, and 100,000,000 invertebrates have been collected, but ancestors for the theoretical first fish—a series of fossils showing an invertebrate changing into a fish—are unknown.
- Over 1,000 fossil sea lions have been collected, but not a single ancestor of sea lions has been found.
- Nearly 5,000 fossilized seals have been collected, but not a single ancestor has been found.

If this was not enough, one more key consideration should clearly convince. What if, after countless millions of hours spent by researchers mining the crust of the Earth for fossil evidence, the fossil record is essentially *complete*? That is, it stands to reason that the millions of fossils we have collected over the last 150 years *exhaustively* record all basic life forms that ever lived, with only a few additional "big surprises" to be found. Given this, can we say that the question of transitional forms has been *asked and answered*?

One way to find out is to "calculate the percentage of those animals living today that have also been found as fossils. In other words, if the fossil record is comprised of a high percentage of animals that are living today, then the fossil record could be viewed as being fairly complete; that is, most animals that have lived on the Earth have been fossilized and discovered."[108] Carl Werner provides a chart demonstrating the results of such an investigation:[109]

- Of the 43 living land animal *orders*, such as carnivores, rodents, bats, and apes, nearly all, or 97.7%, have been found as fossils. This means that at least one example from each animal order has been collected as a fossil.
- Of the 178 living land animal *families*, such as dogs, bears, hyenas, and cats, 87.8% have been found in fossils.

Evolution has had its chance—over 150 years and millions of fossils—to prove itself, and it has come up wanting. The theory has been weighed, tested, measured, and falsified. Aren't 200 million opportunities and one and one-half centuries enough time to answer the issue that *confounded* Darwin himself?

> Why, if species have descended from other species by fine gradations, do we not everywhere see innumerable transitional forms? Why is not all nature in confusion, instead of the species being, as we see them, well defined?…But, as by this theory innumerable transitional forms must have existed, why do we not find them embedded in countless numbers in the crust of the earth?…But in the intermediate region, having intermediate conditions of life, why do

we not now find closely-linking intermediate varieties? This difficulty for a long time quite confounded me. [110]

Strike Three!—Evolutionary "Divergent Forms" Never Existed

Darwinian evolution predicts that as phyla continue to diverge or branch out from their ancestral, evolutionary stock, their numbers should increase just as tree limbs radiate from a central trunk and then multiply outward from each other. According to Wells, "Some biologists have described this in terms of 'bottom-up' versus 'top-down' evolution. *Darwinian evolution is 'bottom-up,' referring to its prediction that lower levels in the biological hierarchy should emerge before higher ones. But the Cambrian explosion shows the opposite*" (emphasis added).[111] The fossil record evidence indicates that the number of phyla in fact decreases from about 50–60 at the "Cambrian Explosion" to approximately 37 living phyla. Extinction—the opposite of evolution's required new phyla—have certainly occurred.[112] *"Clearly the Cambrian fossil record explosion is not what one would expect from Darwin's theory. Since higher levels of the biological hierarchy appear first, one could even say that the Cambrian explosion stands Darwin's tree of life on its head"* (emphasis added).[113]

Rather than a "bottom-up" continuum of ever-morphing divergent forms, the fossil record clearly reveals definite gaps between and "top-down" hierarchical variation within phyla. In fact, these anatomical differences separating major design themes make biological classification of organisms (taxonomy) possible![114] Without these clear-cut gaps between organism kinds, biologists would not be able to divide plants and animals into their respective kingdoms, phyla, classes, orders, families, genera, and species.

Those familiar with the Bible will recognize that one would expect these gaps between biological kinds if all terrestrial life reproduced "after its own kind," a truth that the

Scriptures declares *ten times* in its first chapter (Genesis 1:11, 12, 21, 24, 25). In fact, even the New Testament affirms that "All flesh is not the same flesh, but there is one kind of flesh of men, another flesh of beasts, another of fish, and another of birds" (1 Corinthians 15:39). Obviously, since God's written Word lists different creature groupings as separate kinds with anatomically unique "flesh," biological classification ultimately describes "a created arboretum" of various types of trees, and not a single "evolutionary tree of life" that connects all organisms as Charles Darwin proposed.

With No Fossil Evidence to Support It, Gradualism Strikes Out!

Those who have scientifically examined the fossil record firsthand are justifiably adamant that it completely falsifies all three of the essential evolutionary elements needed to substantiate the concept of an integrated "tree of life." The fossil record bears witness that there are (1) *no ancestral roots*—no "primitive" organisms between microfossils and visible life, (2) *no transitional trunk*—no anatomically-intermediate creatures with structurally-transitional features (e.g., partially-evolved organs, limbs, etc.), and (3) *no divergent branches*—no new phyla being genetically descended from less-evolved "common ancestors."

Explaining the Fossil Record—A Creation Model Home Run!

Well, if the fossil record does not support the evolutionary predictions of ancestral roots, transitional trunk, and divergent branches with regard to the major categories of life, what does it show? To summarize thus far, the fossil record clearly reveals the following about the major classification divisions of organisms:

1. Separation from other phyla by definite, unbridgeable gaps with no ancestor-descendant/bottom-to-top transitional-relationship;
2. All forms suddenly appear as unique body plans with fully-formed characteristic structures;
3. All phyla are represented from the beginning by fossil forms, thus demonstrating fossil-record completeness;
4. All are complex, functional, and were or still are able to survive;
5. All show no innovative change in their basic anatomical form after they first appear as fossils—only minor, top-down variation within a blueprint design;
6. Nearly all (95%) are phyla of marine invertebrates;
7. Many of these are found throughout the fossil record, not restricted to a certain vertical range of rock; and
8. Extinction has decreased the number of sub-kingdom plant and animal classification divisions from 50–60 phyla to nearly 37 phyla—the opposite direction of evolution.

In addition, the fossil record confirms Biblical Creation/global Flood predictions by showing the following:

9. Polystrate fossils cutting across multiple rock layers, supporting rapid sedimentation and catastrophic burial of life-forms;
10. Fossil graveyard deposits;
11. Mass killing and the violent death of creatures;
12. Mixed groupings of organisms from various ecological zones of different habitat and elevation;
13. Highly energetic, destructive processes capable of burying organisms alive, ripping creatures apart, and/or transporting their carcasses great distances;
14. Rock formations with mostly ocean-dwelling creatures catastrophically fossilized;
15. All fossils in continental rocks, not ocean-bottom sediments;

16. Some geologic deposits covering hundreds of thousands of square miles and spanning several continents.

With this being the case, it should therefore be quite obvious that the fossil record is not at all like Charles Darwin's interpretation of an evolutionary "tree of life" preserved in stone. The fossil record has indeed had the last word!

Chapter 6: Natural Selection and Evolution: Do Darwin's Finches Prove Evolution?
Roger Patterson

As you open the typical biology textbook, you will be confronted with an evolutionary view of the world on almost every page. "Evolutionary processes" supposedly turn a single cell floating in an imaginary primordial ooze into a zebra fish or a zebra, and require billions of years to do so. Without these billions of years, natural selection and mutations would not have enough time to "work together" to bring about wholesale creature design changes—assuming they could do that even given an eternity. To accept the evolutionary development of life is to reject the clear meaning of God's description of the creation of life in Genesis 1. In this chapter you will learn of the differences between what evolutionists claim time and chance can accomplish and what we really know to be true from actual scientific studies and the description of God's creative acts in the Bible. Contrary to textbook assertions, you and I are far more than highly evolved animals, but special creations of God made in His image.

If you were to ask the typical person to explain biological evolution, the ideas of natural selection and mutations would surely be a part of their description. But is natural selection really able to accomplish what evolution needs it to accomplish? Can mutations account for the change of an amoeba into a horse? Has any of this actually been observed, or is there a lot of speculation involved? These are the kinds of questions that need to be answered as we sort through the claims found in textbooks and various video programs designed to teach the evolutionary view of how life came to exist on this planet.

The Naturalistic Worldview

Whenever we consider complex ideas like biological evolution, there are many assumptions that have to be made, or at least accepted, for the sake of discussion. The typical person who believes in an evolutionary process embraces a chain of assumptions—whether they realize it or not.

The explanations you will find in textbooks, various teaching videos, and hear in the classroom are almost always based on the worldview called naturalism. Those with a naturalistic worldview believe that everything we see in the universe can be explained by natural processes. To them, everything is a result of the laws of nature acting over time to produce what we see. Humans are simply the result of gravity, time, thermodynamics, natural selection, mutations, and chemical reactions. To a naturalist, there is no need for miracles or a god or anything we can't see and measure to produce the universe as we see it today—including every creature alive or extinct. In fact, the textbook you use might just include a statement like that in the early chapters that talk about what science is. In truth, we must assume uniformity of natural laws in order to achieve scientific discoveries about how things work. However, we must not assume that natural laws are all that ever existed, for, as discussed in the introduction, those very laws had their origin in a God entirely apart from nature.

A famous evolutionist, Dr. Richard Dawkins, admits that there are many elements of the natural world that look like they were designed. But he rejects the idea that there was a designer. Dawkins has said, "The illusion of purpose is so powerful that biologists themselves use the assumption of good design as a working tool"[115] and many other similar statements. When was the last time you saw a building or a watch and thought, "You know, I bet that just happened as a result of the random interactions of various natural laws?" Never. Take a look at your hand and flex your fingers. Move your eyes quickly around the room and consider how fast your eyes focus and take in new information. Next consider your hearing, and how air impulses from sound waves are converted into electrical impulses by your brain then interpreted as speech, almost in "real time." Now consider your whole body working together. Could an engineer design such an intricate machine? And could even the best of human engineers build it to repair and reproduce itself? Not a chance.

God has designed each of the kinds of living things that live on this planet. They did not arise from random events and natural laws. In order for those laws of nature to exist, there must have been a supreme Lawmaker, and He has told us in the Bible how He made all creatures. These creatures were not accidents. God purposefully designed each one in a supernatural act of creation. Every kind of creature was created by the powerful command of Jesus Christ (John 1:3; Colossians 1:16–17). Naturalism cannot offer a satisfactory explanation for how even a single-celled bacterium could have arrived on this planet without a designer. After all, the very laws of nature, such as diffusion and decay, tear away at life. Only the high-tech, ultraminiaturized programs and tools within living cells constantly battle against diffusion, decay, and other life-unfriendly "natural" laws.

Formula for Life

If evolution could be written as a formula, its simplest form would be Natural Selection + Mutations (changed to the genetic code) + Time = Evolution. But let's examine this idea a bit more carefully. For evolution to be a valid scientific theory, it has to be able to explain how the first life reproduced with variety so that future generations would be able to change into new kinds of organisms. Supposedly a bacterium changed into an amoeba, which changed into a sponge, which changed into a fish, which changed into a reptile, which changed into a human—and every other life form we see today. How scientific is this fantastic story?

All life has information inside of it encoded in its DNA. The DNA contains the genetic building and maintenance instructions for all of the parts of an organism. Plants can't make ears (other than corn!) because they don't have the right sequence of DNA instruction to produce ears. So if animals and plants have some common ancestor, at some point the information to make ears had to be added to the genes of some animal. So how did that extra information get there?

In order to exclude God from their thinking, most evolutionists must assume that information initially comes from a natural process in the first place. Otherwise, the first living cell would never have been able to make itself, let alone duplicate itself, without a miracle. This is one of the major hurdles in the hypothesis of chemical evolution—the origin of the first life. But let's assume that information in the DNA was present. If the DNA of an imaginary first organism was simply copied, evolution couldn't move forward in gaining new instructions because no differences would arise in future generations. The gene pool—all of the available genes in a population—would be stagnant.

Mutations

Enter mutations! If there were occasional mistakes in copying the information in the DNA, then differences could arise in future generations. The gene pool would have variety and slightly different organisms could be produced. Another way to introduce variety into the gene pool is through sexual reproduction, where each parent contributes half of the genetic information in its offspring, with different coding combinations possible. However, these processes occur according to very specific cellular and whole organism instructions. Where did those precise instructions come from?

DNA is made up of two molecular chains loosely bonded together. Each chain has a specific sequence of four chemical bases that pair up in specific ways. Adenine always bonds to Thymine, and Guanine always bonds to Cytosine. The DNA sequence is often represented by a series of As, Ts, Cs, and Gs. A particular strand of DNA might have the sequence

ATTCGCATAATGAACCGTC. The sequence of letters serves as a template to produce proteins and other cellular products. The code is read in sets of three: ATT.CGC.ATA.ATG.AAC.GTC in the string above. If one of the letters is incorrectly copied when a cell is reproducing itself, the new cell gains a "point mutation." Other forms of mutations can involve letters being inserted into the code or sections of the code being deleted. In each of these cases, the mutation can cause the cell to die or it may not have any immediate impact at all.

  Mutations are a measurable, observable process in cells—part of observational science. Understanding how a mutation impacts a given cell is an important part of biology and has helped us understand many diseases. Mutations resemble copying errors, like when we miss a letter or punctuation mark when we copy instructions from our teacher's marker board. An evolutionist takes these observable changes in cell's coding and tries to use them to explain how a bacterium could have changed into a bullfrog. This "origins exercise" involves assumptions. Evolutionary scientists try to make careful studies and perform experiments, but they start from the wrong place. They assume all life evolved from a single ancestor and then test their ideas to see if they are reasonable. In many cases, the explanations seem to make sense, but they leave God out of the picture and further investigation reveals how they violate scientific principles. Other chapters in this book give examples, revealing exciting discoveries that totally debunk evolutionary assertions that once sounded reasonable.

  If we start from the Bible, we better understand why mutations do not add the coded instructions for life that evolution requires. Mutations are actually a product of the Fall of man described in Genesis 3. When Adam and Eve sinned against God, it brought death, disease, and the struggle for survival into the world. Mutations began to impact living things and cause disease. Mutations that cause cancer would never have been present before sin entered the world. In contrast, the evolutionary view teaches that mutations and the struggle for life are good because they brought about all of the life forms today. The Bible teaches us that God created the world as a perfect place and that sin has corrupted the world and that death and mutations are a part of that corruption. Our starting points always impact the way we understand the world, including mutations.

Natural Selection

Mutations produce variety—there is no doubt about that. As animals struggle to survive in the wild, some varieties will be able to survive better than others in certain environments. A mutation can lead to a variation of a trait that is beneficial in one environment and harmful in another. Imagine a dog that had a mutation in the hair-producing genes that caused the dog to have long hair. If that dog lived in a cold climate, it might be better able to survive the cold winters and would be more likely to reproduce more offspring with long hair. If it lived in a desert environment, the long hair mutation might cause it to overheat and die. After several generations, that mutation would disappear from the gene pool (or turn dormant).

This is an overly simple explanation of the process of natural selection. However, even if it works the way we imagine it, natural selection can only select from trait variations available within each organism. Natural selection cannot cause new traits to come about any more than climate changes can write new computer codes. Mutations can and do alter pre-existing biological code, however.

Like mutations, evolutionists use natural selection to attempt to explain how organisms could have adapted to different environments and changed from fish into amphibians over the course of millions of years. But this origins science question involves many assumptions about the past that can never be verified. The mutations and natural selection processes from the past can never be observed, measured, or repeated. These two processes are supposed to be able to cause one kind of animal to change into another, but scientists have not witnessed this. In other words, mutations change existing traits within a reproducing kind, but they don't change one kind into another—a distinction that textbooks always ignore. Let's look at some of the classic examples and see if they really demonstrate that new information can be added to the genome through these processes.

Finch Beaks

If you open just about any biology textbook to the section on natural selection and evolution, you are almost certain to find two examples that illustrate Natural Selection + Mutations + Time = Evolution. The first involves some very detailed research conducted over a long period of time on the Galapagos Islands. Peter and Rosemary Grant began their studies in the 1960s. They measured several aspects of the different finches living on the islands in the Pacific Ocean. One thing they noticed was that the shape of the finch beaks changed with different long-term climate changes.

In periods of drought, the island's seeds had thicker shells, so birds with thicker beaks were better able to crack the thick shells. Because they could eat, they survived and passed their genes on to their offspring. When the weather was wetter, the average finch beaks got more slender. They have clearly documented the process of changing variation in the beak sizes and shapes that matched prevailing weather patterns. If this was natural selection, was it also evolution in action? No, and here is why.

The size of the beaks goes up and down over the years, but it never permanently changes, and it certainly doesn't change into something other than a beak. In order for this to be "evolution in action," we should see some type of new physical feature or biological process. But all the Grants observed were skinny beaks changing into wide beaks and vice versa. Beaks remained beaks on birds that were previously birds. How is that evolution in action? Dr. John Morris sum it up this way:

The two scholars, Drs. Peter and Rosemary Grant, observed how, under drought conditions, birds with larger beaks were better adapted than others, thus their percentage increased. But this trend reversed when the cyclical conditions reversed. Furthermore, in times of drought, the normally separate species were observed to cross-breed. They are related after all. Darwin was right! [in this part of the matter]. But is this really evolution? Even after the changes there is still the same array of beak sizes and shapes. This is variation and adaptation, not evolution. Actually, de-evolution has occurred; the observation is that there are larger groupings of species into what may be more reminiscent of the originally created kind. Creation agrees with Darwin's observations and with the newer observations, but evolution doesn't, even though the Grants interpret this as rapid evolution. Wonderful study—great data, wrong interpretation.[116]

"Evolving" Bacteria

Another very popular example found in textbooks and news articles has to do with bacteria becoming resistant to antibiotics. Textbooks don't mention that what is happening in bacterial biology actually opposes what is needed for molecules-to-man evolution to happen.

Here is one common way that antibiotics interact with bacteria. When a bacterium absorbs an antibiotic, a bacterial enzyme breaks it down and turns it into a poison that kills the cell. Certain bacteria in a population may have a mutation that damages or diminishes the enzyme. When they absorb the antibiotic, they can't turn it into the poison so they survive—they are resistant to the antibiotic. So this is survival of the fittest, right? Well, yes—but the mutants are only more 'fit' when swimming in antibiotic. Normally, non-mutants grow much faster than the mutants because the enzyme in question actually performs a life-enhancing task when not used to convert antibiotics to poison. The bacteria that had a mutation survived in that environment. That is the formula for evolution, right?

Well, not exactly. In order for evolution to happen, there has to be an increase in information—new information has to be added to the genome. That is not what happens with these bacteria. The mutations have caused a *loss* of information—the ability to make a proper enzyme. Losing information can't lead to a gain in information. Antibiotic resistance is a great example of natural selection—observational science—but it is not an example of evolution over millions of years—historical science—because it does not generate so much as a single new gene, let alone a new organism.

A Biblical Alternative

Biology books often show a "tree of life" when describing the history of life on Earth. Their evolutionary authors believe that a single organism evolved into different kinds of organisms, branching out into different forms through mutations and the process of natural selection (despite the hurdles described above). One branch of the tree might show a palm and another an orangutan. But no one has seen this tree in actual life—it is a drawing to explain an idea that they believe. It is an idea that follows a certain philosophy—the philosophy of naturalism—and into which they force the evidence.

If we begin our thinking from the Word of God, as we should if we are to honor Christ, we have a very different way of interpreting the evidence. God describes how He created living things in the first chapter of the Bible—Genesis 1. He tells us, as an eyewitness to His own work, that He created plants and animals according to their kinds to reproduce after their kinds. Genesis 1:11 makes this clear: "Let the earth bring forth grass, the herb that yields seed, and the fruit tree that yields fruit according to its kind, whose seed is in itself, on the earth." God supernaturally and specially created the different kinds of plants with seeds to produce more of the same kind. A coconut will never sprout a plum tree. The passages describing animals teach the same thing (Genesis 1:20–25; 6:19–20).

So rather than a single tree of life, we could draw an orchard of trees each representing a distinct kind of plant or animal.[117] All of the branches on the tree represent the variation within those kinds that have resulted from different expressions of the initial genetic variation God programmed in the original organisms as well as later mutations and other forms of genetic mixing. This orchard model is also an idea developed from a certain philosophy—Biblical creation.

Both of these views offer explanations for the evidence that we have in the present, but only one can be correct. Each attempts to apply observational science to understand the history of life on earth. One problem with the evolutionary worldview is that it must rely on unprovable assumptions. In contrast, biblical creation begins from the eyewitness testimony of the Creator God as described in His trustworthy Word—the Bible. You can trust that God has created life on this Earth. He did it for a reason. And that means that He created you for a reason. You are not simply the result of random accidents and the laws of nature—God created you and offers you the opportunity to know Him through His Son, Jesus Christ (Colossians 2:1–10).

Though textbooks portray evolution as a natural process whereby naturally selected mutations build new and more complicated creatures over vast eons from old and simple ones, we have seen this formula fail. Nature can only select from the options organisms already possess, and mutations do not generate the options required to turn bacteria into finches, for example. The alternative origins explanation—biblical creation—fits the evidence just fine by explaining the original biological programming as having been created, and the constantly corrupting mutations as God's consequence for man's original sin.

Chapter 7: Did Hippos Evolve into Whales?
Jonathan Sarfati, Ph.D. & Daniel A. Biddle, Ph.D.

Biology textbooks use illustrations of "ancient" land-dwelling mammals turning into modern whales over millions of years to illustrate their version of history—evolution. For example, Miller & Levine's high school biology textbook prominently displays six creatures leading up to modern whales.[118] This section will review how these "pre-whale" animals don't line up in any such fashion. We will show instead that these fossils represent extinct marine or land animals that never evolved into whales. Further, we will review some impossibilities with the idea in secular circles that some wolf-sized animals evolved into 360,000-pound sea-dwelling whales. Even evolutionists' own models show that these changes cannot be made given their own timescale. In the end, we wish our readers to gain confidence in the fact that so-called "whale evolution" falls far short of what its proponents say about it. In fact, we hope you will see not only how evolution fails whales, but how well the fossils fit into Biblical history.

Overview

Whales are one of God's most magnificent creations. They are even mentioned specifically in the King James Bible translation: "And God created great whales, and every living creature that moveth, which the waters brought forth abundantly, after their kind..." (Genesis 1:21).[119] To begin our discussion on the evolution of whales, let's begin with a quick description of what makes whales so unique.

Let's start first with the obvious—whales are massive. They are the largest animals on Earth, with the 100-foot long female blue whale at the top of the list. This animal weighs in at 360,000 pounds (the equivalent of 2,000 people), has a tongue that is the size and weight of an African elephant, and a heart that is the size of a small car that pumps 2,640 gallons of blood.[120]

Baleen whales have specially designed comb-like bristles in their mouths called "baleen" that enable them to eat tiny krill as they move through the ocean at speeds up to 30 miles per hour (requiring over 1,000 horsepower to do so!). Much of this power is generated by a tail that is 25 feet wide. Blue whales can dive over 1,500 feet and communicate with each other up to 1,000 miles away. Baleen whales feed by the enormously energetic process of 'lunge feeding,' and have a unique sensory organ to coordinate this so their jaws don't shatter. This organ senses the "dynamic rotation of the jaws during mouth opening and closure [and] provides the necessary input to the brain for coordinating the initiation, modulation and end stages of engulfment."[121]
To say the least, these are amazing creatures.

Evolutionists insist that these wonderful marine creatures, outfitted as they are with an array of specifications precisely targeted for successful life in water, evolved from ancestors that once had none of those specifications. These people write state-sponsored textbooks, yet have plenty of explaining to do. How, step-by-step, and without using words like "evolution," "selection," or "emerged," could whales have evolved in the manner they describe?

Evolution faces a whale of a challenge, not just from a theoretical basis but from the standpoint of observational science. What creature kinds have served as the best candidates for evolutionary whale ancestry? The founder of the theory of evolution himself, Charles Darwin, had an idea. In the first edition (1865) of his well-known book, *The Origin of Species*, Darwin wrote:

> In North America the black bear was seen...swimming for hours with widely open mouth, thus catching, like a whale, insects in the water. Even in so extreme a case as this, if the supply of insects were constant, and if better adapted competitors did not already exist in the country, I can see no difficulty in a race of bears

being rendered, by natural selection, more and more aquatic in their structure and habits, with larger and larger mouths, till a creature was produced as monstrous as a whale.[122]

While this section was removed from later editions of the book, documents revealed in 1903 demonstrated that he still maintained his position of bears evolving into whales: "I still maintain that there is no special difficulty in a bear's mouth being enlarged to any degree useful to its changing habits."[123] Clearly, Darwin believed that any creature has an unlimited potential to change its form. He was wrong about this, and other places in this book tell why.

Fast-forward to the 1970s. Bears are now *out* of the evolutionary "whale line" and textbooks report other animal candidates as whale ancestors such as *Mesonychids,* known from fossils.[124] Then in the 1980s *Pakicetus* took first position.[125] Twenty years later, a large group of evolutionists selected the *hippopotamus,* while another group placed pigs into the "evolving" evolutionary ancestry of whales.[126]

What's next? Fortunately, from a biblical creation standpoint, God made whales on the Day 5 of Creation, each creature after their own *kind*, and this view hasn't changed since these words of Scripture were penned about *3,500 years ago*!

If whale evolution is true, then we would expect many other transitional "in-between" whale-like animals, either living or fossil, each stepping up along the evolutionary tree. Just take a look at the differences between some of these "starter" animals, which were land mammals, and the whales into which they supposedly evolved. As Dr. Carl Werner points out:

> Consider how miraculous it would be for a wolf or a bear or any such creature to evolve into the 13 families and 79 species of whales, from the finless porpoise measuring about four feet long, to the blue whale measuring 100 feet. The latter weighs 360,000 pounds (the equivalent of 2,000

people); its tongue is the size and weight of an African elephant; its heart is the size of a small car; its heart pumps 2,640 gallons of blood; and a human could swim through its massive aorta.[127]

A prominent evolutionary biologist now known for expressing doubt about some Darwinist claims, Dr. Richard Sternberg, studied whale evolution in depth. He concluded that there is simply not enough time within evolutionary time stamps to make *even a few of the changes* necessary to reorganize a land creature into a whale.[128] Some of these changes had to include:

- Counter-current heat exchanger for intra-abdominal testes (to keep them cool)
- Ball vertebra (to enable the tail to move up and down instead of side to side)
- Tail flukes and musculature
- Blubber for temperature insulation
- Ability to drink sea water (reorganization of kidney tissues)
- Fetus in breech position (for underwater head-first birth)
- Nurse young underwater (modified mammae)
- Forelimbs transformed into flippers
- Reduction of hindlimbs
- Reduction/loss of pelvis and sacral vertebrae
- Reorganization of the musculature for the reproductive organs
- Hydrodynamic properties of the skin
- Special lung surfactants
- Novel muscle systems for the blowhole
- Modification of the teeth
- Modification of the eye for underwater vision
- Emergence and expansion of the mandibular fat pad with complex lipid distribution
- Reorganization of skull bones and musculature

- Modification of the ear bones
- Decoupling of esophagus and trachea
- Synthesis and metabolism of isovaleric acid (toxic to terrestrial mammals)

In a debate regarding the origins of life, Dr. Sternberg stated, "How could this process alone have produced fully aquatic cetaceans (whales) with their multiple, anatomical novelties, requiring many hundreds, even thousands of adaptive changes in less than 2 million years—even less than 9 million years?...I'm saying it doesn't add up."[129] We would need thousands of in-between examples of fossils demonstrating *each* of these requirements developing through time.

Making this evolutionary process even more difficult to believe, the jawbone of an ancient whale found in Antarctica in October 2011 was "dated" to 49 million years, which would imply that the first fully-developed whales now date to about the same time as one of the supposed whale "ancestors," named *Ambulocetus*.[130]

It is clear that what we have on Earth is a *created* "kind" of whales that have existed since Day 5 of Creation, and not some evolutionary line of land-mammals leading to the largest creature on Earth—a 360,000 pound blue whale that is able to swim up to 30 miles per hour, has a tongue that weighs as much as an elephant, a heart the size of a car, eats 4–8 tons of krill each day, and dives to depths of over 1,500 feet while holding its breath. By now, it should become clear that it takes more faith to believe in evolution than it does in whale Creation.

With this background in mind, we will next review and reject each of the animals that are supposedly linked together in the successive train of whale evolution.

Animals (that Don't Belong) in the Progression of Whale Evolution

Several high school and college biology textbooks display the supposed "whale evolution" model by putting several pictures of extinct and living animals side-by-side and bonding them together in a hypothetical evolutionary explanation that one animal led to the next, on up the evolutionary tree. For example, the first two in Miller & Levine's line-up (Ancient artiodactyls and *Pakicetus*) are land-dwelling mammals (similar to wolves), the next two (*Ambulocetus* and *Rodhocetus*) allegedly started developing fins and tails/flippers, the next two (*Basilosaurus* and *Dorudon*) are early whales, followed by the two suborders of modern whales: Mysticeti (baleen whales) and Odontoceti (toothed whales).[131] Lined up this way, they seem to tell a neat evolutionary story. But as we will show, this arrangement follows more from an underlying philosophical commitment to evolution than to scientific data.

From a biblical creationist standpoint, these eight mammals are not related and have not evolved. Rather, the first two are simply extinct wolf-like creatures most likely buried and later fossilized by Noah's Flood, the next four are extinct whale-like creatures (which also likely died in the Flood), and the last two are obviously whales that still exist today.

Asserting that these eight animals are somehow all tied to the same evolutionary tree is similar to digging up a golf ball, baseball, and soccer ball in your backyard and saying, "See! This must be proof of ball evolution!" Just because animals shared some similar features or habitats does not mean that they are related, or that one led to the other! After all, nobody has ever observed a progression of one kind evolving into another. As discussed in previously, animals can and do *adapt* by making certain adjustments, such as "Darwin's Finches," but they do not change from one kind of animal to another. Indeed, Darwin's Finches are still finches—they differ only by beak size and shape. The same is true with whales.

Each of these "evolving whale" creatures will be discussed below, along with some amazing recent admissions made by the evolutionists who originally touted them as "proof" of evolution.

Ancient artiodactyl

"Artiodactyl" is a collective term used to mean "even-toed" animals, referring to their two or four hoofs per foot. According to evolutionary fossil-age assignments, they date back some 54 million years. Animals in this category include goats, sheep, camels, pigs, cows, and deer. Other than just saying so, there is no evidence connecting this entire group of animals to whales. By suggesting that whales evolved from some "ancient artiodactyl," they implicitly admit that they do not have a real fossil connecting whales to other mammals, instead reaching for an imaginary, not-yet-found "ancestor."

Pakicetus

Pakicetus means "whale from Pakistan," but it looked nothing like a whale. It was originally represented by a few elongated *wolf-like skull fragments* that were first discovered by paleontologist Philip Gingerich in the early 1980s.[132] Based on these skull fragments, Gingerich asserted that the *Pakicetus* was a "perfect intermediate" between land animals and whales.[133] Drawings of the *Pakicetus* swimming in the ocean as a sea creature soon adorned standardized textbooks.[134] At the time, it was easy to pretend that *Pakicetus* had a whale-like body, since we had no body fossils.

About ten years later, more *Pakicetus* fossils were discovered, including additional body fossils associated with skull material. "All the postcranial bones indicate that pakicetids were land mammals… Many of the fossils' features…indicate that the animals were runners, moving with only their digits touching the ground," according to the prestigious journal *Nature*.[135] These led to the conclusion that the *Pakicetus* was "no more amphibious than a tapir"[136] Tapirs are modern browsing mammals living in South America, similar to pigs but with longer snouts. Once new fossils showed that it had well-organized, fast-running legs, was *Pakicetus* immediately removed from its iconic whale ancestry position in evolutionary textbook diagrams? Surprisingly, texts often still include *Pakicetus*. This is just bad science. Tapirs are alive today, and no one has seen these animals evolving at all, much less to anything close to a sea-dwelling whale. A recent article in *National Geographic* reports that Gingerich now believes that whales are related to antelopes based on a "single piece of fossil" found in 2000.[137]

Just viewing the illustration of the *Pakicetus* in common biology textbooks shows these animals to have simply been extinct, wolf-like mammals.

Ambulocetus

Ambulocetus is based on a set of fossil fragments that was discovered in Pakistan in 1993. To date there have been *only two Ambulocetus* fossils found.[138] One high school biology textbook includes this creature in whale evolution by stating: "The limb structure of *Ambulocetus* 'walking whale' suggests that these animals could both swim in shallow water and walk on land."[139]

Alligators and crocodiles are reptiles that look similar to the mammal *Ambulocetus*, and they can swim and walk on land. Why have they not also been lined up in the evolutionary train leading to whales?

In his book, *Evolution: A Theory in Crisis*, evolutionary biochemist, Dr. Michael Denton, points out that *Ambulocetus*' backbone ends in the pelvic bone (from which powerful leg bones extend), which is typical for land mammals. In whales, on the other hand, the backbone continues right down to the tail and there is no pelvic bone at all. *Basilosaurus*, thought to have lived up to 10 million years after *Ambulocetus*, possesses a typical no-pelvis whale anatomy. There is no intermediate form between *Ambulocetus*, a typical terrestrial animal, and *Basilosaurus*, a typical whale. Note also that *Basilosaurus* is about 10 times longer than *Ambulocetus*, although evolutionary textbooks often draw them side-by-side to make the 'transitional series' look better. *Basilosaurus* and sperm whales have small bones independent of the backbone in their lower bodies. Some evolutionists claim that these are shrunken leg bones. However, the bones in question more likely had functional uses in reproduction in *Basilosaurus*, whereas in sperm whales they support the reproductive organs.[140] Why would they have evolved into legs if they were already useful in their present state?

Dr. Carl Werner points out that the evolution "evidence" involving *Ambulocetus* consists of nothing more than *just by saying so*:

> According to Dr. Annalisa Berta, an expert in aquatic mammal evolution, "*Ambulocetus is a whale by virtue of its inclusion in that lineage.*" In other words, *Ambulocetus* was defined as a "walking whale" not because it had a whale's tail or a whale's flippers or a blowhole, but because [some] evolution scientists believed it was on the line to becoming a whale, it became a "whale." And since it was a land animal with four legs, it was then called a "walking whale." Scientists who oppose evolution are quick to point out that this reasoning is circular and therefore specious.[141] (emphasis added)

Dr. Werner also pointed out that because *Ambulocetus* has eyes on the top of its head (like a crocodile) it should be clearly classified as a mammal with legs, having nothing to do with whales.

Rodhocetus

Rodhocetus was also found in Pakistan in 1992, and is now represented by three fossils.[142] The most well-known *Rodhocetus* is made up of two partial skeletons that make up an "early whale" that had short limbs, long hands, and feet.[143] The Levine & Miller biology textbook states that its hind limbs were "short and probably not able to bear much weight. Paleontologists think that these animals spent most of their time in the water."[144]

Many of the textbook illustrations of the *Rodhocetus* show it with legs and a dolphin or a common whale tail. For example, the *Proceedings of the National Academy of Sciences* showed *Rodhocetus* with a fluked tail similar to a typical whale.[145] Several other textbooks followed the practice, making for a convincing presentation that this animal (all three of them) was some type of transition step along the way to today's whales.

Dr. Phil Gingerich, the paleontologist most responsible for the reconstruction and presentation of *Rodhocetus,* added a prominent tail and "fluke" (the wide fin at the end of the tail) to *Rodhocetus* when it was displayed at the Natural History Museum at the University of Michigan. When interviewed about why he added a whale fluke on *Rodhocetus*, Dr. Gingerich answered, "Well, I told you we don't have the tail in *Rodhocetus*. So, we don't know for sure whether it had a ball vertebrae indicating a fluke or not. So, I speculated it might have had a fluke."[146]

During this same revealing interview, Dr. Gingerich also acknowledged that the flippers were drawn on the diagram without fossil representation! Today he no longer believes that this animal had flippers, stating, "Since then we have found the forelimbs, the hands, and the front arms of *Rodhocetus*, and we understand that it doesn't have the kind of arms that can spread out like flippers on a whale." Without flippers or tail, *Rodhocetus* should be removed from its evolutionary lineup. The way its features had been imaginatively added, like those of *Pakicetus* before more complete fossils were found, clearly show whale evolution to be a product of researchers' minds and not of scientific observation.

Basilosaurus

A total of over 100 *Basilosaurus* fossils have been found around the world including Egypt, Jordan, Pakistan, and in the United States (Mississippi and Alabama). One of the features that led evolutionists to believe that the *Basilosaurus* should be included in the "whale evolution line" are its hind "limbs."[147] Evolutionists frequently represent these limbs as "leftovers" from a supposed land-dwelling past. They supposedly lost their legs, evolved flippers, and became whales.

However, many leading evolutionists are now admitting that these limbs, like the small "leftover" limbs in "modern" whales, "could only be some kind of sexual or reproductive clasper."[148] These "claspers" are necessary to join multi-ton animals tightly together while mating in water and swimming, a design found in numerous other sea creatures. Whale evolutionist Dr. Gingerich wrote:

> Hind limbs of *Basilosaurus* appear to have been too small relative to body size... to have assisted in swimming, and they could not possibly have supported the body on land. However, maintenance of some function is likely... The pelvis of modern whales [not a limb-supporting "pelvis"] serves to anchor reproductive organs, even though functional hind limbs are lacking. Thus hind limbs of Basilosaurus are most plausibly interpreted as accessories facilitating reproduction.[149]

It is also interesting that apparently no transitional fossils between current whales and the *Basilosaurus* have been found, even though hundreds of each have been found. If evolution is true, one would think that over 35 million years of evolution would have produced some fossilized examples of transitions, but the fossil record "jumps" from *Basilosaurus*, which was a fully aquatic animal, to modern whales, with nothing in between.[150] In actuality, God created whales and *Basilosaurus* separately.

Dorudon

There have been over 50 *Dorudon* fossils discovered around the world. These animals are simply extinct whales. They had nostril openings (blowholes) on top of their skulls, measured about 50 feet long, and lived in the water full-time. I described them in an online article that I wrote in 2008:

> The *Dorudon* was once classified as a juvenile *Basilosaurus*, since they are very similar, long, slender marine mammals, but *Dorudon* was 5 m long and *Basilosaurus* 18 m. They are now classified as separate subfamilies of Basolosauridae. They are most likely varieties of the same created kind, much as the false killer whale (*Pseudorca crassidens*) and a bottlenose dolphin (*Tursiops truncatus*) are the same biological species given that they can produce a fertile hybrid called a wholphin…the serpentine body structure, cheek teeth and nasal bones mean that it could not have been an ancestor to modern whales. Also, the allegedly vestigial hind limbs actually had an important function as reproductive claspers.[151]

Finally, Mysticetes include grey, blue, and humpback whales, and Odontocetes include toothed whales like dolphins and sperm whales. These modern whales are already whales, so have no place in whale evolution.

Summary

One of the certain facts that we can know from fossils is that *the animal died*. However, fossils do not come with tags showing the year they were created or buried in mud. When the evolutionist assumptions are removed, we no longer have a string of animals that led one to the other. Rather, we have various created kinds of animals that died by rapid muddy burials and then fossilized when the mud later dried.

What we can know for certain regarding the supposed story of whale evolution is that its theories have often changed—bears, mesonychids, *Pakicetus*, and now hippopotamuses have rotated through. The biblical viewpoint, however, remains *unchanged* since penned about 3,500 years ago: Whales were created as whales that can express variations within each of their kinds: some died off (many did not survive the Flood), and many are still alive today.

Finally, considering the number of changes that are needed to turn a wolf, bear, hippopotamus, or pig into a 360,000 pound, 100-foot blue whale doesn't even pass the common sense test. It takes more faith to believe in that type of evolution than it does to believe in biblical creation. The multiple families of whales we have were simply created that way. Dr. Duane Gish describes such "incredible faith in the evolution" this way:

> Evolutionists are forced to believe that whatever the need may be, no matter how complex and unusual, random genetic errors were able to produce the structures required in a perfectly coordinated manner... It requires an enormous faith in miracles, where materialist philosophy actually forbids them, to believe that some hairy, four-legged mammal crawled into the water and gradually, over eons of time, gave rise to whales, dolphins, sea cows, seals, sea lions, walruses, and other marine mammals via thousands and thousands of random genetic errors. This blind

hit and miss method supposedly generated the many highly specialized complex organs and structures without which these whales could not function, complex structures which in incipient stages would be totally useless and actually detrimental. Evolution theory is an incredible faith.[152]

Few of the members depicted in textbook illustrations of whale evolution belong there. Each shows evidence that it was a uniquely created creature, having no anatomical link to whales. Instead of showcasing evolution, the wonderful and integrated design features that make whale life possible should showcase their great Creator, the God of the Bible.

Chapter 8: A Brief History of Human Evolution in Textbooks
Daniel A. Biddle, Ph.D.

Evolution's Beginnings

The standard line-up of the four ape-to-human icons that public school textbooks most often feature today is quite different from the evolutionary story of apes progressing to humans described in the past. The standard lineup presented in textbooks changes at least every couple of decades. If ideas of human evolution are false, we would expect them to shift frequently, just as history has proven happens. To demonstrate this, let's journey through time and review the once best but now discarded evolutionary ideas that perhaps your grandparent's textbooks promoted.

In **1829**, Neanderthal skulls were first discovered in Belgium, and dozens have been found since. Originally classified as "pre-humans" or "sub-humans," they are now believed to be human in every practical sense. These ancient humans had unique features, but none that lie outside the range of modern men and women. Nevertheless, Neanderthal's peculiarities were too tempting for those anxious to find a missing link. They thought they found it. However, recent discoveries prove that Neanderthals were fully human—descendants of Adam just like us. They buried their dead, made instruments, practiced burial rituals, and made and used advanced tools. They have even been found buried alongside modern-looking humans.[153] Their skulls were close to 200 cc greater than that of present-day humans—hardly an intermediate form between humans and apes! Neanderthal expert Erik Trinkhaus admitted, "Detailed comparisons of Neanderthal skeletal remains with those of modern humans have shown that there is nothing in Neanderthal anatomy that conclusively indicates locomotor, manipulative, intellectual, or linguistic abilities inferior to those of modern humans."[154] If textbook writers of yesteryear waited until evolutionists examined Neanderthal fossils enough to see that they were fully human, they would not have been able to illustrate human evolution very well.

Figures 19 and 20 show this changing position on Neanderthals—from pre-human "brute" to human.

Figure 19. Previous Idea of Neanderthal Man (Credit: This reconstruction of the La Chapelle-aux-Saints Neanderthal skeleton—discovered in France in 1908—was published in L'Illustration and in the Illustrated London News in 1909).

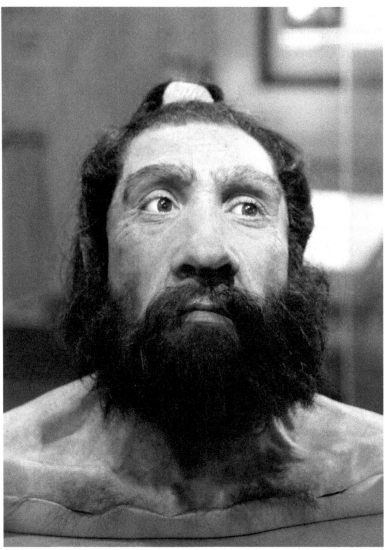

Figure 20. Current Idea of Neanderthal Man. Once considered an ape-like caveman, Neanderthal remains have proven their identity as fully human. Give him a shave, haircut, and button-down shirt and this Neanderthal would blend right into a city crowd (Credit: Wikipedia).

In **1859**, Charles Darwin published the *Origin of Species by Means of Natural Selection*. This book did not broach the topic of how evolution might apply to humans. Darwin only stated that future research would reveal the origin of man: "light will be thrown on the origin of man and his history" (Chapter 14).

In **1863**, famous promoter of evolution Thomas Henry Huxley laid out his best case to show that humans evolved from apes in a book titled *Evidence as to Man's Place in Nature*.[155] In his book, Huxley concluded, "it is quite certain that the Ape which most nearly approaches man, in the totality of his organization, is either the chimpanzee or the gorilla." Huxley presented one of the earliest "March of Man" images used to suggest human evolution (Figure 21).

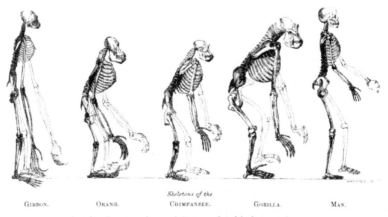

Figure 21. Huxley's Comparison of Ape and Human Skeletons (Evidence as to Man's Place in Nature, 1863). In contrast to Huxley's original caption, the "MAN" skeleton is smaller in relation to chimp and orangutan. Also, these drawings depict awkward postures that make them look more similar than their natural postures would suggest (Credit: Wikipedia).

In **1871**, Darwin published *The Descent of Man,* where he laid out his theories that humans are descended from ape-like creatures. Darwin supported his ideas from three main categories: similarities between humans and other primates, similarities in embryological development, and vestigial organs (which are parts of our bodies that are supposedly "leftover" from evolution). Darwin concludes that we are closely related to either gorillas or chimpanzees: "In each great region of the world the living mammals are closely related to the extinct species of the same region. It is, therefore, probable that Africa was formerly inhabited by extinct apes closely allied to the gorilla and chimpanzee; and as these two species are now man's nearest allies, it is somewhat more probable that our early progenitors lived on the African continent than elsewhere" (Darwin, *Decent of Man*, 1871).

Darwin's ideas bolstered racist thought and ideas of the 19th and 20th centuries, and in some cases still today. Darwin's infamous book *Origin of the Species* was originally released in 1859 under the full title, *On the Origin of Species by Means of Natural Selection or the Preservation of Favoured Races in the Struggle for Life*. This title was shortened in 1872 (with the release of the sixth edition) to simply, *The Origin of Species*. Darwin's second book, *The Descent of Man*, included one chapter titled "The Races of Man." In this chapter, Darwin stated:

> At some future period not very distant as measured by centuries, the civilized races of man will almost certainly exterminate and replace the savage races throughout the world. At the same time, the anthropomorphous apes...will no doubt be exterminated. The break between man and his nearest Allies will then be wider, for it will intervene between man in a more civilized state, as we may hope, even than the Caucasian, and some ape as low as the baboon, instead of as now between the Negro or Australian and the gorilla.[156]

In chapter 7 he noted:

> Their mental characteristics are likewise very distinct; chiefly as it would appear in their emotional, but partly in their intellectual faculties. Everyone who has had the opportunity of comparison must have been struck with the contrast between the taciturn, even morose, aborigines of S. America and the light-hearted, talkative negroes.

Darwin's belief in racial superiority was obvious: If man evolved then so did the various races, and the "Caucasian" race evolved farther than others. The impact of these philosophies is enormous according to historians who have traced Darwin's ideas to Hitler's death camps during World War II.[157]

In **1874**, Ernst Haeckel published *The Evolution of Man* which included a famous figure showing humans evolving from Amoeba to modern man through 24 stages.

Figure 22. 1874 Human Evolution Ideas. The figure shows humans evolving through 24 stages, from Amoeba (1) to Worm (7) to Jawless fish (lamprey) (10), to a plesiosaur (14), to Monkey (20), to Modern human (24) (Credit: The modern theory of the descent of man, by Ernst Haeckel, published in *The Evolution of Man*, 1874).

While Biblical Creation continued as the predominant teaching in public schools, evolutionary ideas began their first introductions into school textbooks between 1888 and 1890.[158] Darwin published his last work in 1882, the same year he died. Two complete Neanderthal skeletons were found in 1886 in a cave in Belgium, giving naturalists fuel for more evolutionary imaginings.

In **1891**, Ernst Haeckel updated his ideas about human evolution by publishing a new book titled *Anthropogeny*,[159] which included one of the earliest "trees" of human evolution. The trees change with almost every new paper or research study, whether evolutionists use DNA sequences or body forms to guess at "relatedness." As you read this section, pay careful attention at how this "tree" changes.

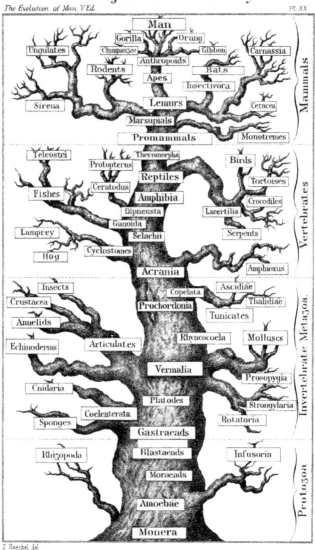

Figure 23. Ernst Haeckel's late 19th century (1891)[160] idea of which animal forms may have evolved into which over imagined eons.

Java Man

Even bigger news came in **1891** when Eugene Dubois enlisted the help of the colonial government, two engineers, and fifty convicts to manually tear through tons of earth on the Indonesian island of Java in an attempt to find "the missing link" between apes and humans.[161] In addition to numerous animal fossils, Dubois' team discovered a tooth, a skullcap, and a femur (thighbone) in East Java. While the femur was found a year later and about 50 feet from the skullcap, he assumed they were from the same creature. Dubois named the collection "Java Man" and gave it the scientific name Pithecanthropus *erectus*.

Immediately after he published his finds, the science community opposed them. When Java Man was presented before the Berlin Anthropological Society in January 1895, German Dr. W. Krause unhesitatingly declared that the tooth was a molar of an ape, the skull was from a gibbon, and the femur was human. Krause said, "The three could not belong to the same individual."[162] Despite reasonable objections, almost 80 books or articles had been published on Java Man within ten years of Dubois' find, explaining them as missing links for human evolution.

Decades of hype finally began to topple in 1939 when two experts, Ralph von Koenigswald and Franz Weidenreich, revealed that Java Man looked similar to a set of fossils found in 1923–1927 called "Peking Man," or *Sinanthropus pekinensis*. Both were actually normal human beings.[163] The final nail was hammered into the coffin of Java Man as a transitional form in 1944. Harvard University professor Ernst Mayr, the leading evolutionary biologist of the 20th century, classified both of these finds as human.[164]

Interestingly, Dubois found two definitely human skulls called the Wadjak skulls, which were discovered in strata at the same level as the "Java Man" fossils. Why did he keep them secret for 30 years? During that time, the international scientific community accepted Java Man as a real missing link.[165] Near the end of his life, however, Dubois publicly conceded that Java Man was extremely similar to—though he believed not identical with—a large gibbon. Dubois wrote, "Pithecanthropus was not a man, but a gigantic genus allied to the Gibbons,"[166] a statement over which both Creationists and Evolutionists are still quarreling.

What were the Java Man remains? They probably consisted of a human femur and extinct ape bones including a gibbon's skull remains. These simply show that some people and some apes were fossilized as distinct kinds. Java Man never really existed. Unfortunately, the next generation of public school textbooks did not admit this. Instead, they slyly replaced the "Java Man" story with a new hopeful evolutionary link.

Figure 24. Reconstruction of Java Man.[167] The white parts of the skull and the facial reconstruction was based only on the skullcap, which is the dark part on the top.

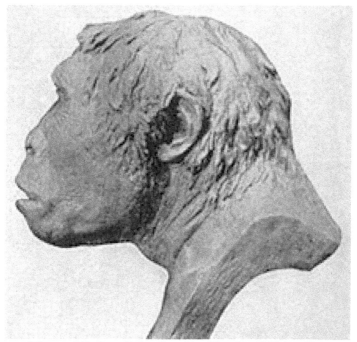
Figure 25. Java Man Profile (Credit: Wikipedia)

This Java Man profile has been prominently displayed in books and other media for decades.

Figure 26. Java Man Statue.[168] A statue of an imaginary reconstruction of a "Java Man" skull marks the land of its discovery, even though most evolutionists finally determined that it was no missing link at all.

What was fishy about this ape man?

Howard E. Wilson points out some interesting facts about Java man—some that are not widely known.[169] Apparently, DuBois did not enjoy having people come view the actual Java Man fossils. He kept them under tight lock-and-key for 30 years. When others finally viewed them, the bones turned out to be vastly different than the copies displayed and analyzed around the world! The well-known journal *Science* published an article[170] that stated:

> There is a "skeleton in the closet" of man's evolutionary history, and Prof. E. DuBois... holds the key. The "closet" is said to be a good stout safe in Haarlem, Holland, and the skeleton is none other than that of *Pithecanthropus erectus*, the famous ape-man who [supposedly] lived in Java over a half million years ago. For thirty years scientists from all over Europe have besieged Dr. DuBois for permission to examine the remains, while eminent anthropologists have crossed the ocean for that purpose only to be turned away at the door.

After being largely hidden away for 30 years, Dr. Alex Hrdlicka of the Smithsonian Institute wrote, "None of the published illustrations or the casts now in various institutions is accurate. Especially is this true of the teeth and the thigh bone. The new brain cast is very close to human. The femur is without question human."[171] Now that's an amazing statement! "None of the published illustrations of the cast now in various institutions is accurate." How can Java Man be trusted as a "transition" between apes and man if none of the casts were accurate?

Some have argued that Java Man's brain was too small to be human. The cranial capacity of Java Man was estimated at 1000 cc. This would be small, but fits within the range of modern humans. Apes never exceed 600 cc.[172] While 1000 ccs is not a large cranial capacity, some people groups also have smaller brains (in the 900 to 1,000 cc range),[173] but this does not make them any less human or less intelligent.[174]

When the 20th century began, biblical creation continued as the primary teaching on origins. Evolution teaching was scarcely taught in public schools. Oscar Richards more recently conducted a study of six of the most commonly used textbooks in the U.S. published between 1911 and 1919 (representing 75% of all U. S. schools). Using word counts, he estimated that only 1.68% of these textbooks was devoted to evolution.[175]

Piltdown Man

"Piltdown Man" is a fraudulent composite of fossil human skull fragments plus a modern ape jaw with two teeth that Charles Dawson supposedly discovered in a gravel pit at Piltdown, east Sussex, England. History testifies, as summarized by Pat Shipman, that "the Piltdown fossils, whose discovery was first announced in 1912, fooled many of the greatest minds in paleoanthropology until 1953, when the remains were revealed as planted, altered—a forgery."[176]

The New York Times.

SUNDAY, DECEMBER 22, 1912.

DARWIN THEORY IS PROVED TRUE

English Scientists Say the Skull Found in Sussex Establishes Human Descent from Apes.

THOUGHT TO BE A WOMAN'S

Bones Illustrate a Stage of Evolution Which Has Only Been Imagined Before.

Figure 27. Piltdown Man Announced in the New York Times[177] (1912) Major media outlets have a long history of splashing headlines that support evolution, but burying news that refutes it. Piltdown Man was later proven a 100% fraud.

Consider the following deliberate (and desperate) measures some have used to promote belief in macro-evolution:

> Piltdown Common had been used as a mass grave during the great plagues of A.D. 1348–9. The skull bones were quite thick, a characteristic of more ancient fossils, and *the skull had been treated with potassium bichromate* by Dawson to harden and preserve it... The other bones and

stone tools had undoubtedly been planted in the pit and had been treated to match the dark brown color of the skull. *The lower jaw was that of a juvenile female orangutan. The place where the jaw would articulate with the skull had been broken off to hide the fact that it did not fit the skull.* The teeth of the mandible [lower jaw] were filed down to match the teeth of the upper jaw, and the canine tooth had been filed down to make it look heavily worn… The amazing thing about the Piltdown hoax is that at least twelve different people have been accused of perpetrating the fraud… what has been called *the most successful scientific hoax of all time.*[178] (emphasis added)

In **1915,** Sir Arthur Keith, Conservator of the Royal Medical College in England and President of the Royal Anthropological Institute of Great Britain and Ireland in the early 1900s, wrote the most definitive human evolution text of that era, *The Antiquity of Man.*[179] This 500+ page book prominently displayed a gold embossed skull of the Piltdown Man.

Over 100 pages of Arthur Keith's *The Antiquity of Man* book[180] is devoted to Piltdown Man, which was revealed as a fraud just two years before Keith died in 1955.[181] Keith placed so much trust in Piltdown Man as a "proof of evolution" that he called it: "one of the most remarkable discoveries of the twentieth century."[182] Boy was he wrong! But it was too late. He had convinced his readers that human evolution had scientific backing, when it never did.

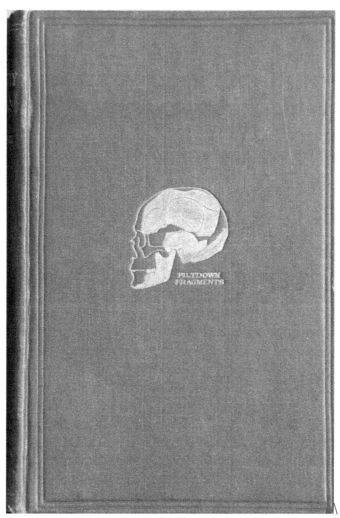

Figure 28. Sir Arthur Keith's Leading Human Evolution Book of the Early 1900s with Piltdown Man on the Cover[183] (Volume I, "The Antiquity of Man" by Sir Arthur Keith. Philadelphia: J.B. Lippincott Company, 1925. Second Edition, Sixth Impression. Illustrated).

Figure 29. Group Portrait of the Piltdown Skull Examination. Back row (from left): F.O. Barlow, G. Elliot Smith, Charles Dawson, Arthur Smith Woodward. Front row: A.S. Underwood, Arthur Keith, W. P. Pycraft, and Ray Lankester. Painting by John Cooke, 1915. (Credit: Wikipedia).

For over 40 years, Piltdown models were displayed around the world as proof of human evolution, and more than 500 articles and memoirs are said to have been written about Piltdown man.[184] How did this fraud continue for so long before being exposed? Harvard paleontologist (and evolutionist) Stephen Gould suggests wishful thinking and cultural bias on the part of evolutionists was one reason.[185]

Figures 30–32 below show Piltdown's prominent place in leading human evolution "trees."

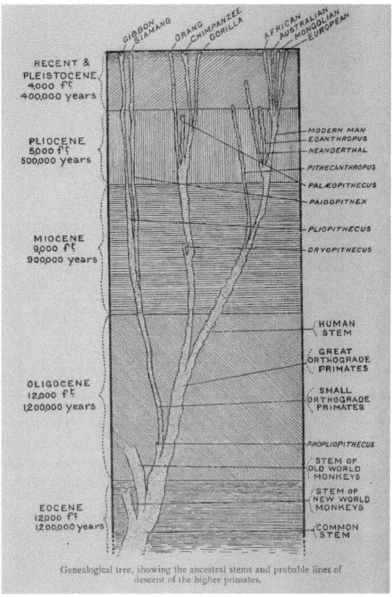

Figure 30. 1915 Human Evolution Ideas (Credit: Sir Arthur Keith, The Antiquity of Man. London: Williams & Norgate, 1915).

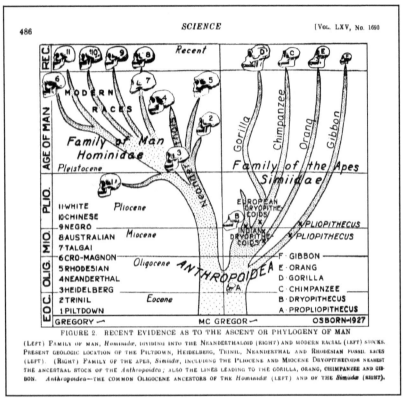

Figure 31. 1927 Evolutionary Tree Showing Fraudulent Piltdown Man.[186] Note Piltdown featured in the middle-left.

Figure 31 demonstrates Piltdown Man's prominent place in the supposed progression of human evolution. Piltdown models were displayed around the world as proof of human evolution for over 40 years, and illustrations including Piltdown Man in the chain of human evolution were used for decades in school textbooks.

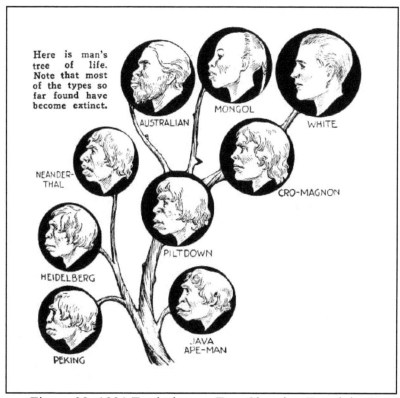

Figure 32. 1931 Evolutionary Tree Showing Fraudulent Piltdown Man.[187] Piltdown Man, although completely faked, became standardized evidence for evolution.

167

Nebraska Man

From **1917** to **1928**, yet another icon came on the scene as "certain proof" of human evolution. Geologist Harold Cook found a ***single molar tooth*** in Nebraska which later was named Hesperopithecus, or "Nebraska Man."

Figure 33. Nebraska Man (Credit: Wikipedia)

In **1922**, the head of the American Museum of Natural History (Henry Fairfield Osborn) proclaimed that the single molar found by Harold J. Cook in 1917 belonged to the first *pithecanthropoid* (ape-man) of the Americas, hence the name "western ape." The globally-distributed *Illustrated London News* broadcast British evolutionist Grafton Elliot Smith's receiving knighthood for his efforts in publicizing "Nebraska Man." This imaginative "reconstruction" of the tooth's owner is a club-carrying ape-man walking upright. It shows primitive tools, possibly domesticated animals, and a brutish bride gathering roots. An artist derived all this from a single tooth! In July 1925, the Nebraska Man tooth was used to prove man evolved from ape-like creatures in the Scopes "Monkey Trial" held in Dayton, Tennessee.

This all changed when excavations continued in 1927–1928 at the same place the tooth was found. These excavations revealed that the tooth belonged neither to man nor ape, but to a wild pig![188] Then, in 1972, living herds of this same pig were discovered in Paraguay, South America.[189] According to the late renowned creation scientist Duane T. Gish, "this is a case in which a scientist made a man out of a pig, and then the pig made a monkey out of the scientist!"[190]

Scopes Trial

Next, the Scopes Trial of **1925** (Tennessee v. John Scopes) tested the state of Tennessee Butler Act, which prohibited the teaching of "any theory that denies the story of the Divine Creation of man as taught in the Bible, and to teach instead that man has descended from a lower order of animals." In other words, the Tennessee Butler Act made it illegal to teach human evolution in public school.

The Scopes Trial was one of the most famous trials of the 20th century, and public high school students still study it today—or at least watch the counterfactual black and white movie version titled *Inherit the Wind*. The famous criminal lawyer Clarence Darrow, known for believing that God was not knowable, represented John Scopes, a substitute high school teacher who was brought to trial for teaching evolution against State law. Three-time Democratic Presidential candidate and Christian William Jennings Bryan led the prosecution. The movie portrays him as a raving mad lunatic, but in real life he was calm, reasonable, and winsome. Scopes was found guilty under the Butler Act and was fined $100.

We bring up the Scopes Trial for three reasons. First, the case shows the growing tension in the creation-evolution debate and the extent to which each viewpoint was taught in school about 100 years ago. Second, both Nebraska Man (a pig's tooth) and Piltdown Man (a complete forgery) were used as evidence to prove evolution at the Scopes Trial.[191] Third, legal battles regarding these issues resonate to this day. For example, removing the Ten Commandments, Crosses, and Nativity Scenes from public spaces makes big news.

Progressing through the early- to mid-1900s, students continued to learn biblical creation, even in public schools.[192] While some might find this difficult to believe because evolution theory is taught so widely in today's public schools, browsing public school textbooks from this era easily confirms this fact. For example, in 1941 John Cretzinger investigated evolution teaching in 54 biological textbooks published between 1800 and 1933. He wrote, "The theory of Evolution was finally formulated by Charles Darwin in 1858, but it was destined to have little acceptance in secondary school books until after 1900 when the convincing evidence of Wallace and Haeckel made that theory acceptable as on the secondary science level."[193] Evolution theory was still only minimally represented in textbooks about 100 years ago, with only token representations in junior high and high school texts.

In the 1950s, G.D. Skoog wrote, "… there was a continued increase in the emphasis on evolution in the textbooks from 1900 to 1950. This trend was reversed in the 1950s when the concept was deemphasized slightly."[194] A recent analysis of high school biology textbooks shows that emphasis on the topic of evolution decreased just before the 1925 Scopes Trial. The relative priority of evolution teaching retuned to pre-Scopes levels by 1935 and did not decrease significantly in the decades that followed.[195]

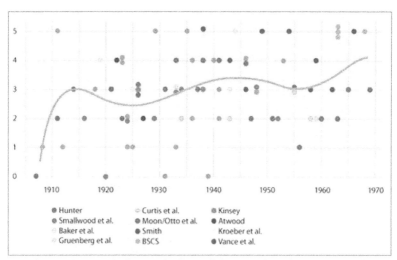

Figure 34. Relative Priority of the Topic of Evolution in Biology Textbooks 1907–1969.[196] The data in this image included 82 American high school biology textbooks published between 1907 and 1969. Each textbook was assigned a rating between 0 and 5 based on a qualitative assessment of the presentation of the topic of evolution.

Figure 34 shows a clear decline in the priority of the topic of evolution in the years ahead of Scopes trial in 1925, restoration of the topic to earlier levels by 1935, a secondary decline from about 1945 to 1955 and then a rise into the 1960s. A different analysis of 93 biology textbooks done by G.D. Skoog revealed:

> Analysis of the 93 biology textbooks revealed that prior to 1960, evolution was treated in a cursory and generally noncontroversial manner. However, there was a continued increase in the emphasis on evolution in the textbooks from 1900 to 1950. This trend was reversed in the 1950s when the concept was deemphasized slightly. In the 1960s the activities and influence of the Biological Sciences Curriculum Study

(BSCS) resulted in several textbooks that gave unprecedented emphasis to evolution. Accordingly, 51% of the total words written on the topics concerned with the study of evolution in the 83 textbooks published between 1900-1968 appeared in 17 textbooks published in the 1960s.[197]

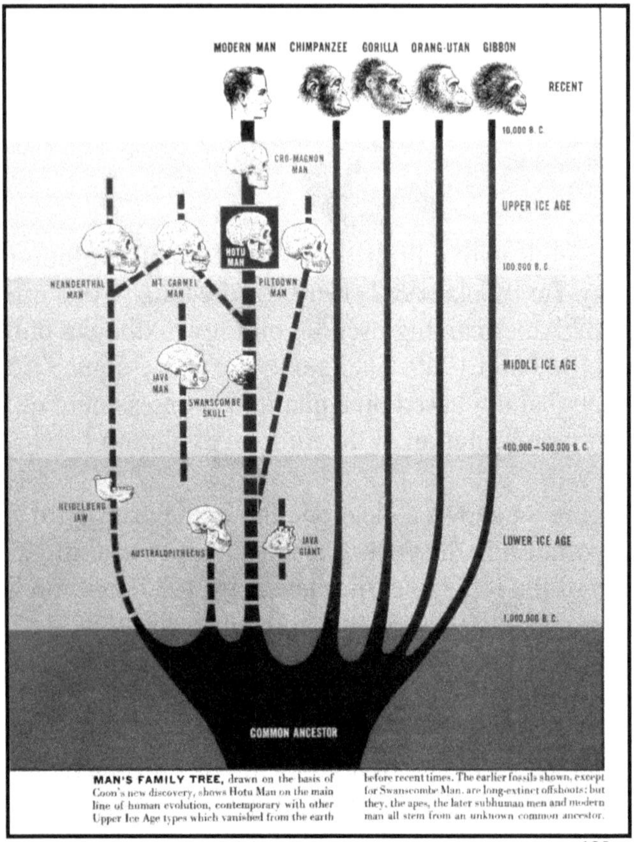

Figure 35. 1951 Life Magazine Evolutionary Tree[198] (still showing Java Man and Piltdown Man). This drawing shows a typical idea of human evolution in the 1950s, published in the well-known Life Magazine in 1951.

In **1959** a new fossil find filled a much-needed gap, since by then Nebraska and Piltdown frauds left nothing but a gaping hole that countless fossils should have filled if human evolution really happened. Enter *Zinjanthropus boisei*. National Geographic featured "Zinj," for short, as "Nutcracker Man" and framed it as "our real ancestor." Today, "virtually no evolutionist believes anymore that Zinj was our ancestor, but the images remain deep in millions of subconscious minds, reinforced by successive waves of other, often similarly temporary, "ape ancestor" images."[199] What happened? Further investigation revealed they were just extinct apes. Scientists have renamed them *Paranthropus*, and decided that they evolved alongside humans, not as our ancestors.

Next, in 1960 anthropologists uncovered remains from various locations at Olduvai Gorge in northern Tanzania and cobbled them together to make *Homo habilis*. *Homo habilis*, discussed in detail below, clearly does not fit in the line-up of human ancestry.

The concept of evolution became easier to believe in **1965** when Time-Life Books published the infamous "March of Progress" illustration in *Early Man*.[200] This book included a foldout section (shown in Figure 36) that displayed the sequence of figures drawn by Rudolph Zallinger.

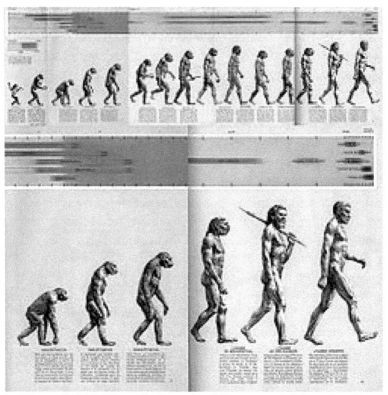

Figure 36. Zallinger's March of Progress (1965) (Credit: Wikipedia)

The year **1974** welcomed the famous "Lucy," a fossil form that bears the name *Australopithecus afarensis*. Lucy is arguably the most famous human evolution icon ever displayed in public school textbooks. Pictures and dioramas of Lucy inhabit countless museums and thousands of articles and dissertations. Lucy will be extensively discussed in the next section, where we expose details showing that it was merely an extinct ape.

Figure 37. National Geographic "March of Progress" (1985). Moving into the 1980s, this image provides an example of the current thinking about human evolution. (Credit: National Geographic magazine, 1985)

While Figure 37 was designed to show the alleged progression of "the evolution of running," it demonstrates the amazing imagination that artists have when taking scant fossil evidence and making them look increasingly human by lining them up side-by-side and altering their anatomies to fit the story. One such artist admitted: "I wanted to get a human soul into this ape-like face to indicate something about where she was headed."[201] Medical doctor Matthew Thomas wrote, "If today's police detectives obtained and interpreted evidence following these same principles/guidelines there would be chaos... yet we're supposed to accept this in science—paleontology—a field that seems to produce such abundant returns from such few fragments of fact![202]

Evolution Teaching in Today's Public Schools

Fast forward to today, where human evolution along with evolution theory in general, are taught as fact in public schools. The map shown in Figure 38 shows the creation-evolution teaching by state and school type (private/public). This map reveals that only two states (Louisiana and Tennessee) allow the Biblical view of Creation to be widely taught in public schools. The state of Texas has several charter schools that allow Creation curricula and nine states have private schools that accept tax-funded vouchers or scholarships that provide creation-based curricula.

Figure 38. Creation-Evolution Teaching by State.[203]

Amazingly, all states taught creation 100 years ago. It is even more shocking when considering the fact that about 70% of Americans profess Christianity,[204] and 46% of Americans believe that God created humans miraculously less than 10,000 years ago (see below). Wow—why do 96% of the states (48 of 50) teach "evolution as fact" in public schools, while 70% of America is "Christian" and 46% believe that God recently (and miraculously) created humans? We offer some spiritual answers to this complex question below. Fortunately, the vast majority of homeschoolers in the U.S. use creation-based curriculum, and most private Christian schools use creation-based curricula that treat Genesis historically.

History Tour Wrap-up

While going through the 150-year "tour" through man's ideas of human origins, did you notice that the story changes substantially every few decades? Neanderthals were used to prove the "pre-human" myth from **1829 until the 1950s** when it was shown that they were human in almost every practical sense—burying their dead, making instruments, practicing burial rituals, using advanced tools, and even being buried alongside humans.[205] Java Man fooled the world from **1891 to 1939.** Nebraska Man (a pig's tooth) filled the gap from **1917 until 1927.** Piltdown Man (a fraud) reigned from **1912 until 1953.** It seems like when one icon deceives a generation, a new one is introduced to save the day, and carry the evolutionary ideas for another generation.

Biblical creation, however, fits both "reality" and the fossil record much better. In reality, apes reproduce after their own kind and humans after theirs. And in the fossil record we see apes (including some extinct apes) and humans in a variety of shapes, and sizes. Why would you want to put your faith and understanding of our origins in a "science" that clearly changes its mind every 20 years? The Biblical position has fit the facts since the beginning and has never changed.

Why is Evolution Taught in Public Schools?

The following chart shows the percentage of all Americans who hold the creationist view that God created humans in their present form within the last 10,000 years. This has been the predominant view since the question has been tracked by the Gallup Poll for the past 30 years. About one-third of Americans believe that humans evolved, but with God's guidance; 15% say humans evolved, but that God had no part in the process.

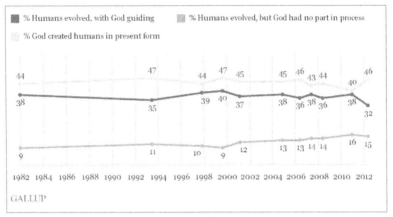

Figure 39. American Positions on Human Origins: 1982 to 2012[206]

If the majority position on human origins is "Divine Creation less than 10,000 years ago," then why do the majority of secular institutions today teach that humans evolved, a position which is held by only 15% of the U.S. population? Some might answer this question by stating, "Separation of church and state" or by offering some plausible political explanations. Some might say that "apathetic Christians" are to blame. While these and other explanations might seem to fit, we offer a different reason—a *spiritual* reason.

The Bible gives the purpose behind a strong delusion that will arise. "They perish because they refused to love the truth and so be saved. For this reason, God sends them a powerful delusion so that they will believe the lie and so that all will be condemned who have not believed the truth but have delighted in wickedness" (2 Thessalonians 2:10–12). Could the "powerful delusion" be evolution and "the lie" be that God does not exist? This delusion is sent to those who chose not to believe the Gospel of Christ. It takes more faith to believe in evolution than Creation, and Romans 1 makes it clear that everyone will be held accountable to the Creator because of His Creation:

> The wrath of God is being revealed from heaven against all the godlessness and wickedness of people, who suppress the truth by their wickedness, since what may be known about God is plain to them, because God has made it plain to them. For since the creation of the world God's invisible qualities—his eternal power and divine nature—have been clearly seen, being understood from what has been made, so that people are without excuse. (Romans 1:18–20)

This passage continues to explain that God allows those who disregard and reject Him to earn their own condemnation. This process is happening in America at a record pace—showing that some prophesies in Scripture are increasingly relevant today:

> Above all, you must understand that in the last days scoffers will come, scoffing and following their own evil desires. They will say, "Where is this 'coming' he promised? Ever since our ancestors died, everything goes on as it has since the beginning of creation." But they deliberately forget that long ago by God's word the heavens came into being and the earth was formed out of water and by water. By these waters also the world of that time was deluged and destroyed. (2 Peter 3:3–6)

Peter warns that these scoffers would "willfully forget" about the biblical creation account and the catastrophe of the Flood. Just how does someone "willfully forget" about something? By *teaching the opposite*—which is exactly what's happening in today's public schools. Creation deniers replace the worldwide Flood with long-age geology, just as Peter foretold. Indeed, the mission that was started by Charles Lyell in 1830—to "free science from Moses" [207] (meaning the

Genesis creation and Flood accounts)—has made incredible progress.

Each person has a choice. We can accept and believe the truth of Jesus Christ as presented in the Scriptures—that His death paid our sin debt, and that His resurrection paved the way to everlasting life for believers. "This is love for God: to obey His commands" (1 John 5:3). He commands everyone everywhere to turn from their sins and go to Him. Conversely, to know the truth and not obey it earns the wrath of God: "The wrath of God is being revealed from heaven against all the godlessness and wickedness of men who suppress the truth by their wickedness" (Romans 1:18). Frankly, there is no more dangerous condition for man than to know the truth and refuse to obey it. To do so is to harden the heart and make God's condemnation sure.

"Professing themselves to be wise they became fools."
– Romans 1:22

"Why is not every geological formation and every stratum full of such intermediate links? Geology assuredly does not reveal any such finely graduated organic chain; and this is the most obvious and serious objection which can be urged against the theory."
– Charles Darwin, Origin of Species, 1872.

"There is a popular image of human evolution that you'll find all over the place ... On the left of the picture there's an ape ... On the right, a man ... Between the two is a succession of figures that become ever more like humans ... Our progress from ape to human looks so smooth, so tidy. It's such a beguiling image that even the experts are loath to let it go. But it is an illusion."
– Bernard Wood, Professor of Human Origins, George Washington University[208]

"Fossil evidence of human evolutionary history is fragmentary and open to various interpretations. Fossil evidence of chimpanzee evolution is absent altogether."
– Henry Gee, Senior Editor of Nature Magazine[209]

"Modern apes, for instance, seem to have sprung out of nowhere. They have no yesterday, no fossil record. And the true origin of modern humans—of upright, naked, tool-making, big-brained beings - is, if we are to be honest with ourselves, an equally mysterious matter."
– Dr. Lyall Watson, Anthropologist[210]

Chapter 9: Typical Ape-to-Human Progression in Public School Textbooks
Daniel A. Biddle, Ph.D. & Dave Bisbee

The four "stages" of human evolution typically presented in Sixth Grade Social Studies (World History) classes looks like this:

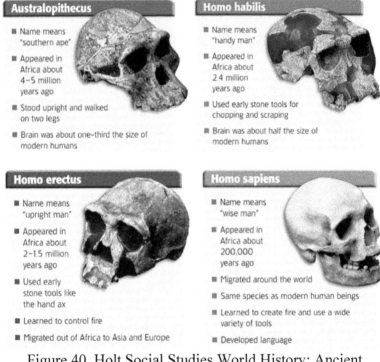

Figure 40. Holt Social Studies World History: Ancient Civilizations[211](Credit: Holt Social Studies World History: Ancient Civilizations, Holt, pages 24-35, 2006)

Next we'll review each of these "ape-to-human" icons one at a time, starting first with "Lucy."

Australopithecus afarensis ("Lucy")

In 1974, Donald Johanson discovered a fossil in Ethiopia, Africa that he declared was the "missing link" between man and ape. The fossil was nicknamed "Lucy" and given the scientific name *Australopithecus afarensis*. Australopithecus simply means "southern ape." Southern ape is a very appropriate name because, as you'll learn below, Lucy was just that—an ape!

Although public school textbooks often state that Lucy was our ancestor and feature human-like drawings of her, the fossil evidence tells quite a different story. Now, after 40 years of research on Lucy and other Australopithecine fossils, here is what scientists have found (Note: because more Australopithecine fossils have been found since Lucy, some of the references below refer to *Australopithecines* in general):

- **Entire Skeleton:** Even though many of the first reports that came out after Lucy was discovered stated that Lucy's skeleton was "40% complete,"[212] Lucy's discoverer clarified in a book published 22 years after[213] Lucy was found stating: "Lucy's skeleton consists of some 47 out of 207 bones, including parts of upper and lower limbs, the backbone, ribs and the pelvis. With the exception of the mandible [lower jaw] the skull is represented only by five vault fragments, and most of the hand and foot bones are missing." This computes to actually **22.8%** of the complete skeleton (47 ÷ 206), not "about 40%." Generations of artists have drawn Lucy with human feet even though the fossil lacked both hand and foot bones. Frustratingly for those who care about truth, illustrations continue to ignore subsequent finds, revealing that *Australopithecines* had curved ape fingers and grasping feet.

- **Skull:** Even though only a few fragments of Lucy's skull were found, they revealed that her skull was about the same size as a chimpanze. As Donald Johanson himself said, "Her skull was almost entirely missing. So knowing the exact size of Lucy's brain was the crucial bit of missing evidence. But from the few skull fragments we had, it looked surprisingly small."[214] Later estimates reveal that Lucy's brain was just one third the size of a human's, which is the same size as the average chimpanze brain.[215] Sir Solly Zuckerman, chief scientific advisor to the British government, said that the "Australopithecine skull is in fact so overwhelmingly ape-like, as opposed to human that the contrary position could be equated to an assertion that black is white."[216]
- **Height:** Lucy was about 3.5 feet tall (and most other Australopithecine fossils found since are similar in height).
- **Walking Upright:** Even evolutionists strongly disagree over whether or not Lucy walked upright like humans.[217] Lucy's hip was found broken and was reconstructed, so it's difficult to tell how she (and other *Australopithecines*) moved. Her bones seemed to show that she was a "real swinger… based on anatomical data, *Australopithecines* must have been arboreal [tree-dwelling]…Lucy's pelvis shows a flare that is better suited for climbing than for walking."[218] Most likely, Australopithecine apes could walk in their own unique way—unlike chimps or humans.
- **Fingers and Limbs:** Other examples of Australopithecine apes had curved fingers and ape-like limb proportions that point toward her kind as living in trees, so we can assume the same was true of Lucy.[219]
- **Locking Wrists:** Lucy had locking wrists like quadruped apes, not like humans.[220] This was even

reported in the San Diego Union Tribune: "A chance discovery made by looking at a cast of the bones of 'Lucy,' the most famous fossil of *Australopithecus afarensis*, shows her wrist was stiff, like a chimpanzee's, Brian Richmond and David Strait of George Washington University in Washington, D.C., reported. This suggests that her ancestors walked on their knuckles."[221] Another study revealed: "Measurements of the shape of wristbones (distal radius) showed that Lucy's type were knuckle walkers, similar to gorillas."[222]

- **Teeth:** The wear on Lucy's teeth indicate she ate tree fruit.[223] Penn State University professor of anthropology and biology Alan Walker has studied paleontological fossils to learn how to reconstruct their ancient diets. In speaking of Alan Walker's material, Johanson noted: "Dr. Alan Walker of Johns Hopkins has recently concluded that the polishing effect he finds on the teeth of robust [thick-boned] *Australopithecines* and modern chimpanzees indicates that *Australopithecines*, like chimps, were fruit eaters.... If they were primarily fruit eaters, as Walker's examination of their teeth suggests they were, then our picture of them, and of the evolutionary path they took, is wrong."[224]

- **Ribs:** Lucy's rib cage is not shaped like a human's, but was cone shaped like an ape's.[225] Peter Schmid, a paleontologist at the Anthropological Institute in Zurich, Switzerland, studied a replica of Lucy and noted: "When I started to put the skeleton together, I expected it to look human. Everyone had talked about Lucy being very modern. Very human. So I was surprised by what I saw. I noticed that the ribs were more round in cross section. More like what you see in apes. Human ribs are flatter in cross section. But the shape of the ribcage itself was the biggest surprise of all. The human ribcage is barrel shaped. And I just couldn't get Lucy's ribs to fit this kind of shape. But I could get them to make a conical-shaped ribcage, like what you see in apes."[226]

- **Ears:** Earlier in this book we learned that an animal's semicircular canals help reveal its identity. After extensive research, it has been concluded that the semicircular canals of *Australopithecines* resemble an ape's, not a human's or a transitional creature's.[227]
- **Gender:** A great deal of debate has emerged even over Lucy's gender, with some scientists arguing that the evidence shows she was actually a male! Articles with catchy titles have emerged such as "Lucy or Lucifer?[228] and more recently, "Lucy or Brucey?"[229]
- **Toes:** The toe bones of *Australopithecines* were long and curved, even by ape standards.[230] Their fossils thus show no evidence that they walked like humans, and strong evidence that they did not.

It is because of these recent findings that leading experts in Australopithecine fossils conclude that Lucy and other *Australopithecines* are *extinct ape-like creatures*:

- Dr. Charles Oxnard (professor of anatomy) wrote, "The *Australopithecines* known over the last several decades … are now irrevocably removed from a place in the evolution of human bipedalism…All this should make us wonder about the usual presentation of human evolution in introductory textbooks."[231]
- Dr. Solly Zuckerman heads the Department of Anatomy of the University of Birmingham in England and is a scientific adviser to the highest level of the British government. He studied Australopithecus fossils for 15 years with a team of scientists and concluded, "They are just apes."[232]

- Dr. Wray Herbert admits that his fellow paleoanthropologists "compare the pygmy chimpanzee to 'Lucy,' one of the oldest hominid fossils known, and finds the similarities striking. They are almost identical in body size, in stature and in brain size."[233]
- Dr. Albert W. Mehlert said, "the evidence… makes it overwhelmingly likely that Lucy was no more than a variety of pygmy chimpanzee, and walked the same way (awkwardly upright on occasions, but mostly quadrupedal). The 'evidence' for the alleged transformation from ape to man is extremely unconvincing."[234]
- Marvin Lubenow, Creation researcher and author of the book *Bones of Contention,* wrote, "There are no fossils of Australopithecus or of any other primate stock in the proper time period to serve as evolutionary ancestors to humans. *As far as we can tell from the fossil record, when humans first appear in the fossil record they are already human*[235] (emphasis added).
- Drs. DeWitt Steele and Gregory Parker concluded: "Australopithecus can probably be dismissed as a type of extinct chimpanzee."[236]

In reality, these ape-like creatures' remains occur in small-scale deposits that rest on top of broadly extending flood deposits. They were probably fossilized after Noah's Flood, during the Ice Age, when tremendous rains buried Ice Age creatures.[237] Donald Johanson, the discoverer of Lucy, admits: "The rapid burial of bones at Hadar, particularly those of the 'First Family,' are related to a geological catastrophe suggesting, perhaps, a flash flood. Bones are fragmented and scattered because individuals fell into a river, or were washed into a river, rapidly transported, broken up, and scattered. These are all products of a depositional process."[238]

Despite these recent findings, Lucy continues to be displayed more human-like than her fossils would justify. Some examples of these exaggarations at public museums and in textbooks are below. First, let's look at what they actually found:

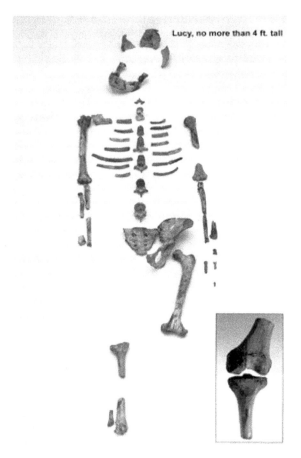

Figure 41. Actual Lucy Fossil
(Credit: Answers in Gensis Presentation Library)

Before viewing some renditions that superimpose human characteristics on Lucy, let's start with what she probably looked like.

Figure 42. What Lucy Most Likely Looked Like
(Credit: Answers in Genesis Presentation Library)

Next, let's look at how Lucy is represented at public exhibits, such as those found at the St. Louis Zoo and Denver Museum of Nature and Science.

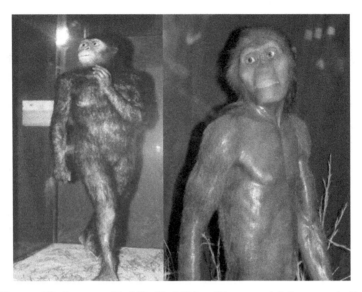

Figure 43. Lucy at Public Exhibits (Zoos and Museums). Lucy at the St. Louis Zoo (left) (Credit: Answers in Genesis) and at the Denver Museum of Nature and Science (Credit: Brian Thomas)

Most Lucy reproductions show her with white sclera (eyeballs), even though 100% of all apes alive today have dark eyes. Do you think this was done to make her look more human-like?

Figure 44. Lucy with White Sclera (Eyeballs). Like similar Hollywood characters, this imaginative version of Lucy presents it with human eyes, though eyes don't fossilize. (Credit: Wikipedia)

Now let's view how Lucy is typically represented in public school textbooks:

Figure 45. Lucy in Public School Textbooks [Credit: Australopithecus afarensis (History Alive! The Ancient World (Palo Alto, CA: Teachers Curriculum Institute, 2004)].

Next, let's take a look at where 100% of the Australopithecus fossils have been found (see circles in Figure 46).

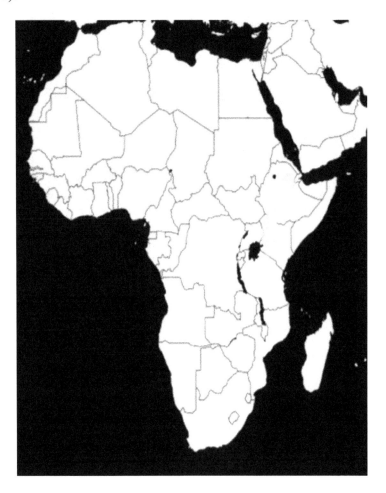

Figure 46. Map Showing where Australopithecus Fossils have been Found [239] (Credit: *www.fossilworks.com*)

Here is one interesting fact that you won't likely learn about from school textbooks: At the specific site where Lucy was found, 87 other animal types were discovered—a wide collection that included just about every animal you would expect to see with ape-like creatures, including elephants, rhinoceros, hippopotamus, antelope, and numerous other African-native animals. In fact, this specific area (the Hadar Valley formation) has yielded nearly 6,000 specimens representing as many as 4,000 different animals.[240] It certainly makes sense that apes in Lucy's day were living with similar creatures in a similar habitat as ape-like creatures today! Now if Lucy's fossil looks like an ape, she lived with other apes, lived in an environment like apes today, and lived with 87 other animal types that live around apes, what do you think she was?

How many Australopithecus afarensis fossils have been found?

An online research tool known as the Global Biodiversity Information Facility (GBIF) tabulates various fossil specimens found around the world. This free tool provides a single point of access to more than 500 million records, shared freely by hundreds of institutions worldwide, making it the biggest biodiversity database on the internet, with information regarding more than 1.5 million species.[241]

Using GBIF to research *Australopithecus afarensis* fossils reveals a total of 47 "occurrences" (individual findings or dig sites where multiple specimens have been found). Browsing through these "occurrences" reveals just how limited the findings are for this species. The biggest occurrence is called the "First Family" where 260 bones and bone pieces were found representing between 13 to 17 creatures.[242] The vast majority of the bones were found within the top few feet of the surface, indicating they likely died at the same time.[243]

Some recent estimates place the total count of *Australopithecus afarensis* fossils at only 362 fragments,[244] which likely represents only a few dozen individual creatures. With only 260 of these fragments coming from one "family," and another 47 from Lucy, one wonders where all the leftovers are from supposedly millions of years of

Lucy populations. If human evolution really occurred as the textbooks state, wouldn't we expect to find, as Charles Darwin stated, "innumerable transitional forms"[245] and "every geological formation full of intermediate links"? Clearly, as Darwin himself admitted, "Geology does not reveal any such finely-graduated chain; and this is the most obvious and serious objection against the theory."[246]

Even though earth layers have revealed precious few Australopithecine fossils, they reveal all we need to know: Lucy was an ape. Even the most recent Human Family Tree from the Smithsonian Institute shows that *Australopithecines* are not even on the same "branch" of the tree that includes *Homo habilis* and *Homo erectus*!

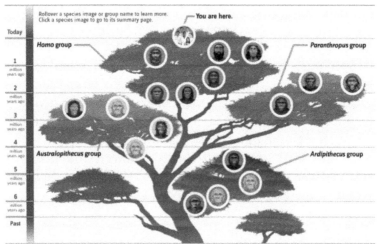

Figure 47. Smithsonian Institute Human Family Tree[247]

Homo habilis

Homo habilis or "handy man" is often shown in public school textbooks as a "transitional" form between apes and humans. Textbooks state that this evolutionary ancestor supposedly lived around 1.4–2.4 million years ago[248] and was one of the "stepping stones" in the line of human evolution. In reality, *Homo habilis* is not just one fossil, but rather a *very* small collection of fossils that have been the center of intense controversy and confusion for decades. With so many now agreeing that Lucy was almost all ape, and with so many agreeing that the other species in genus Homo, including Neanderthals, are modern man, evolutionists are desperate for a genuine link between apes and man. Frankly, if *Homo habilis* fails to connect apes to humans, then human evolution fails with it.

The name *Homo habilis* was officially given to a set of fossils that were discovered by a team led by scientists Louis and Mary Leakey between 1960 and 1963 at Olduvai Gorge in Tanzania. In 1964, this team announced *Homo habilis* as a "new human ancestor." The original fossils were said to be 1.8 million years old and consisted of scattered skull parts, hand bones, and foot bones from four young specimens. According to Louis Leakey, the foot bones showed signs that *Homo habilis* may have been able to walk upright on two feet, and the hand bones indicated they were skillful with their hands. However, since these bones were not found next to the skull fragments, there was no way to be sure that they belonged to the same creature. Some evolutionary scientists even believe that the *Homo habilis* fossils were just a mixture of Australopithecine (ape) and *Homo erectus* (human) fossils—not a new species at all, and certainly not a missing link.[249]

The Leakey's also found some primitive stone tools at the site. Originally scientists claimed these tools belonged to another supposed missing link known as *Zinjanthropus,* which turned out to be just an ape. Louis Leakey claimed the tools were used by their newfound individuals. This was the reason for naming these fossils "*Homo habilis*" or handy man. But because we weren't there to observe these creatures, we don't know if the creatures used the tools, or if the tools were used on them!

In 1986, Tim White and Don Johanson discovered a partial adult skeleton. Since the fossil was discovered in Olduvai Gorge, it was designated "Olduvai Hominid 62" and was dated (by evolutionists) at 1.8 million years old. Because the skull and teeth were similar to the original *Homo habilis* fossils found in 1964, the new fossil was said to belong to the same species. This presented three big problems for evolutionists:

1. The body of Olduvai Hominid 62 was rather ape-like and even smaller than the famous Australopithecine fossil known as Lucy.[250] Since Lucy was about 3.5 feet tall, and *Homo erectus* individuals grew to be about six feet, Olduvai Hominid 62 should have been somewhere in between them if it truly links the two.
2. Since the body of Olduvai Hominid 62 was ape-like, it seemed to support the belief that the original *Homo habilis* fossils found in 1964 were actually a mixture of Australopithecine parts and human bones, most notably human hands and feet.
3. If the fossilized hand and feet bones found in 1964 were actually human, then the tools found at that site were probably used by people living there—not by ape-like people, or people-like apes, but the descendants of Adam and Eve.

Despite the bold statements made about *Homo habilis* in many school textbooks, paleoanthropologists are still trying to make sense out of this odd collection of fragments. Here is how evolutionist Richard Leakey described the problem: "Of the several dozen specimens that have been said at one time or another to belong to this species, at least half of them don't. But there is no consensus as to which 50% should be excluded. No one anthropologist's 50% is quite the same as another's."[251] The same could be said of every proposed missing link. For every evolutionist who asserts that a particular fossil belongs in human ancestry, another one counter-asserts that it evolved parallel to the unknown evolutionary ancestors of man. What a mess.

Some studies have revealed that the ears of the *Homo habilis* specimens studied prove they were just apes. Of course, these results don't cover the fossil bits attributed to this name that actually belong to another. Anatomy specialists Fred Spoor, Bernard Wood, and Frans Zonneveld compared the semicircular canals in the inner ear of humans and apes, including several Australopithecus and *Homo habilis* specimens. Because the semicircular canals are involved in maintaining balance, studying them can reveal whether an animal was inclined to walk upright or on all fours. Their study concluded: "Among the fossil hominids [apes or humans] the earliest species to demonstrate the modern human morphology is *Homo erectus*. In contrast, the semi-circular canal dimensions in crania from southern Africa attributed to Australopithecus and *Paranthropus* resemble those of the extant great apes."[252] The authors wrote that *Homo habilis* "relied less on bipedal behavior than the *Australopithecines*," meaning that the *Homo habilis* specimen was even more ape-like than the Australopithecus samples. They concluded that the *Homo habilis* specimen they studied "represents an unlikely intermediate between the morphologies seen in the *Australopithecines* and *Homo erectus*."[253] In other words—the *Homo habilis* is a "mixed bag" classification that includes some ape bones and some human bones. In summary, their study resulted in two very important findings:

1. These *Homo habilis* fossils do not actually belong to the "human" group, but rather to an ape category, and probably Australopithecus.
2. Both *Homo habilis* and Australopithecus walked stooped over like an ape and not upright like a man.

The claim that *Australopithecus and Homo habilis* walked upright was disproved by inner ear analyses carried out by Fred Spoor. He and his team compared the centers of balances in the inner ears, and showed that both moved in a similar way to apes of our own time.

Figure 48. Semicircular Canals[254]

So was *Homo habilis* really our ancestor? Even evolutionists disagree. Dr. Bernard Wood of George Washington University, an expert on evolutionary "trees," suggests that none of the *Homo habilis* fossils represent human ancestors. He wrote, "The diverse group of fossils from 1 million years or so ago, known as *Homo habilis*, may be more properly recognized as *Australopithecines*."[255]

In a more recent article titled, "Human evolution: Fifty years after *Homo habilis*," Dr. Wood summarizes more than one-half of a century of research on *Homo habilis* by concluding that:

> Although *Homo habilis* is generally larger than Australopithecus *africanus*, its teeth and jaws have the same proportions. What little evidence there is about its body shape, hands and feet suggest that *Homo habilis* would be a much better climber than undisputed human ancestors. So, if *Homo habilis* is added to Homo, the genus has an incoherent mishmash of features. Others

disagree, but I think you have to cherry-pick the data to come to any other conclusion. My sense is that handy man should belong to its own genus, neither australopith nor human.[256]

Although evolutionists keep trying to convince themselves (and others) that humans evolved from ape-like creatures, interpretations of the fossil record have been filled with mistakes, fraud, and fantasy, with almost every major pronouncement denounced by another expert. Why don't textbooks tell these truths? Perhaps before even examining the evidence, textbook writers reject the truth that we were created by God on day six of creation week. Since the beginning, humans have always been humans and apes have always been apes. And since Adam and Eve sinned, humans have worked extra hard to ignore our Creator.

Homo erectus

Homo erectus means "erect or upright man." Typically, school textbooks claim that *Homo erectus* fossils fill the gap between *Australopithecines* (apes) and both Neanderthals and modern humans.

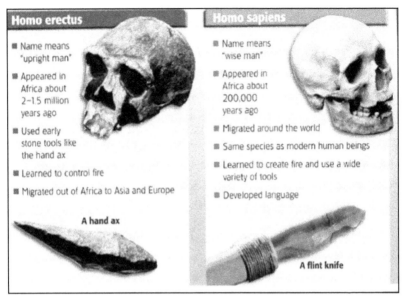

Figure 49. Homo erectus in School Textbooks [Credit: Holt Social Studies World History: Ancient Civilizations (Holt, 2006, pages 24-35)]

Here is an example of what a middle school textbook (Holt, 2006) teaches about *Homo erectus*:

- The name *Homo erectus* means "upright man."
- Scientists agree that *Homo erectus* was not fully human and was the evolutionary link between *Homo habilis* and *Homo sapiens*.
- *Homo erectus* first "appeared" in Africa 2 to 1.5 million years ago and migrated to Asia and Europe.
- *Homo erectus* used early stone tools and learned to control fire.

Although school textbooks (like the one shown above) often teach that we evolved from primitive, sub-human ancestors known as *Homo erectus*,[257] the growing creationist (and evolutionist) view is that *Homo erectus* and all Homo *sapien* forms should be considered not as separate species but as a single human species that represent a wide range of diversity. In the Biblical Creation view there was no evolution from apes, nor was there any "ascent" from an inferior human type to a more advanced kind.[258] A total of about 280 *Homo erectus* fossils have been found to date[259] They include bones, bone fragments, and teeth.

Some evolutionists claim that the size of the skulls helps determine how far along a creature is in its journey towards becoming human. The skulls designated *Homo erectus* fall within the cranial capacity range of modern humans (700 cc to 2100 cc).[260] Marvin Lubenow, an expert on human fossils, comments: "My own conclusion is that *Homo erectus* and Neanderthal are actually the same: *Homo erectus* is the lower end, with regard to size, of a continuum that includes *Homo erectus*, early *Homo sapiens*, [who looked just like people today] and Neanderthal. The range of cranial capacities for fossil humans is in line with the range of cranial capacities for modern humans."[261]

One study compared modern humans to *Homo erectus* fossils including Java Man, Peking Man, and East African Man. What they found was a big surprise to many evolutionists: A group of 202 modern day Australian aborigines share an astonishing 14 of the 17 *Homo erectus* traits.[262] The most recent evidence indicates that only a handful of features distinguish these two presumed species of man, and even these are doubtful.[263] Nobody should doubt the fully human status of Australian aborigines, so why doubt the fully human status of most fossils designated as *Homo erectus*?

Although *Homo erectus* is supposed to represent an evolutionary link between *Homo habilis* and *Homo sapiens*, its fossils occur throughout most layers thought to contain human evolution remains. The dates evolutionists assigned to these fossils show that *Homo erectus* lived during the **same time periods** as both *Homo habilis* (a category that includes a mixture of both Australopithecine and human fossils) and modern humans.[264] How could *Homo erectus* be an evolutionary link if they lived at the same time?

Table 10. Secular Homo erectus dates overlap with modern humans[265]

Homo erectus Fossil Name	Date Assigned by Evolutionists
Swartkrans SK-15, 18a and 18b	1.8 million years
KNM-WT15000 Kenya	1.6 million years
Kow Swamp Fossils	9,500 years
Cossack Skull	6,500 years
Mossgiel Individual	6,000 years

Many of the artifacts found with *Homo erectus* fossils show that they intelligently used tools, built shelters, controlled fire and even carved quartzite rocks into human figurines.[266] During the early 1800s, many Native Americans lived in a similar manner. In other words, although they were not as technologically advanced as some other cultures, they were fully human. The bones in the *Homo erectus* classification are really nothing more than an example of human variability. The next time you visit a public place, take a good look at the people around you (politely, of course). You'll see humans come in a wide variety of shapes and sizes.

Homo sapiens

Homo sapiens means "wise man" in Latin and is the scientific name for mankind. The human genus "Homo" includes Neanderthals and *Homo sapiens sapiens* ("wise, wise man"). Some sources show Neanderthals (Homo *neanderthalensis*) as a subspecies of modern man by accepting the name *Homo sapiens neanderthalensis*.[267] While evolutionary thinkers search for tiny differences on which to base their pre-judgment of ape ancestry, creation-based thinking sees fossil and modern variations as expressions of wide genetic potential that God built into Adam.

School textbooks often place "stone-age men" and "cavemen" into the *Homo sapiens* category. Even the term "cavemen" is somewhat misleading because it assumes that ape-like men had not yet evolved enough intelligence to construct homes. However, throughout history people have lived in caves wherever caves exist—even to very modern times. Sometimes their homes were permanent, sometimes they were temporary, and sometimes people found temporary shelter or buried their dead in caves.

The term caveman, however, typically refers to people who lived before or during the Ice Age. Five groups fit this definition: Neanderthals, early *Homo sapiens* (Cro-Magnon man), *Homo erectus*, Denisovans, and Homo *floresiensis*. The latter two groups were recently added.[268] Researchers discovered these remains in caves. Who were these people?

A biblical view on cavemen is simple: they were people who lived soon after the Flood, which left behind the rock layers and caves in which they found temporary shelter. Perhaps some cave-dwellers represented those who first scattered around the world from the Tower of Babel dispersal that Genesis chapter 11 describes. They sought caves as temporary and sometimes permanent shelters, especially during the post-Flood Ice Age.

According to Scripture, humans have been bright, innovative, and capable from the very beginning. We have seen the science of archaeology confirm this, as even cave-living humans left behind well-crafted tools. According to Genesis chapter 4, fifth generation humans like Tubal-cain worked with metals including copper and iron. People were gardening, farming, working with different types of metal and even building cities before the Flood. Cain was a tiller of the ground. (Gen. 4:2). Later in Cain's life he built a city. Cain's eighth generation Jubal "was the father of all those who play the harp and flute."

After the Flood, much of this technology and know-how was lost, especially after people scattered around the world from the Tower of Babel dispersion. Let's take a closer look at the two most common "cavemen" described in public school textbooks to see which expectation their remains most closely match: that of less-than-human evolutionary ancestors or fully human early wanderers.

Neanderthal Man[269]

Neanderthal man was named after the Neander Valley near Dusseldorf in West Germany where the first fossils were found in 1856. It gained its name because of the frequent visits by hymn writer Joachem Neander + *tal*, or *thal* in Old German, meaning "valley." Just as "Thomas" is pronounced "Tomas," so we pronounce "Neanderthal" as "Neandertal." Confusingly, experts use either spelling. The story of how evolutionists have classified Neanderthal from true man to "missing link" and then to variant forms of modern humans is as interesting as the people themselves. Originally, "when the first Neanderthal was discovered in 1856, even 'Darwin's bulldog,' Thomas Henry Huxley, recognized that it was fully human and not an evolutionary ancestor."[270] Nevertheless, evolutionary bias helped anatomist William King reinterpret the fossils, concluding they were a separate, primitive species of man called Homo *neanderthalensis*. This designation easily fit the assertion that modern humans evolved from Neanderthals. More and better evidence, including burial sites that held Neanderthals and modern men in the same tombs, forced some evolutionists to change its name in 1964. Today, with more than 200 known specimens representing 40+ discovery sites in Europe, Asia, and Africa, "Neanderthal fossils are the most plentiful in the world [of paleoanthropology]."[271] In recent decades this mound of data has testified to the fact that, "while the Neanderthals may not have been as culturally sophisticated as the people who followed . . . the Neanderthal people were not primitive but the most highly specialized of all the humans of the past."[272] "Evolutionists now admit that the Neanderthals were 100% human; they are classified as *Homo sapiens neanderthalensis*, designating them as a [subspecies] variety of modern humans."[273] Their skeletons were a bit thicker in places than most modern humans. They were up to 30% larger in body mass and had more than 13% larger brain volumes.

However, "the strongest evidence that Neanderthals were fully human and of our species is that, at four sites [3 in Israel and 1 in Croatia], Neanderthals and modern humans were buried together," indicating that "they lived together, worked together, intermarried, and were accepted as members of the same family, clan, and community" since generational "reproduction is on the species level."[274] Neanderthal burials include jewelry and purses, showing they had nothing to do with any ape-kind. Strikingly, the Neanderthal burial practice of using caves as family burial grounds or tribal cemeteries exactly parallels that of the post-Babel patriarchs of Genesis, for example Abraham (Genesis 23:17–20), Isaac (Genesis 25:7–11), and Jacob (Genesis 49:29–32.)

The lifespan of the Neanderthal people also looks astonishingly similar to the lifespan of those living in the post-Flood generations including Peleg (Genesis. 11:12–17). Using recent dental studies and digitized x-rays, computer-generated projections of orthodontic patients have illustrated the continuing growth of their craniofacial bones. These show a Neanderthal-like profile of the skull as the patient advances into their 300th, 400th, and even 500th year of simulated life.[275] Career dentist Dr. Cuozzo analyzed teeth and jaw development in children. He wrote, "studies on aging reveal that the older we get, the more our faces begin to look like those of Neanderthal man. The most accurate assumption that can be made about these strange-looking skeletons that are not old enough to be fossilized is that they have been alive long enough for their bones to change into those shapes—they are skeletons of patriarchs who lived hundreds of years, but have only been dead for thousands of years, not millions!"[276]

Creation researchers have been saying for decades that Neanderthal man was wholly human, with no hint of a single evolutionary transitional feature. Neanderthal DNA sequences published in 2010 confirmed this, showing that certain people groups today share bits of Neanderthal-specific DNA sequences.[277]

Cro-Magnon Man

Cro-Magnon Man is known as the "big hole man" in the French dialect local to the initial 1868 discovery site, a cave in the Dordogne area of Les Eyzies in southwest France. Once regarded as our most recent evolutionary ancestors on the "ape-to-man" illustrations, "evolutionists now admit that Cro-Magnons were modern humans. Cro-Magnons are classified as Homo *sapien sapiens* [wise, wise man'], the same classification assigned humans today."[278] Creation writer Vance Ferrell echoed this consensus when he wrote, "the Cro-Magnons were normal people, not monkeys; and they provide no evidence of a transition from ape to man."[279] With interests ranging from stone tools, fishhooks, and spears to more sublime activities like astronomy, art, and the afterlife, "every kind of evidence that we have a right to expect from the fossil and archeological record indicates that the Cro-Magnon and Neanderthal peoples were humans in the same ways that we are human."[280]

Contrary to popular belief, most Cro-Magnon people used caves for rituals, not residences. In addition, authenticated etchings on the cave walls at Minetada, Spain in 1915, and La Marche, central France (1937), depict Cro-Magnon men with clipped and groomed beards while the women display dresses and elegant hair styles.[281] Advanced not only in manner but also in the way they looked: "the Cro-Magnons were truly human, possibly of a noble bearing. Some were over six feet tall, with a cranial volume somewhat larger (by 200cc–400cc) than that of man today."[282] Brain size should not be exclusively used to judge whether or not a given specimen was human or not, but it can, in combination with other skull features, add its testimony. In any case, just as with Neanderthal man, Cro Magnon men were wholly human. Why do illustrations of human evolution show them walking up behind modern men if they showed no real differences after all?

Chapter 10: What about the Different "Races" of People?
Jerry Bergman, Ph.D.

Genesis teaches that God pronounced the first two created people *very good* when He created them at the very beginning. "Then God said, 'Let us make man in our image, in our likeness.' So God created man in His own image, in the image of God He created him; male and female He created them. God blessed them and said to them, 'Be fruitful and increase in number; fill the earth and subdue it.' God saw all that He had made, and it was very good" (Genesis 1:26-31 NIV).

Soon after, Adam openly violated God's command not to eat of the forbidden fruit, and as a result, sin entered into the human race. God had to curse all of creation, and on that day Adam and Eve began the process of aging that always ends in death. As a result, an originally perfect created man began accumulating genetic mutations both in his body cells and in his germ cells.

Every generation has suffered from these mutations ever since. They degenerate each person's body, sometimes causing death through cancer and other diseases. Mutations in the germ line over many generations have caused degeneration of the entire human race. This process has continued until today. Geneticists have identified the mutations that cause over 5,000 specific diseases in humans. Although a rare few mutations bring a benefit in very limited circumstances, 99.99% either cause harm or make virtually undetectable changes. But these small changes accumulate. After hundreds of generations, every person today inherits thousands of these mutations that now cause all kinds of damage.

Mutations in eggs and sperm cells are either lethal, harmful (disease-causing), or nearly neutral, having no immediate effect. As in body cells, near-neutral mutations cause miniscule damage. After enough of these accumulate, they cause a genetic meltdown leading to extinction of the species. The text *Principles of Medical Biochemistry*[283] under the subtitle "Mutations Are an Important Cause of Poor Health" states:

> At least one new mutation can be expected to occur in each round of cell division, even in cells with unimpaired DNA repair and in the absence of external mutagens [mutation-causing agents]. As a result, every child is born with an estimated 100 to 200 new mutations that were not present in the parents. Most of these mutations change only one or a few base pairs … However, an estimated one or two new mutations are "mildly detrimental." This means they are not bad enough to cause a disease on their own, but they can impair physiological functions to some extent, and they can contribute to multifactorial diseases [when many causes add up to cause illness]. Finally, about 1 per 50 infants is born with a diagnosable genetic condition that can be attributed to a single major mutation (p. 153).

The authors concluded that, as a result:

> Children are, on average, a little sicker than their parents because they have new mutations on top of those inherited from the parents. This mutational load is kept in check by natural selection. In most traditional societies, almost half of all children used to die before they had a chance to reproduce. Investigators can only guess that those who died had, on average, more "mildly detrimental" mutations than those who survived (p. 153).

If macro-evolution is true, it is *going the wrong way!* It does not cause the ascent of life by adding new and useful biological coding instructions, but rather the descent of life by eroding what remains of the originally created biological codes. Should we call it devolution instead?

What do mutations have to do with "races?" Geneticists have studied DNA sequences in all kinds of different people groups. These studies reveal that each people group—which is most easily identified on a cultural level by sharing a specific language—shares a set of mutations. They must have inherited these "race" mutations from their ancestors after the Tower of Babel, since their ancestors freely interbred for the several hundred years between the Flood and the Tower. Amazingly, however, all these mutations make up less than one percent of all human DNA in the human genome. This means that no matter how different from you someone looks, they are 99.9% genetically identical to you. For this reason, even evolutionary geneticists admit that the term "race" has virtually no biological backing. It comes from cultural and mostly language differences. Bottom line: all peoples have the same genetic basis to be considered fully human, while expressing interesting cultural and subtle physical variations.

The DNA Bottleneck

According to the chronologies in Genesis 5 and 11, the Genesis Flood occurred about 1,656 years after Creation. From possibly millions of pre-Flood peoples, only three couples survived the Flood and had children afterward. This caused a severe DNA bottleneck. Genetic bottlenecks occur when circumstances suddenly squeeze populations down to small numbers. They concentrate mutations and thus accelerate diseases. This occurs, for example, when people or animals marry or mate with close relations. Children or offspring from these unions have a much higher chance of inheriting mutations and the damage they cause. The genetic bottleneck of the Flood accelerated the decay of the human genome from Adam and Eve's once perfect genome.

Then, not long after the Tower of Babel a major dispersion of humans occurred, leading to diverse ethnicities tied to languages. The Bible records 70 families left the Tower. Many of them have gone extinct. Those few original languages have diversified into over 3,000 languages and dialects today. For example, English descended from the same basic language as German, while Welsh and Mandarin descended from fundamentally different original languages. Details from genetics and linguistics confirm Paul's statement in Acts 17:26, "He has made from one blood every nation of men to dwell on all the face of the earth."

Charles Darwin grouped these "nations" into "races," then organized races into those he believed were less human—less evolved—than others. He was completely wrong. Genetically, people in each ethnicity or nation share equal standing with other men. Biblically, they share equal standing before God, "For all have sinned and fallen short of the glory of God," according to Romans 3:23.

Physical Differences

As noted, all of the differences between the human races are all very superficial, such as differences in skin, hair, and eye color. These traits account for less than 0.012% of human genetic differences, or 1 gene out of 12,000.[284] The two major racial differences that our society uses to label races are hair shape and skin color differences. One reason why we have two very distinct racial groups in America today, commonly called blacks and whites, is because the original immigrant population in the United States 350 years ago included primarily light-skinned people from Northern Europe and dark-skinned people from Africa. However, when dark-skinned people marry those with light skin, their children usually show medium-tone skin. Adam and Eve must have had medium tone skin. Sometime in history—probably at Babel—those with darker skin took their languages one direction, while those with lighter skin took theirs in another. Of course, they almost never remained in total isolation. Genetic tests reveal that probably everybody contains a mixture of ethnic-identifying mutations. Many dark Americans descended from dark-skinned African tribes that were kidnapped to be sold as slaves. Most people in the world have skin tones in between these two extremes, having brown skin and brown hair. Others have a mixture of traits.

Hair

Subtle genetic differences develop different shaped hair follicles that produce from straight to curly human hairs. Round hair follicles manufacture tube-like, straight hair. Oval-shaped hair follicles produce flattened hair shafts, which curl. Flatter hairs make tighter curls.

SHAPE OF THE HAIR

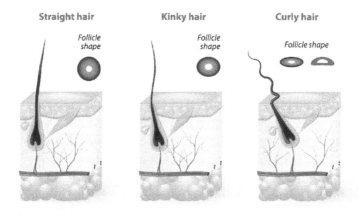

Figure 50. The Shape of the Hair (Credit: Dreamstime)

Human hair also shows a range of tones, from white to black, all depending on the amount of the pigment called melanin in hair. White hair, usually found in the elderly, almost totally lacks pigment. Brown hair contains a medium level, and black hair has the most amount of pigment. Red hair contains an iron oxide pigment which gives it the red-brown color similar to iron rust.

Special cellular machinery manufactures melanin pigments from the amino acid tyrosine. In humans, melanin serves mostly to add color to skin, hair, and eye irises. The chemical structure of melanin is so complex that so far it has defied detailed chemical analysis. In a similar way to how each snowflake differs from another, pigments like melanin are large enough to often include subtle molecular differences.

Eye color

Melanin is responsible for the color of our eyes, which actually comes from the color that coats the iris diaphragm. The small black pupil of the eye is a hole that allows light to enter the inside of the eyeball, so it has no pigment. Light-sensitive photocells, called rods and cones, register light waves that enter the eyeballs. Variation in eye color from brown to green depends on the amount of melanin on the iris, which is determined genetically. However, it involves dozens of genes, each with its own inheritance pattern, so it is difficult to pinpoint the exact color of a child's eyes by the genes alone. Individuals with black or brown eyes have more melanin, which is important to block the sun's damaging ultraviolet rays. Blue eyes filter less ultraviolet light, which commonly damages retinas. Blue eyes are actually a result of a mutation that prevents adding the pigment necessary for proper eye protection. Persons with light blue, green, or hazel eyes have little protection from the sun, and often experience discomfort, irritation, burning, and tissue damage if the eyes are not protected by sunglasses when exposed to bright light. What does this have to do with ethnicities? First, eye color again illustrates how mutations cause damage. They are the biological enemies of human evolution. Second, the wide varieties and often stunning beauty in eye colors showcases God's creativity.

Apes' and other animals' eyes are often simply dull in comparison.

Skin color

Like eye color, skin color depends on the level and type of melanin that special cells called melanocytes produce in the skin. In addition to showing variation, melanin protects the cell's nuclear DNA. It does not shield the entire cell, but covers the nucleus like a protective umbrella. Cells have molecular machines that detect and measure DNA damage caused by radiation. When excess damage occurs, they send their message to other systems that switch on melanin production. This causes skin to darken, or tan. No matter how dark one's skin normally is, if all the body systems work properly, skin will become darker after exposure to the sun's rays.

Figure 51. Skin Color tends to be a Major Factor in Determining Race (Credit: Shutterstock)

Melanin reduces ultraviolet type B (UVB) damage by absorbing or scattering the ultraviolet radiation that otherwise would have been absorbed by the DNA, causing mutations. This protects against skin cancer. The specific wavelengths of light that melanin absorbs match those of DNA, thus protecting DNA from the sun's damaging radiation. Skin color also depends upon the size, number, shape, and distribution of melanocytes, as well as the chemical nature of their melanin content.

Modern genetics reveals that Adam and Eve could have had within their created genes almost all the pigmentation varieties seen today. If the trait of human skin color follows the "polygenic" inheritance pattern, then Adam and Eve's children could have appeared either very dark or very light, although most were probably medium brown, like their parents.

Vitamin D Triggered by Sunlight

A melanin balance is necessary to protect the skin's DNA from UV damage, yet allow the light skin to "trigger" its benefits. Skin harvests UVB sunlight and uses it to process vitamin D, which the body requires. Vitamin D helps to promote proper bone density and growth by helping to regulate calcium and phosphorus in the body. Vitamin D deficiency leads to bones that lack the required calcium levels, causing rickets and even contributing to cancer, cardiovascular disease, mental impairment in older adults, and severe asthma in children.

What does all this have to do with the origin of people groups? As people migrated away from Babel in modern-day Iraq to northern latitudes, they had less exposure to sun. Others migrated to the tropics. Each person inherits their skin tone, and different skin tones interact differently with various climates.

Light-skinned people from the frozen north who visit lower latitude sunny locations have less melanin to block the sun's UVB rays. Without this protection, they may experience sunburn, which dramatically increases the odds of skin cancer. On the other hand, dark-skinned people visiting areas of dim sunlight may not produce enough vitamin D. They may need vitamin D supplements or obtain additional vitamin D from foods. For this reason, foods such as milk and bread are vitamin D fortified.

As global geographical distribution of various peoples shows, skin color variation is not determined by distance from the equator. Nevertheless, the skin tones we inherit can have different fits in different environments, and basic genetics reveal God could easily have programmed all human skin variation into the first created couple.

Eye Shape

Another example of superficial racial differences are the so-called almond eyes of Oriental people groups. The Asian eye has a fat layer in the upper eyelid that pushes the lid down, causing the eye to appear to be more closed. No Caucasian or Middle-Eastern ethnicities have this eye design, but two rare African tribes do. These tribes plus Asians must have inherited the trait from their ancestors at Babel. The information that codes for this trait was lost to Caucasians, Arabs and others who migrated away from those who retained it.

All of these are normal variations and examples of the remarkable variety that exists in all life—even within each created kind. Genetics confirm that only two people, Adam and Eve, contained all of the genes required to produce all of the variety seen across cultures today. In the end, as these people groups illustrate, race is not a biological, but a sociological construct.

Darwin's Conclusions about Race and Sex

Charles Darwin, the founder of modern evolutionary theory, openly expressed racist and gender sentiments that make modern readers cringe. As mentioned above, although the title of Darwin's most important book is often cited as *The Origin of Species*, the complete title is *The Origin of Species of Means of Natural Selection, or the Preservation of Favoured Races in the Struggle for Life*. The favored races, he argued in a later book titled *The Descent of Man* and *Selection in Relation to Sex*,[285] were supposedly Caucasians.

Darwin also taught that the "negro race" would become extinct, making the gap between whites and the lower apes wider. In his words:

> At some future period, not very distant as measured by centuries, the civilized races of man will almost certainly exterminate and replace throughout the world the savage races ... The break will then be rendered wider, for it will intervene between man in a more civilized state ... than the Caucasian, and some ape as low as a baboon, instead of as at present between the negro or Australian and the gorilla.[286]

Darwin did not begin racism, but his ideas bolstered it big time.[287] No science supports Darwin's ideas, and the Bible treats all people as equally human in God's sight.

Darwin also taught that women were biologically inferior to men, and that human sexual differences were due, in part, to natural selection. As Darwin concluded in his *Descent of Man* book: "the average mental power in man must be above that of women." Darwin argued that the intellectual superiority of males is proved by the fact that men attain:

> a higher eminence, in whatever he takes up, than can women—whether requiring deep thought, reason, or imagination, or merely the use of the senses and hands. If two lists were made of the most eminent men and women in poetry, painting, sculpture, music composition and performance, history, science, and philosophy,

with half-a-dozen names under each subject, the two lists would not bear comparison ...We may also infer... that if men are capable of a decided preeminence over women in many subjects, the average of mental power in man must be above that of women.[288]

Modern society has proved this naïve assumption to be not only wrong, but irresponsible. Darwin used many similar examples to illustrate the evolutionary forces that he concluded produced men to be of superior physical and intellectual strength, and women that were docile. Thus, due to "...success in the general struggle for life; and as in both cases the struggle will have been during maturity, the characters thus gained will have been transmitted more fully to the male than to the female offspring. Thus man has ultimately become superior to woman."[289] All this imaginative drivel ignores God's Word entirely. Genesis one extols the equality of genders by telling us that God created both husband and wife together as a married couple to reflect His image. It takes both to reflect His image. As a divinity student, Darwin surely read this. Did he deliberately ignore it?

Chapter 11: Are Humans and Chimps 98% Similar?
Jeffrey Tomkins, Ph.D. & Jerry Bergman Ph.D.

> "As most people know, chimpanzees have about 98% of our DNA, but bananas share about 50%, and we are not 98% chimp or 50% banana, we are entirely human and unique in that respect."
> –Professor Steve Jones, University College, London[290]

Introduction

One of the great trophies that evolutionists parade to prove human evolution from some common ape ancestor is the assertion that human and chimp DNA are 98 to 99% similar.[291] A quick Internet search reveals this quip in hundreds of textbooks, blogs, videos, and even scientific journals. Yet, any High School student can debunk the "Human and Chimp DNA is 98% similar" mantra that this chapter covers.

Why does this matter? If we are genetically closely related to chimps, then, since we know that genes determine much of our nature, from our sex to our hair color, then some may conclude that animal behavior by humans is expected, with no fear of divine judgment. But if we are all descended from Adam, not from animals, common animal behavior such as sexual promiscuity, cannot be justified on these grounds as some do.[292]

We will now review the major evidence that exposes the 98% myth and supports the current conclusion that the actual similarity is closer to 88%, or a difference of 12%, which translates to 360 million base pairs' difference, an enormous difference that produces an unbridgeable chasm between humans and chimpanzees.

If human and chimp DNA is nearly identical, why can't they interbreed?[293] Furthermore, such an apparently minor difference in DNA (only 1%) does not account for the many obvious major differences between humans and chimps.

Claiming that "because humans and chimps share similar DNA, they both descended from a recent common ancestor" is as logical as claiming that, "Because watermelons, jellyfish, and snow cones consist of about 95% water, therefore they have a recent common ancestor."

If humans and chimps are so similar, then why can't we interchange body parts with chimps? Over 30,000 organ transplants are made every year in the U.S. alone, and currently there are over 120,000 candidates on organ transplant lists—but *zero* of those transplants will be made using chimp organs!

Table 11. Organ Transplants[294]

Organ Transplants (2016)			
Organs	# Currently Waiting	% of Transplants Made Using	
		Human Organs	Chimp Organs
All Organs	121,520	100%	0%
Kidney	100,623	100%	0%
Liver	14,792	100%	0%
Pancreas	1,048	100%	0%
Kid./Panc.	1,953	100%	0%
Heart	4,167	100%	0%
Lung	1,495	100%	0%
Heart/Lung	47	100%	0%
Intestine	280	100%	0%

A Basic Overview

The living populations of the chimp kind include four species that can interbreed. From the beginning, they were *soulless* animals created on Day 6 of creation. Later that Day, God made a single man in His own image, then gave him an eternal *soul* (Genesis 2:7), and commanded him to "rule over the fish in the sea and the birds in the sky, over the livestock and all the animals," including chimps (Genesis 1:26).

If the creation narrative from the Bible is true, we would expect *exactly* what we see in today's ape-kinds. First, all varieties of chimps have no concept of eternity. For example, they do not bury their dead nor conduct funeral rituals. Secondly, apes use very limited verbal communication—they cannot write articles or even sentences. Thirdly, they do not display *spiritual or religious practices* as humans do. In other words, they show no capacity for knowing their spiritual creator through worship or prayer. This fits the biblical creation account that humans are created, spiritual beings with a soul.

It is logical that God, in His desire to create diverse life forms on Earth, would begin with the same building materials, such as DNA, carbohydrates, fats, and protein, when making various animal kinds. Research has revealed that He used similar building blocks for all of the various physical life forms that He created. Genetic information in all living creatures is encoded as a sequence of only 4 nucleotides (guanine, adenine, thymine, and cytosine, shown by the letters G, A, T, and C). We also see this principle in nature—such as many plants sharing Fibonacci spirals (clear numerical patterns) and sequences as basic building blocks and patterns.

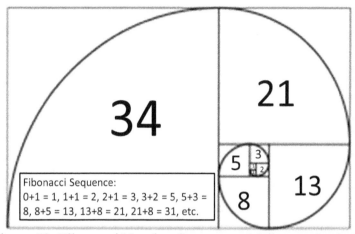

Figure 52. Fibonacci Number Sequence. A Fibonacci spiral approximates the golden spiral using quarter-circle arcs inscribed in squares of integer Fibonacci-number side, shown for square sizes 1, 1, 2, 3, 5, 8, 13, 21, 34 etc.

Figure 53. Examples of the Fibonacci Sequence in Nature (Credit: Wikipedia)

    Chimp and human DNA share many similarities, but this does not prove that those similarities came from shared ancestors. **They are similar due to design constraints that require an engineer to use many of the same raw materials and building plans to produce two very different types of** "**machines.**" For example, an automotive engineer could make a Volkswagen bug and a Porsche Carrera framework out of steel, glass, and plastic but not diatomic oxygen, carbon dioxide, and H_2SO_4. Next, let's take a look at just how different chimps and humans are, even though they share some similar DNA.

Comparisons of Chimps and Humans

    A child that sees a chimpanzee can immediately tell that it is radically different from a human. Compared to chimps, humans are about 38% taller, 80% heavier, live 50% longer, and have brains that are about 400% larger (1330 ccs compared to 330 ccs).[295] Look at someone next to you and roll your eyes at them. Chimps can't do that because their sclera, like most other animals, is hidden behind their eyelids. Now tap your fingertips with your thumb. Chimps can't do that either—their fingers are curved, their thumbs are both tiny and set further back on their wrists than humans, and they are missing the flexor pollicis longus—the major muscle that controls thumb dexterity in humans. Plus their knees point out, whereas ours point forward. Humans can build space shuttles and write songs. Chimps cannot.

    Scientists now know that chimpanzees are radically different than humans in many different ways besides their outward appearance. Humans and chimpanzees have different bone structures, different brain types, and other major physiological differences. Humans also have the ability to express their thoughts abstractly in speech, writing, and music, as well as developing other complicated systems of expression and communication. This is why humans stand above all other types of creatures. **The claimed small genetic differences between human and chimp DNA (1 to 2%) must account for these and many other major differences!** The difference between humans and chimpanzees is major and includes about 350 million different DNA bases. **In fact, it is hard to compare the two genomes because they are so different.**

The chimp genome is much longer than the human genome: The chimp genome is not 98% of the length of the human genome. According to the latest data, there are 3,096,649,726 base pairs in the human genome and 3,309,577,922 base pairs in the chimpanzee genome (a 6.4% difference).[296] Telomeres in Chimps and other apes are about 23 kilobases (a kilobase is 1,000 base pairs of DNA) long. Humans are unique among primates with much shorter telomeres only 10 kilobases long.[297] The human Y chromosome is a very different size and has many markers that do not line up when the human and chimpanzee chromosome is compared.[298] Even if human and chimpanzee DNA sequences are as similar as some evolutionists claim, the DNA coding makes two entirely different creatures!

Humans have 46 chromosomes, chimps have 48, and the fusion theory, the claim that human chromosome 2 was created by the fusion of two smaller chimpanzee chromosomes, has now been refuted. In fact, this claim has been used as "demonstrable proof of common ancestry" and a "direct fulfillment of an evolutionary prediction."

Research by Dr. David A. DeWitt has revealed new stunning insights regarding the major differences between human and chimp DNA: There exist 40–45 million bases [DNA "letters"] in humans missing from chimps, and about the same number present in chimps that are absent from man. These extra DNA nucleotides are termed "insertions" and "deletions" because they are assumed to have been added or lost from the original common ancestor sequence. These differences alone put the total number of DNA differences at about 125 million. However, since the insertions can be more than one nucleotide long, about 40 million total separate mutation events would be required to separate the two species. Such research continues to reveal that we are genetically far more different from chimps than the textbooks reveal! To put this number into perspective, a typical 8½ x 11-inch page of text has about 4,000 letters and spaces. It would require 10,000 such pages of text to equal 40 million letters! These "10,000 pages" of different DNA programming are also enough to fill 20 full-sized novels.

The difference between humans and chimpanzees includes about 45 million base pairs in the human that are absent from the chimp, and about 45 million in the chimp absent from the human.[299] More research has left no doubt that a specific set of DNA programming exists for humans, and another for chimps. Despite clear differences between humans and apes, we are repeatedly told by an array of mainstream outlets including textbooks, that human and chimpanzee DNA is 98 to 99% similar. Are we really just a few genetic changes away from being an ape? And what is the field of modern genetics research actually revealing?

Biology textbooks typically explain that humans descended from some common ancestor related to the great apes. This animal group consists of orangutans, gorillas, and chimpanzees. Of these apes, evolutionists claim that humans are most closely related to chimpanzees based on comparisons of human DNA to chimp DNA. The real world consequences of this ideology involve concluding humans are not special creations, but are evolved animals.

This has been a primary foundation for the mistreatment of humans worldwide by genocidal political leaders and governments over the past 150 or so years. One highly reputable study showed that the leading cause of death in the 20th century was "Democide"—or "murder by government," which has claimed well over 260 million lives.[300] All of the totalitarian murderous tyrannies the world over, despite their different political variations, maintained the same Darwinian evolutionary philosophy that humans are higher animals to be herded and culled in wars, death-camps, abortions, mass starvations, and outright slaughter.[301]

Do the new sciences of DNA sequencing and genomics justify the evil ideology that comes from believing that some humans are more evolved while others are nothing but common animals? Genetics research exposes human evolution as a total misrepresentation of reality. If this question is important to you—and it should be as a member of the human family—you will find this section very important. Once you understand that the new DNA evidence debunks the alleged human evolution paradigm, you will appreciate that you are a unique creation whom the Creator made in His own image—special and unique compared to all of creation.

When experts talk about DNA similarity, they refer to a variety of different features. Sometimes they talk about humans and chimpanzees having the same genes. At other times, they talk about certain DNA sequences being 98 to 99% similar. First, let's consider why human and chimpanzee DNA sequences are actually closer to 88% than 98% similar. Then, describing the concepts of genes and gene similarity will reveal much insight into human and chimp DNA dissimilarity.

Reality of DNA and Genome Similarity

Human, plant, and animal DNA is packaged into separate packages called chromosomes. Each one contains millions of the four different DNA bases (T, A, C, G), stacked like rungs on a ladder. Their specific order forms a complex set of instructions called the "genetic code." Humans have two copies of each chromosome; one set of 23 from the mother and one set of 23 from the father. Each chromosome set contains over 3 billion base pairs of information. Therefore, a total of 6 billion DNA bases are in our 46 chromosomes that are inside of nearly every cell in our body. When scientists talk about a creature's genome, they are only referring to one set of chromosomes. Thus, the reference genome in humans is the sum total of one complete set of 23 chromosomes.

The "initial draft" of DNA sequences in the human genome was initially published in 2001. In 2004, scientists published a more complete version, but there were still small parts that remained to be sequenced, so researchers kept updating the human genome as DNA sequencing technologies improved and more data were acquired. The human genome is now one of the most complete of all known genome sequences–mostly because considerably more research money has been spent on it compared to other life forms. In order to organize 3 billion bases, researchers use unique DNA sequences as reference markers. Then they determine where these short sequences are located on each chromosome. They assumed that comparing sequences between related creatures would help locate them. Scientists initially chose chimpanzees as the closest creature to humans because they knew that their proteins and DNA fragments had similar biochemical properties.[302] However, some researchers for various reasons chose gorillas or orangutans as being closest to humans and compared their DNA instead. In fact, a recent research paper made the claim that orangutan DNAs were more similar to humans' in structure and appearance than chimpanzee, and thus should be considered our closest ancestor. Nevertheless, the consensus opinion among evolutionary scientists is that chimpanzees are closest to humans on the hypothetical evolutionary tree. For this reason, most genetics studies assume this relationship before they even begin analyzing DNA.

    In the early days of DNA sequencing in the 1970s, scientists were able to sequence only very short segments of DNA. For this reason, they focused on DNA segments that they knew would be highly similar between animals, such as blood globin proteins and mitochondrial DNA (DNA which is inherited from the mother). They selected similar regions for comparison, because you cannot glean any meaningful comparisons between two DNA sequences that exist only in one and not the other. Researchers discovered that many of the short stretches of DNA genetic sequences that code for common proteins were not only highly similar in many types of animals, but nearly identical between humans and apes.[303]

    Before the true levels of similarity between human and chimp genomes can be determined, a basic understanding of what DNA sequencing actually entails is helpful. While the basic DNA sequencing techniques have not changed much since they were developed, the use of small-scale robotics and automation now enable researchers to sequence massive amounts of small DNA fragments. The DNA of an entire organism is too long to be sequenced, thus millions of small pieces, hundreds of bases in length are sequenced. Computers are then used to assemble the small individual pieces into larger fragments based on overlapping sections.[304] DNA regions that have hundreds of repeating sequences are for this reason very difficult to reconstruct, yet we now know that they are important for cell function.

Enter New Technology

Despite the early discoveries of apparently high DNA similarity between humans and chimps, large-scale DNA sequencing projects began to present a very different picture. In 2002, a DNA sequencing lab produced over 3 million bases of chimp DNA sequence in small 50 to 900 base fragments that were obtained randomly from the entire chimp genome.[305] The short sequences must then be assembled, and the physical arrangement of chimp DNA sequences are largely based on the human genomic framework.[306] This turned out to be only one of many problems. When the chimp DNA sequences were matched with the human genome by computers, only two-thirds of the DNA sequences could be lined up with human DNA. While many short stretches of DNA existed that were very similar to human DNA, more than 30% of the chimp DNA sequence was not similar to human DNA!

In 2005 the first rough draft of the chimpanzee genome was completed by a collaboration of different labs.[307] As a rough draft, even after the computational assembly based on the human genome, it still consisted of thousands of small chunks of DNA sequences. The researchers then assembled all of the small sequences of chimp DNA together to form a complete genome. They did this by assuming that humans evolved from a chimp-like ancestor, so they used the human genome as the framework to assemble the chimp DNA sequences.[308] At least one lab that helped to assemble the chimp sequence admitted that they inserted human DNA sequences into the chimp genome– based on the evolutionary assumptions. They assumed that many human-like sequences were missing from the chimp DNA so added them electronically. The published chimp genome is thus partly based on the human genome. Because it contains human sequences, it appears more human than the chimp genome in fact is.

A large 2013 research project sequenced the genomes of chimpanzees, gorillas, and orangutans to determine their genetic variation. They then assembled all of these genomes using the human genome as a framework![309] Much shorter lengths of DNA fragments are produced by new technologies, providing faster results, but smaller sections are more difficult to assemble.

Unfortunately, the research paper describing the 2005 chimp draft genome avoided the problem of overall average genome similarity with humans by analyzing the regions of the genomes that were already known to be highly similar. This deceptively reinforced the mythical 98% similarity notion. However, enough data were in the 2005 report to allow several independent researchers to calculate overall human-chimp genome similarities. They came up with estimates of 70 to 80% DNA sequence similarity.[310]

This result is important because evolution has a difficult time explaining how only 2% of 3 billion bases could have evolved in the 6 million years since they believe chimps and humans shared a common ancestor. They want to avoid the task of explaining how 20 to 30% of three billion bases evolved in such a short time! Natural processes cannot create 369 million letters of precisely coded information in a billion years, let alone a few million years.[311]

Thus, the commonly reported high levels of human-chimp DNA similarity were actually based on highly similar regions shared by both humans and chimps and exclude vastly different regions of these separately created genomes. Cherry-picking of data is not valid science. Other published research studies completed between 2002 and 2006 compared certain isolated regions of the chimp genome to human DNA. These also seemed to add support to the evolutionary paradigm, but reinserting dissimilar DNA sequence data where it could be determined that evolutionists had omitted it from their analyses, significantly changed the results.[312] The results showed that the actual DNA similarities for the analyzed regions varied between about 66% to 86%.

One of the main problems with comparing DNA segments between different organisms that contain regions of strong dissimilarity is that the computer program commonly used (called BLASTN) stops matching DNA when it hits regions that are markedly different. These unmatched sections consequently are not included in the final results, raising significantly the overall similarity between human and chimp DNA.

In addition, the computer settings can be changed to reject DNA sequences that are not similar enough for the research needs. The common default setting used by most evolutionary researchers kicks out anything less than 95% to 98% in similarity. In 2011, Tompkins compared 40,000 chimp DNA sequences that were about 740 bases long and already known to be highly similar to human.[313] The longest matches showed a DNA similarity of only 86%.

If chimp DNA is so dissimilar to human, and the computer software stops matching after only a few hundred bases, how can we find the actual similarity of the human and chimp genomes? A 2013 study resolved this problem by digitally slicing up chimp DNA into the small fragments that the software's algorithm could optimally match.[314] Using a powerful computer dedicated to this massive computation, all 24 chimp chromosomes were compared to humans' 23 chromosomes. The results showed that, depending on the chromosome, the chimp chromosomes were between 43% and 78% similar to humans. Overall, the chimp genome was only about 70%[315] similar to human. This data confirmed results published in secular evolutionary journals, but not popularized by the media or evolutionists.

Although textbooks still contain the 98% DNA similarity claim, scientists in the human-chimp research community now recognize the 96% to 98% similarity is derived from isolated areas. However, while the 96–98% similarity is crumbling, geneticists rarely make public statements about overall estimates because they know it would debunk human evolution. Although the human and chimpanzee genomes overall are only about 88% similar, some regions have high similarity, mostly due to protein-coding genes. Even these high similarity areas actually have only about 86% of matching sequences overall when the algorithm used to analyze them is set to produce a very long sequence match.[316]

The regions of high similarity can be explained by the fact that common genetic code elements are often found between different organisms because they code for genes that produce proteins with similar functions. For the same reason that different kinds of craftsmen all use hammers to drive or pry nails, different kinds of creatures use many of the same biochemical tools to perform common cellular functions. The genome is a very complex system of genetic codes, many of which are repeated in organisms with similar functions. This concept is easier to explain to computer programmers and engineers than biologists who are steeped in the evolutionary worldview.

Gene Similarities—the Big Picture

If two creatures have the same genes, usually only a certain part of a gene sequence is shared. The entire gene could be only 88% similar, while a small part of it may be 98% similar. In fact, the protein-coding regions called "exons" are on average in humans only about 86% to 87% similar to chimps. Much of this is due to human exon sequences completely missing in chimps.

The original definition of a gene describes it as a DNA section that produces a messenger RNA that codes for a protein. Early estimates projected that humans contained about 22,000 of these protein-coding genes, and the most recent estimates are about 28,000 to 30,000.[317] We now know that each of these protein-coding genes can produce many different individual messenger RNA variants due to gene regulation of gene section splicing variations. Consequently, over a million protein varieties can be made from 30,000 or fewer genes! Nevertheless, less than 5% of the human genome contains actual "exon" protein-coding sequences.

Humans have a high level of DNA/gene similarity with multiple other creatures

The human body has many molecular similarities with other living things, because they are all made up of the same molecules, all use the same water and atmosphere, and consume foods consisting of the same molecules. Their metabolism and therefore genetic make-up would resemble one another. This, however, is not evidence that they evolved from a common ancestor because, likewise, all building construction uses common materials (brick, iron, cement, glass, etc.).

The same holds for living beings. DNA contains much of the information necessary for the development of an organism, and if two organisms look similar, we would expect there to be some DNA similarity. The DNA of a cow and a whale should be more alike than the DNA of a cow and a bacterium. Likewise, humans and apes have many morphological similarities, so we would expect there would be many DNA similarities. Of all known animals, chimps are most like humans, so we would expect that their DNA would be most like human DNA.[318]

This is not always the case, though. Some comparisons between human DNA/genes and other animals in the literature including cats have 90% of homologous genes with humans, dogs 82%, cows 80%,[319] chimpanzees 79%, rats 69%, and mice

67%.[320] Other comparisons found include fruit fly (Drosophila) about 60%[321] and chickens about 60% of genes correspond to a similar human gene.[322] One should keep in mind that these estimates suffer from the same problems that the human-chimp do.

The Myth of "Junk" DNA

The 30,000 or so genes occupy less than 5% of the 3 billion base pairs in the human genome. Because evolutionary scientists did not know what the other 95% of the genome does, and because they needed raw genetic material for evolution to tinker with over millions of years, they labeled it "junk DNA." However, new research from different labs all over the world has documented that over 90% of the entire human genome is transcribed into a dizzying array of RNA molecules that perform many different important functions in the cell.[323] This phenomenon, called "pervasive transcription," was discovered in an offshoot of the human genome project called ENCODE, which stands for ENCyclopedia of DNA Elements.[324]

While refuting "junk" DNA, the ENCODE project has also completely redefined our concept of a gene. At the time of this writing, experts estimate that non-protein-coding RNA genes called *long noncoding RNAs* or "lncRNAs" outnumber protein coding genes at least 2 to 1.[325] They have similar DNA structures and control features as do protein-coding genes, but instead they produce functional RNA molecules that do many things in the cell.

Some regulate the function of protein coding genes in various ways and remain in the cell nucleus with the DNA. Others are transported into the cell cytoplasm to help regulate various cellular processes in collaboration with proteins. The cell exports other lncRNAs outside of the cell in which they are produced. There they regulate other cells. Many of these lncRNA genes play important roles in a process called epigenetics, which helped to regulate many aspects of how chromosomes are organized and the genome functions.

In contrast to many evolutionary studies that compared only the highly similar protein-coding regions of the genome, the lncRNA regions are only about 67 to 76% similar—about 10 to 20% less identical than the protein-coding regions. Chimp and human lncRNAs are very different from each other, but critical to each life form kind.

Clearly, the *entire genome* is a storehouse of important information. Using the construction project analogy, the protein-coding genes are like building blocks and the noncoding regions regulate and determine how and where the building blocks are used. This is why the protein-coding regions tend to show more similarities between organisms and the noncoding regions show fewer similarities. Protein-coding regions specify skin, hair, hearts, and brains, but "noncoding" regions help organize these components into the different but distinct arrangements that define each creature's body plan. Given all these facts, it is not surprising that humans and chimps are markedly different!

Chromosome Fusion Debunked

One of the main arguments that evolutionists have used to support their human-chimp story is the supposed fusion of two ape-like chromosomes to form human chromosome number two. The great apes actually contain two more (diploid) chromosomes than humans—humans have 46 and apes have 48. Large portions of two small ape chromosomes look somewhat similar to human chromosome 2 when observed under a microscope after special staining. Evolutionists attempt to argue that they look so similar because they have descended from a common ancestor, namely two ancient chromosomes from an ape-like ancestor fused during human evolution.[326]

Supposedly, the modern chimp's chromosomes look like the imaginary ape-human ancestors' did. Taking their cues from evolutionary assumptions, these two chimp chromosomes are called 2A and 2B. Gorillas and orangutans also have a 2A and 2B chromosome like chimps. Could the similarities between these two ape chromosomes and human chromosome 2 come from some cause other than common ancestry? What detailed features would we expect to see if these chromosomes fused to become one in humans?

In 1991, scientists found a short segment of DNA on human chromosome 2 that they claimed was evidence for fusion. It looked to them like a genetic scar left over from two chromosome ends that were supposedly stitched together, even though it was not what they should have expected based on the analysis of known fusions in living mammals.[327] The alleged fusion sequence consisted of what looked like a degraded head-to-head fusion of chromosome ends called "telomeres."

Telomeres contain repeats of the DNA sequence TTAGGG over and over for thousands of bases. Human telomeres are typically 5,000 to 15,000 bases long. If these actually fused, then they should have thousands of TTAGGG bases.[328] The alleged fusion site, however, is only about 800 bases long and only 70% similar to what would be expected. Plus, telomeres are specifically designed to prevent chromosomal fusion, and this is why a telomere-telomere fusion never has been observed in nature!

This fusion idea has for many years been masquerading as a solid argument proving human evolution from a chimp-like ancestor, but has now been completely refuted by genetic research. It turns out the alleged fusion site is actually a *functional* DNA sequence inside an important noncoding RNA gene.[329] Though, based on the old and mistaken belief in junk DNA, it is commonly referred to as "noncoding" these sequences, in fact, code for useful, often critically important, RNAs.

In 2002, researchers sequenced over 614,000 bases of DNA surrounding the supposed fusion site and found that it was in a gene-rich region. Also, the fusion site itself was inside of what they originally labeled a pseudogene, which are supposedly damaged "dysfunctional relatives" of formerly real protein-coding genes.[330] They are supposed to represent more genetic junk from a messy evolutionary past. However, continual discoveries of important cellular roles for "pseudogenes" keep surprising evolutionists. They expect junk, but keep finding functional genetic design.

New research using data from the ENCODE project now shows that part of the so-called "fusion site" is part of a noncoding RNA gene that is expressed in many different types of human cells. The research also shows that the alleged fusion site encodes a location inside the gene that binds to proteins that regulate the gene expression. Even more clear evidence for creation is the finding that not one of the other genes within 614,000 bases surrounding the alleged fusion site exists in chimpanzees. Although many evolutionists, unaware of the recent research, still promote it, the facts reveal that human chromosome 2 was a unique creation showing none of the expected signs of a chromosome fusion.

Beta-globin Pseudogene Debunked

Another story that evolutionists use to promote human-ape ancestry is the idea of shared mistakes in supposedly broken genes called pseudogenes noted above. Supposedly, the ape ancestor's genes were first mutated. Then, after its descendants diverged, both its chimp and human descendant genomes have retained those old mutations. After all, they argue, how else could two different but similar species have the same mutations in the same genes unless they evolved from the same ancestor?

If this story were true, if we evolved from apes, then we obviously were not created in God's image. Fortunately, exciting new research shows why science supports Scripture. As noted, many so-called "pseudogenes" are actually very *functional*. They produce important noncoding RNAs discussed previously.[331] This means that the shared DNA sequence "mistakes" were actually purposefully created DNA sequences all along.

One example is the beta-globin pseudogene, actually a functional gene in the middle of a cluster of five other genes. The other five genes code for, and produce, functional proteins.

Evolutionists originally claimed that the beta-globin gene was broken because it did not produce a protein and because of its DNA similarity to chimps and other apes. Now multiple studies have shown that it produces long noncoding RNAs and is the most genetically networked gene in the entire beta-globin gene cluster, meaning it is transcribed often, likely for multiple purposes.[332]

Genes do not act alone, but like computer servers are connected to each other to produce the internet, are functionally connected to many other genes in the genome. Not only do other genes depend on the proper function of the beta-globin pseudogene, but over 250 different types of human cells actively use the gene! Why do chimps and humans share this very similar sequence? Not because they both inherited it from a common ancestor, but because they both use it for very similar purposes, like bricks can be used to build either a house or a library.

GULO Pseudogene Debunked

Another case of so-called evidence for evolution is the GULO pseudogene, which actually looks like a broken gene. A functional GULO gene produces an enzyme in animals that helps to make vitamin C. Evolutionists claim that humans, chimps and other apes share GULO genes that mutated in the same places because the mutations occurred in their common ancestor.

However, broken GULO pseudogenes are also found in mice, rats, bats, birds, pigs, and famously, guinea pigs. Did we evolve from guinea pigs? When the GULO gene was recently analyzed in its entirety, researchers found no pattern of common ancestry.[333] Instead, it looks like this gene is predisposed to being mutated no matter what creature it is in. Since humans and other animals can get vitamin C from their diet, they can survive without the gene. Also, the other genes in the GULO biochemical pathway produce proteins that are involved in other important cellular processes. Losing them could be disastrous to the organism. So many creatures and humans can tolerate having a damaged GULO gene by consuming plenty of vegetables with vitamin C.

The GULO gene region and the mutational events that damaged it are associated with unique categories of a system that use transposable elements, commonly called jumping genes which can cut themselves out of one location in the genome and splice themselves into another location. The many different types of transposable elements in the human genome serve very important tasks. Sometimes, though, they splice themselves into the wrong location and disrupt genes.

In the case of GULO, the transposable element patterns between humans and each of the ape kinds that were evaluated show unique differences. Therefore, GULO shows no pattern of common ancestry for humans and apes—negating this evolutionary argument. Like the claims of 99% similarity, chromosome fusion, and Beta-globin, evolutionists built the GULO argument based on a prior belief in evolution, plus a lack of knowledge about how these systems actually function in cells.

In reality, the GULO pseudogene data defies evolution and vindicates the creation model. According to the Genesis account of the fall that caused the curse on creation, we would expect genes to mutate as this one did. This process of genetic decay, called genetic entropy, is found everywhere in the animal kingdom. Cornell University Geneticist John Sanford has shown in several studies that the human genome shows no signs of evolving or getting better, but is actually in a state of irreversible degeneration.[334] Perhaps our early ancestors had a working GULO gene that could thus manufacture vitamin C. Today, lacking sufficient vitamin C in our diets causes an illness called "scurvy."

The Human-Chimp Evolution Magic Act

Stage magicians, otherwise known as illusionists, practice their trade by getting you to focus on some aspect of the magician's act to divert your focus from what is really occurring or what the other hand is doing. By doing this, they get you to believe something that isn't true, creating an illusion—a fake reality. The human-chimp DNA similarity "research" works almost the same way.

The evolutionist who promotes the human-chimp fake paradigm of DNA similarity accomplishes the magic act by getting you to focus on a small set of data representing bits and pieces of hand-picked evidence. In this way, you don't see the mountains of hard data that utterly defy evolution. While some parts of the human and chimpanzee genomes are very similar—those that the evolutionists focus on—the genomes overall are vastly different, and the hard scientific evidence now proves it. The magic act isn't working any longer, and more and more open-minded scientists are beginning to realize it.

Confronting Human-Chimp Propaganda

To close this chapter, let's discuss a hypothetical exchange that could take place using the information in this chapter with some human-chimp similarity proponent. This exchange could happen with a teacher, a friend, or a schoolmate. First, the person makes the claim that "human and chimp DNA is genetically 98–99% identical or similar." You can respond, "That's only partially true for the highly similar regions that have been compared between humans and chimps." You can then clarify this response by noting that "recent research has shown that, overall, the entire genome is only about 88% similar on average when you include all the DNA. This is equal to 12 percent difference, or 360 million base pair differences."

You can also add, "Several thousand genes unique to humans are completely missing in chimps, and scientists have found many genes that are unique to chimps are missing in humans." Then ask, "How can you explain these massive differences by evolutionary processes?" In sum, ask, "How is it that such supposedly minor differences in DNA can account for such major and obvious differences between humans and chimps?"

At this point in the conversation, you will rapidly find out if the person is really interested in learning more about the issue of human origins, or if they are so zealous about evolutionary beliefs that they refuse to listen to challenging evidence. In reality, the whole modern research field of genetics and genomics is the worst enemy of evolution. As new genomes of different kinds of organisms are being sequenced, they consistently are shown to be unique sets of DNA containing many genes and other sequences that are specific to that type of creature. Evolutionists call these new creature-specific genes "orphan genes" because they are not found in any other type of known creature.[335] Orphan genes appear suddenly in the pattern of life as unique sections of genetic code with no evolutionary history. Of course, believers in an omnipotent Creator know that each different genome, such as that for humans and that of chimpanzees, was separately, uniquely, and masterfully engineered at the beginning of creation. God created and embedded each creature's orphan genes to network with all the rest of that creature's genetic coding instructions. The scientific data overwhelmingly show that God deserves the credit, and evolution deserves none.

Conclusion

With so much at stake—the answer to life's largest question, "Where did I come from?" —do we want to trust in extremely biased answers? Every high school student can refute 98% similarity dogma by tracking the main points above as outlined below.

1. Overall, the entire genome is only about 88% similar on average when you include all the DNA. This is equal to a 12 percent difference, or 360 million base pair differences, a chasm away from our supposed closest evolutionary relative.

2. The "Junk" DNA claim has long been refuted and most all of it has been found to have clear functions, mostly regulatory in nature.
3. The Chromosome Fusion claim is false. First, telomeres are designed not to fuse, thus, as per their design, telomere to telomere fusion is unknown in the natural world. Telomeres contain repeats of the DNA sequence TTAGGG over and over for thousands of bases. Human telomeres are from 5,000 to 15,000 bases long. If these actually fused, then they should have thousands of TTAGGG bases, but the alleged fusion site is only about 800 bases long and only 70% similar to what would be expected. The claimed fusion site actually contains a gene, and is very different from a telomere.
4. The Beta-globin Pseudogene is not a pseudogene and not proof that a damaged gene was inherited from the human-chimp common ancestor, but actually is a functional gene in the middle of a cluster of five other genes.
5. The GULO Pseudogene is not evidence for common decent, but evidently is due to a hot spot in this gene, meaning that it is in an area of the genome that is very prone to mutate.

Chapter 12: How Modern Genetics Supports a Recent Creation
Jeffrey P. Tomkins, Ph.D.

A substantial amount of convincing evidence exists for a recent creation as described in the Bible using hard scientific data from the disciplines of geology, paleontology, physics, and astronomy.[336] However, what does the field of genetics and modern genomics, one of the most rapidly advancing areas of science have to offer in this regard? As it turns out, new discoveries using the tools of modern biotechnology also showcase recent creation and events associated with the global flood.

One of the first questions we need to ask ourselves to form a hypothesis or model about the origins of human genetics involves comparing the *predictions* of creation science versus evolution. Creation science predicts that the genomes of all of the different kinds of living creatures were created perfect *in the beginning*, but due to the curse on creation related to man's sin and rebellion combined with the damaging effects of time, we should see degradation, corruption, and the loss of information. While evolutionists do recognize that information loss occurs, in the overall grand Darwinian scheme, their model predicts just the opposite of creationists. They believe that over vast amounts of time, genomes evolved and became more complex—gaining new information through random mutational processes. Let's see what the data actually says and which prediction or model is supported by it.

Over time, errors are made by cellular machinery that copies DNA during the standard process of cell division. These errors are called mutations. Sometimes they can lead to serious diseases such as cancer. However, when a mutation occurs in cell division that leads to making sperm or egg cells, these mutations can be inherited and passed on to the next generation. In fact, scientists have actually measured this rate among humans and found it to be about 75 to 175 mutations per generation.[337] An earlier chapter in this book quoted an estimate of between 100 and 200 new mutations. Using this known data about mutation rates, a research group lead by Cornell University geneticist Dr. John Sanford modeled the accumulation of mutations in the human genome over time using computer simulations that accurately accounted for real-life factors. They incorporate the standard observations and theories behind population genetics. They found that the buildup of mutations would eventually reach a critical level and become so severe that humans would eventually go extinct. This process of genome degradation over time and successive generations is called *genetic entropy*. Remarkably, the timeframe of human genome degradation coincides closely with a recent creation of six to ten thousand years ago as predicted by the documented genealogies found in the Bible.[338]

    Amazingly, after the results of the human genome modeling research were published, two different large groups of scientists unwittingly vindicated the idea of genetic entropy and a recent creation.[339] In each study, they sequenced the protein coding regions of the human genome. One study examined 2,440 individuals and the other 6,515. From the DNA sequence data, they discovered many single nucleotide differences (variants) between people in their protein coding genes, with most of these being very rare types of variants. In addition, they found that over 80% of these variants were either deleterious or harmful mutations. Surprisingly, they attributed the unexpected presence of these harmful mutations to "weak purifying selection." This essentially means that the alleged ability of natural selection to remove these harmful variants from human populations was powerless to do so. Sanford's model predicted that natural selection could not remove these slightly harmful mutations, and these studies confirmed exactly that in the real world of human genetics.

    Not only were these studies bad news for the evolutionary idea of mutation and natural selection as the supposed drivers of evolutionary change, but also overwhelmingly illustrated genetic entropy. Most of the mutations resulted in heritable diseases afflicting important protein-coding genes. Protein-coding regions are less tolerant of variability than other parts of the genome. These DNA regions can give us a better idea of the gene sequences of our forefathers because those who have too many mutations to important genes died long ago. Secular evolution-believing scientists usually pin their models of DNA change over time—referred to as molecular clocks—to millions of years before they even approach the data. In other words, they assume millions of years of human evolution and literally incorporate these deep time numbers into their models. The millions of years conclusion does not come from biology experiments.

In contrast, these new genetic variant studies used models of human populations that incorporate more realistic data over known historical time and geographical space. The resulting data revealed a very recent, massive burst of human genetic diversification. Most of it links with genetic entropy. One of the research papers stated, "The maximum likelihood time for accelerated growth was 5,115 years ago."[340] This places the beginning of the period of genetic diversification of humans close to the Genesis Flood and subsequent dispersion at the Tower of Babel, a point in time that the earth began to be repopulated through Noah's descendants. This recent explosion of human genetic variability clearly associated with genetic entropy also follows the same pattern of human life expectancy that rapidly declined after the Flood as also recorded in the Bible.[341]

One more important realm of research demonstrating a recent creation comes from Harvard trained scientist Dr. Nathaniel Jeanson. He has been examining the mutation rates of DNA in mitochondrial genomes.[342] The mitochondria is located outside the cell's nucleus. Mitochondria provide the energy for cells. They also contain their own DNA molecule that encodes a variety of proteins it uses for energy processing. The mitochondrial DNA molecule is typically inherited from the egg cell from a creature's mother. Its mutation rates can accurately be measured to produce a molecular-genetic clock. When these genetic clocks are not calibrated by (theoretical) evolutionary timescales, but by using the organism's observed mutation rate, we can reveal a more realistic and unbiased estimate of that creature's genetic life history. By comparing the molecular clock rates in a few very different animals (fruit flies, round worms, water fleas, and humans), Dr. Jeanson demonstrated that a creation event for these organisms (including humans) occurred not more than 10,000 years ago!

Interestingly, buried deep within a secular research paper in 1997, the same thing regarding human mitochondrial DNA (mtDNA) mutation rate was reported, but received little attention in the media. The authors of this paper wrote, "Using our empirical rate to calibrate the mtDNA molecular clock would result in an age of the mtDNA MRCA [the first human woman] of only ~6,500 years…"[343] One year later, another author wrote in the leading magazine *Science*, "Regardless of the cause, evolutionists are most concerned about the effect of a faster mutation rate. For example, researchers have calculated that "mitochondrial Eve"—the woman whose mtDNA was ancestral to that in all living people—lived 100,000 to 200,000 years ago in Africa. Using the new clock, she would be a mere 6000 years old." The article also noted that the new findings of faster mutation rates pointing to mitochondrial Eve about 6,000 years ago have even contributed to the development of new mtDNA research guidelines used in the forensic investigations "adopted by the FBI."[344] Now, over 17 years later, and using even more human mtDNA data, Dr. Jeanson is spectacularly confirming this previously unheralded discovery.

The combined results of all these different genetic studies fit perfectly with the predictions of a biblical creation, complete with its recent timeframe for creation as provided in the Bible. The unbiased genetic clocks simply cannot have been ticking for millions of years.

In addition, evolution predicts a net gain of information over time, accompanied by natural selection removing harmful genetic variants. But instead, we see a human genome filling up with harmful genetic variants in every generation. Information loss or genetic entropy rules over all genomes. Clearly, the predictions based on Scripture align well with the discoveries being made in the field of genetics.

In the case of humankind, the Bible indicates that Adam and Eve were originally created with pristine error-free genomes. No harmful mutations were present. Then sin entered into the world at the point of man's rebellion against God in the Garden of Eden and the whole of creation became cursed and subject to futility as a result of man's sin. The human genome has essentially been on a steep downhill slide ever since this key point in time. We are not gradually evolving better and improved genomes through random processes. Instead, the recently measured genetic patterns of degradation clearly match the biblical model and timeframe given to us in the Scriptures.

There is no valid science behind human macro-evolution, but well documented empirical science supports biblical creation. This means that you and I have Adam, not apes, in our past. It also means we can trust the Bible's history and whatever else it teaches.

Chapter 13: Vestigial Structures in Humans and Animals
Jerry Bergman, Ph.D.

Most people have heard the common assertion that human bodies have some parts that are "leftover" from the evolutionary process that took "millions of years." Body parts such as the tailbone, tonsils, and the appendix are commonly placed in this category of "extra" or "unnecessary" body parts.

While many evolutionists are just fine with this assumption, many Christian's might ask, "Why would God—who is able to design humans in a complete and perfect fashion—leave such 'extra' or 'unnecessary' parts?" This question is answered by this section by explaining that these supposedly "extra" parts are not extra at all. We do this by providing current medical research that demonstrates just how intentional God was when He designed the human body.

Introduction

One major supposed proof of evolution is the observation that some organs appear to be degenerate or useless, often called vestigial organs. As Professor Senter opines, the "existence of vestigial structures is one of the main lines of evidence for macroevolution."[345] Vestigial organs are usually defined as body structures that were believed to have served some function in an organism's evolutionary history, but are now no longer functional, or close to functionless.[346]

Thus, evolutionists teach that "living creatures, including man, are *virtual museums of structures that have no useful function*, but which represent the remains of organs that once had some use"[347] (emphasis added). Because all of the claimed vestigial organs have now actually been shown to be useful and integral to human function, evolutionists who attempt to salvage their idea have tried to shift gears. They now suggest that some organs have "reduced function," compared to

their function in some undefined past. Thus, a new definition for "vestigial" is being used by some evolutionists. A problem with the revisionist definition is: Just how much reduction is required before the "vestigial" label is appropriate? Is 30% a large enough reduction, or will a 10% reduction suffice? In addition, there are so many putative examples of "reduced size" functional structures that the label "vestigial" becomes meaningless.

For example, an analysis of skull shapes of our supposed evolutionary ancestors shows that our human jaw is vestigial compared to our alleged ancestors, since it is claimed to be much smaller in humans today (and also has a reduced function relative to its strength and ability to chew food).[348] Furthermore, not only the human jaw and nose, but our eyes, eyebrows, front limbs, ears, and even our mouth could also be labeled vestigial when compared to our alleged ancestors. For this reason, the term becomes meaningless when defined in this fashion. Anything could be "vestigial" if it simply suits the writer.

Darwin discussed this topic extensively, concluding that vestigial organs speak "infallibly" to evolution.[349] Darwin asserted that the existence of vestigial organs is strong evidence against creation, arguing that vestigial organs are so "extremely common" and "far from presenting a strange difficulty, as they assuredly do on the old doctrine of creation, might even have been anticipated in accordance with evolution."[350]

The view that vestigial organs are critical evidence for macroevolution was further developed by the German anatomist Wiedersheim, who made it his life's work.[351] Wiedersheim compiled a list of over 100 vestigial and so-called "retrogressive structures" that occur in humans. His list included the integument (skin), skeleton, muscles, nervous system, sense organs, digestive, respiratory, circulatory and urogenital systems.[352] Most of these remnants of (past physical) structures are found completely developed in other vertebrate groups.[353] Therefore, Wiedersheim concluded that the "doctrine of special creation or ... any teleological hypothesis" fails to explain these organs.[354]

For the medically-informed reader, we left most of the technical language in this chapter in-tact. Readers without this background, however, should still be able to read this chapter and gain an understanding that God has an incredible design for each and every part of the human body!

Vestigial Problems in the Textbooks

Let us now examine the most common vestigial organ claims. We hope your appreciation grows for God Who did in fact know what He was doing when He *created us in His image* (Genesis 1:27) and Who ensured we are *fearfully and wonderfully made* (Psalm 139:14).

The Coccyx (tailbone)

Humans lack a tail. All lower primates have tails and the human coccyx (tailbone) is interpreted by Darwinists as a rudimentary tail left over from our distant monkey-like ancestors that supposedly had tails. Specifically, Darwin claimed that the "coccyx in man, though functionless as a tail, plainly represents this part in other vertebrate animals."[355]

A major problem with the conclusion that the coccyx shows evolution is that our supposed "nearest relatives" including chimpanzees, gorillas, orangutans, bonobos, gibbons or the lesser apes such as siamangs all lack tails! Only a few of the over 100 types of monkeys and apes, such as spider monkeys, have tails. The primates that have tails tend to be the small cat-like lemurs and tarsiers.

In fact, the coccyx "is merely the terminal portion of the backbone. After all, it does have to have an end!"[356] The major function of the coccyx is an attachment site for the interconnected muscle fibers and tissues that support the bladder neck, urethra, uterus, rectum, and a set of structures that form a bowl-shaped muscular floor, collectively called the pelvic diaphragm, that supports digestive and other internal organs.[357]

The muscles and ligaments that join to the coccyx include the coccygeus muscle ventrally, and the gluteus maximus muscle dorsally. The coccygeus muscles enclose the back part of the pelvis outlet.[358] The levator ani muscles constrict the lower end of both the rectum and vagina, drawing the rectum both forward and upward.[359] The cocygeus muscle, which is inserted into the margin of the coccyx and into the side of the last section of the sacrum, helps to support the posterior organs of the pelvic floor. The coccygeus muscle is a strong, yet flexible, muscle, often described as a "hammock," that adds support to the pelvic diaphragm against abdominal pressure. The coccyx muscle system expands and contracts during urination and bowel movements, and also distends to help enlarge the birth canal during childbirth.[360]

Another useful structure connected to the coccyx is the anococcygeal raphe, a narrow fibrous band that extends from the coccyx to the margin of the anus.[361] Without the coccyx and its attached muscle system, humans would need a very different support system for their internal organs requiring numerous design changes in the human posterior.[362] Darwin was clearly wrong about the coccyx, and it is way past time that textbooks reflect known science about the well-designed end of the human spine.

The Tonsils and Adenoids

Among the organs long considered vestigial are the tonsils and adenoids. The tonsils are three sets of lymph tissues. The first, called palatine tonsils or "the tonsils," consist of two oval masses of lymph tissue (defined below) attached to the side wall at the back of the mouth. The second pair is the nasopharyngeal tonsils, commonly called the adenoids. The last section contains the lingual tonsils, which consist of two masses of lymph tissue located on the dorsum of the tongue.

The assumption that the tonsils are vestigial has been one reason for the high frequency of tonsillectomies in the past. Decades ago J. D. Ratcliff wrote that "physicians once thought tonsils were simply useless evolutionary leftovers and took them out thinking that it could do no harm. Today there is considerable evidence that there are more troubles of the respiratory tract after tonsil removal than before, and *doctors generally agree that simple enlargement of tonsils is hardly an indication for surgery*"[363] (emphasis added).

In recent years, researchers have demonstrated the important functions of both the tonsils and adenoids. As a result, most doctors are now reluctant to remove either the tonsils or the adenoids. Medical authorities now actively discourage tonsillectomies.[364]

The tonsils are lymph glands. They help establish the body's defense mechanism that produces disease-fighting antibodies. These defense mechanisms develop during childhood, as children sample and record materials through their mouths. The tonsils begin to shrink in the preteen years to almost nothing in adults, and other organs take over this defense function.[365] Because tonsils are larger in children than in adults, the tonsils are important in the development of the entire immune system.[366] For example, one doctor concluded that:

> The location of the tonsils and adenoids allows them to act as a trap and first line of defense against inhaled or ingested bacteria and viruses. The tonsils and adenoids are made up of lymphoid tissue which manufactures antibodies against invading diseases. Therefore, unless there is an important and specific reason to have the operation, it is better to leave the tonsils and adenoids in place. [367]

The tonsils are continually exposed to the bacteria in air we breathe and for this reason can readily become infected. As part of the body's lymphatic system, they function to fight disease organisms.[368] The tonsils "form a ring of lymphoid tissue" that guards the "entrance of the alimentary [digestive] and respiratory tracts from bacterial invasion." Called "super lymph nodes" they provide first-line defense against bacteria and viruses that cause both sore throats and colds.[369] Although removal of tonsils obviously eliminates tonsillitis (inflammation of the tonsils), it may increase the incidence of strep throat, Hodgkin's disease, and possibly polio.[370] Empirical research on the value of tonsillectomies in preventing infection demonstrate that the "tonsillectomy is of little benefit after the age of eight when the child's natural defenses have already made him immune to many infections." [371]

Just like calling the coccyx a useless evolutionary leftover, calling tonsils useless vestiges of organs that were only useful in our supposed distant evolutionary ancestor's bodies totally ignores the facts. These organs are well-designed and useful, just as if God created them on purpose.

The Vermiform Appendix

The appendix was one of the "strongest evidences" used by Darwin to disprove creationism in his *The Descent of Man* (1871) book: "in consequence of changed diet or habits, the caecum had become much shortened in various animals, the vermiform appendage [appendix] being left as a rudiment of the shortened part... Not only is it useless, but it is sometimes the cause of death ... due to small hard bodies, such as seeds, entering the passage and causing inflammation." [372] Since Darwin, this claim has been repeated often in books and journals. The appendix was once commonly cited in many biology texts as the best example of a vestigial organ. [373]

The human appendix is a small, narrow, worm-shaped tube that varies in length from 1 to 10 inches.[374] Its average length is slightly over three inches long, and less than 1/2 inch wide.[375] The small intestine empties into the large intestine above the floor of the cecum at an entrance passage controlled by a valve. The lower right end of the large intestine in humans terminates somewhat abruptly at an area termed the cecum. The vermiform appendix is connected to the lower part of the cecum.

The Safe House Role

Most bacteria in a healthy human are beneficial and serve several functions, such as to help digest food. If the intestinal bacteria are purged, one function of the appendix is to replenish the digestive system with beneficial bacteria. Its location—just below the normal one-way flow of food and germs in the large intestine in a sort of gut cul-de-sac—supports the safe house role by protecting and fostering the growth of "good germs" needed for various uses in the intestines, and enabling the digestive bacteria system to "reboot" after bouts of disease such as cholera, or the use of antibiotics. Diarrhea is designed to flush out all bacteria from the colon, both good and bad. The bacteria in the appendix are not affected by diarrhea and can rapidly repopulate the colon to quickly reestablish healthy digestion.

For years, we noticed few effects of removing the appendix. Evolutionists thought that if people don't need them, they must be useless. And if it's useless, then it must be a remnant of some evolutionary ancestor that did need it for something. However, just because removing a body part does not immediately kill you does not mean that it has no use. One can lose the end of some fingers and still do almost everything that fully fingered people do, but fingertips are still useful. Like fingertips, tonsils and the appendix are useful, and as far as is known, they always have been ever since God created them.

The Functions of the Appendix in Development

The appendix is also involved in producing molecules that aid in directing the movement of lymphocytes to other body locations. During the early years of development, the appendix functions as a lymph organ, assisting with the maturation of B lymphocytes and in the production of immunoglobulin A (IgA) antibodies. Lymph tissue begins to accumulate in the appendix soon after birth and reaches a peak between the second and third decades of life. It decreases rapidly thereafter, practically disappearing after the age of about 60.

The appendix functions to expose white blood cells to the wide variety of antigens normally present in the gastrointestinal tract. Thus, like the thymus, the appendix helps suppress potentially destructive blood- and lymph-borne antibody responses while also promoting local immunity.[376]

In summary, researchers have concluded, "Long thought to be an evolutionary remnant of little significance to normal physiology, the appendix has ... been identified as an important component of mammalian mucosal immune function, particularly B lymphocyte-mediated immune responses and extrathymically derived T lymphocytes."[377] Calling the appendix "vestigial" is a big mistake.

The Thyroid

The thyroid is a two-lobed gland connected by a narrow strip located just below the voice box.[378] German Darwinist Ernst Haeckel long ago asserted that not only is the thyroid vestigial, but that our body contains "many rudimentary organs.... I will only cite the remarkable thyroid gland (thyreoidea)."[379] Because surgeons found that adults could survive after having their thyroid removed, it was assumed by some that it was useless. Wiedersheim listed the thyroid as vestigial because of the "manner in which the thyroid originates."[380] Were they right? Modern medicine has revealed enough about the thyroid for us to find out.

The thyroid is one of the largest endocrine glands, and can grow to as large as 20 grams in adults. The three most important hormones it produces are triiodothyronine (T3) and thyroxine (T4), both of which regulate metabolism, and calcitonin, which regulates calcium levels. Both T3 and T4 stimulate the mitochondria to provide more energy for the body and increase protein synthesis. Without T3 and T4, humans become sluggish, and growth stops. An oversupply (or an undersupply) of thyroxine results in over-activity (or under-activity) of many organs. Defects in this organ at birth can cause a deformity known as cretinism, shown as severe retardation of both physical and mental development.[381] Haeckel was exactly wrong about the Thyroid, but he didn't know its values. Museums and textbook displays still portraying the thyroid as vestigial show an almost criminal disregard of good observational science.

The Thymus

The thymus gland is an example of an important organ that was long judged not only vestigial, but harmful if it became enlarged. Maisel reported that for generations physicians regarded it "as a useless, vestigial organ."[382] Clayton noted that an oversized thymus was once routinely treated with radiation in order to shrink it.[383] Follow-up studies showed that, instead of helping the patient, such radiation treatment caused abnormal growth and a higher level of infectious diseases that persisted longer than normally.

The thymus is a small pinkish-gray body located below the larynx and behind the sternum in the chest.[384] A capsule, from which fingers extend inward, surrounds it and divides it into several small lobes, each of which contains functional units called follicles.

Functions of the Thymus

This once-deemed worthless vestigial structure is now known to be the master gland of the lymphatic system. Without it, the T-cells that protect the body from infection could not function properly because they develop within the thymus gland. Researchers have now solved the thymus enigma, finding that far from being useless, the thymus regulates the intricate immune system which protects us against infectious diseases.

Thanks to these discoveries, many researchers are now pursuing new and highly promising lines of attack against a wide range of major diseases, from arthritis to cancer.[385]

The cortex, or outer tissue layer, of the thymus is densely packed with small lymphocytes surrounded by epithelial-reticular cells. The lymphocytes, also called thymic cells, are produced in the cortex and exit the gland through the medulla.[386] The medulla is more vascular than the cortex, and its epithelial-reticular cells outnumber the lymphocytes.

Besides being a master regulator and nursery for disease-fighting T-cells, the thymus takes a dominant role in reducing autoimmune problems. These occur where the immune system attacks the person's own cells, called the self-tolerance problem.[387] As research on immune tolerance continues, "the multiplicity of mechanisms protecting the individual from immune responses against self-antigens" and "the critical role the thymus plays is becoming better understood."[388] "Evidence now exists that regulatory cells have a role in preventing reactions against self-antigens, a function as important as their role of clonal deletion of high-affinity self-reactive T-cells." [389]

Regulatory T-cells also help to prevent inappropriate inflammatory responses to non-disease-causing foreign antigens. This system plays an essential role in preventing harmful inflammatory responses to foreign antigens that come in contact with mucous membranes, such as in many allergies.

In summary, a primary function of the thymus is to nurse to maturity small white blood cells called lymphocytes, which are then sent to the spleen and the lymph nodes, where they multiply.[390] There is nothing vestigial about the thymus.

The Pineal Gland

The pineal was first described by French psychiatrist Philip Pineal in the 1790s.[391] The pineal body is a cone-shaped gland positioned deep inside the head, near the brain stem. Scientists are now finding out that the pineal gland's functions include regulating hormones:

> Scientists are closing in on a mystery gland of the human body, the last organ for which no function has been known. It is turning out to be a lively performer with a prominent role in the vital hormone producing endocrine system... Medical science is now finding what nature really intended by placing a pea-sized organ in the middle of the head.[392]

Of course, the Creator really deserves credit for the pineal gland, not nature. Nevertheless, the pineal gland also serves in reproduction:

> It has long been known that reduction in the amount of light reaching the eyes stimulates this small gland to synthesize and secrete an anti-gonadotrophic hormone(s) which results in marked attenuation of virtually all aspects of reproductive physiology.[393]

Researchers at the National Institute of Mental Health found that the pineal gland is a very active member of the body's network of endocrine glands, especially during certain growth stages.

The Pineal Gland and Melatonin Production

The pineal gland's most commonly mentioned function is its role in producing the hormone melatonin.[394] Cells in the pineal gland produce a special enzyme that converts serotonin to melatonin.[395] Melatonin is produced mainly in the pineal gland of vertebrates, but is also produced in a variety of other tissues.[396]

Light-dark levels are communicated to the brain from the retina to the pineal gland and help regulate melatonin levels.

Melatonin is also a sleep-inducing hormone. This is why darkness generally promotes sleepiness.[397]

Melatonin also has important immune function stimulatory properties. It enhances the release of T-helper cell type 1 cytokines such as gamma-interferon and IL-2, counteracts stress-induced immunodepression and other secondary immunodeficiencies, protects against lethal viral encephalitis, bacterial diseases, and septic shock, and diminishes toxicity associated with several common chemotherapeutic agents.[398] The administration of melatonin also increases thymus cellularity and antibody responses.[399] Conversely, pinealectomy accelerates both thymic involution and depresses the humeral and cell-mediated immune response.[400]

Pineal and Reproduction

The pineal gland is the primary controller of the timing of the onset of puberty, a critical developmental function. Melatonin regulates the production of anti-gonadotropin hormones. These help block the effects of hormones that stimulate gonad development. Damage to the pineal gland leads to early puberty in males. Conversely, if the pineal gland is overactive, puberty is delayed. Among melatonin's many other reproductive functions is regulation of the estrus cycle in women. Melatonin levels decrease as women age, particularly after they pass child-bearing age.[401] Changes in melatonin levels may be responsible for some sleep difficulties in menopausal females.

Before the advent of modern artificial lighting, the number of hours humans spent in darkness was much greater. Today, bright lighting found in almost all homes and offices may be affecting our reproductive cycle. Exposure to a large amount of light during most of one's waking hours may cause the onset of sexual maturity at an earlier age, and even the higher rate of multiple births.

Studies on "pre-electric" Inuit Indians support the conclusion that light and the pineal gland are important in reproduction. When it is dark for months at a time in their arctic home, Inuit women stop producing eggs altogether and men become less sexually active. When daylight returns, both the women and the men resume their "normal" reproductive cycles.[402]

The "Nictitating Membrane" in the Human Eye

An excellent example of another commonly mislabeled vestigial organ is the so-called nictitating membrane remnant in the human eye. A nictitating membrane, or "third eyelid," is a very thin and transparent structure that small muscles move horizontally across the eye surface to clean and moisten the eye while maintaining sight. It hinges at the inner side of the lower eyelid of many animals. To nictitate means to move rapidly back and forth over the front of the eye.[403] The nictitating membrane is especially important in animals that live in certain environments, such as those that are exposed to dust and dirt like birds, reptiles, and mammals, or marine animals such as fish. Charles Darwin wrote about the "nictitating membrane:"

> …with its accessory muscles and other structures, is especially well developed in birds, and is of much functional importance to them, as it can be rapidly drawn across the whole eyeball. It is found in some reptiles and amphibians, and in certain fishes, as in sharks. … But in man, the quadrumana, and most other mammals, it exists, as is admitted by all anatomists, as a mere rudiment, called the semilunar fold.[404]

Many continue to repeat Darwin's wrong idea about this membrane being a vestigial structure, even though, as we will show, it is clearly important in the human eye. [405]

Its Use in Humans

The classic eye anatomy textbook by Snell and Lemp accurately describes what we now recognize as the misnamed nictitating membrane. The plica semiluminaris, or "plica" for short, is a semilunar fold located on the inner corner of the eye to allow that side of the human eyeball to move further inward, toward the nose.[406] Its anatomy reveals a delicate half-moon-shaped vertical fold. The eye has about 50–55% rotation, but without the plica semilunaris, the rotation would be much less. There exists slack that must be taken up when the eye looks forward or side-to-side; hence the fold. No such arrangement exists for looking up or down, for at this area the fornix is very deep. The absence of a deep medial fornix is required for the puncta to dip into superficial strips of tear fluid.[407] Because the plica allows generous eye rotation, it actually is an example of over-design. [408]

Another function of the plica semilunaris is to collect foreign material that sticks to the eyeball. Stibbe notes on a windy day the eyes can rapidly accumulate dust, but due to the plica they can usually effectively remove it.[409] To do this, it secretes a thick sticky fatty liquid that effectively collects foreign material and, in essence, insulates the material for easy removal from the eye without fear of scratching or damaging the delicate eye surface. The critical role of the plica in clearing foreign objects from the eye surface has been recognized since at least 1927. This should be an embarrassment to those who have thought of it as vestigial since then.

Muscle and Bone Variations as Vestigial Organs

Most of the over 100 vestigial organs and structures listed in Wiedersheim's original 1895 work were small muscles or minor variations in bones, and not glands or discreet organs such as the human appendix.[410] Many of these muscles were labeled vestigial because they were small and made only a small contribution, or supposedly no contribution, to the total muscle force. The problem is, if a muscle is vestigial it would rapidly shrink, as research on living in a weightless situation, such as in outer space, has documented.

Thus, if a muscle has not atrophied it must be functional. It is now known that most small, short body muscles produce fine adjustments in the movement of larger muscles, or serve other roles, such as in proprioception.[411] The proprioceptive system allows the body to rapidly and accurately control limb position. It is why falling cats so often land on their feet. Anatomist David Menton concludes that:

> ...most muscles have a sensory function in addition to their more obvious motor function.
> ...that some of the smaller muscles in our body that were once considered vestigial, on the basis of their small size and weak contractile strength, are in fact sensory organs rather than motor organs.[412]

Certain other muscles and bone variations are also labeled vestigial primarily because they are not present in most (or many) people and are not required for survival. As is clearly evident in human skill differences, these muscle variations help to produce the enormous variety in many abilities so evident in modern humans. An example is the gross body muscle development of the stereotyped computer programmer compared with a football player. More commonly, many muscles are not well developed in most persons today in Western society due to our sedentary lifestyle.

This does not mean that they are vestigial, but only demonstrates their lack of use in modern life. It also demonstrates a very different lifestyle today than in the past. Lifestyle differences could cause many of these "less developed" muscles to be much larger. Would evolutionists have called them vestigial if they saw how much larger they were in a more athletic person's body? The fact that some individuals are superior athletes from a young age is evidence that genetic components clearly play an important role in complex physical activities. DeVries maintains that athletic ability depends on variations of numerous aspects of muscle cell structure and physiology.[413] Certain muscles and muscle types must first be present before they can ever be developed by proper training.

Gifted athletes, such as gymnastic and acrobatic stars, may tend to have certain muscles that some people may not even possess, or they can develop certain muscles to a greater extent. Most human abilities appear to be influenced by genetic differences that result from body structure variations. It follows that the human muscle system would likewise be influenced by heredity.

The argument that some small muscle is vestigial depends heavily on judgments as to the value and the individual use of a particular structure. It is clear that none of the so-called vestigial muscles are in any way harmful. Indeed, if they are developed at all, then those who have them may enjoy an advantage in certain activities, even if it is only an athletic or aesthetic advantage.

Scientist have clearly identified specific and well-designed purposes for every single supposedly vestigial organ so far proposed. Darwinist books, movies, and displays are dead wrong if they promote the concept of vestigial organs, which don't actually exist.

Conclusion

If the God of the Bible is true, we would expect to find clear "evidence trails" described in each chapter:

- Chapter 2 (Can We Trust the Bible?): We would expect to find *inspired content* that withstands the test of time; prophecies that are foretold centuries before they come true; and a consistent description of intelligent design and scientific underpinnings of Creation.
- Chapter 3 (Did Noah's Flood Really Happen?): We would expect to find billions of dead things laid down by water all over the earth, including the high mountains and major "bonebeds" where thousands of mixed and same-species animals are jumbled together, buried by the deluge of the flood; major coal deposits from countless buried forests and animals; evidence of mountain formations made by buckling as the continents shifted catastrophically; and a God-designed Ark that was built to weather the worst storm in history, filled with a feasible number of "kinds" necessary to repopulate the Earth with the animals we see today.
- Chapter 4 (The Age of the Earth, Dating Methods, and Evolution): We would expect to find evidences that disprove "old-age" dating methods and evolutionary "gradualism" assumptions that cannot be relied upon; evidence of young coal deposits; "young" diamonds; and numerous cases of "young bones and flesh" in supposedly old Earth matter; and young ocean.
- Chapter 5 (Do Fossils Show Evolution?): We would expect to find that evolutionary "ancestral forms," "transitional forms," and "divergent forms" never existed; that the fossil evidence does not allow for gradualism; and that Noah's Flood provides the most reasonable and logical explanation for the billions of dead animals in Earth's crust all over the world.

- Chapter 6 (Natural Selection and Evolution): We would expect to find that "Darwin's Finches" are great examples of God-designed adaptation (but not evolution) and that God has a Divine formula for life.
- Chapter 7 (Did Hippos Evolve into Whales?): We would expect to find that several mammal and whale designs died off during the Flood and that several "created kinds" still exist today in the perfectly-designed form necessary for navigating and living in the ocean.
- Chapter 8 (History of Human Evolution in Textbooks): We would expect to find countless mis-identified, over-exaggerated "icons" that carry evolution teaching for each generation. We would also expect to find that the evidence underpinning these icons to fall apart over the years, which is exactly what has happened!
- Chapter 9 (The Typical Line-up of Ape-to-Human Progression in Public School Textbooks): We would expect to find extinct species (e.g., *Australopithecines*), mixed classification (*Homo habilis*), and humans of various types, forms, and ages (e.g., *Homo erectus*, Neanderthal Man, and Cro-Magnon Man) in the fossil records mapped in a way to attempt to prove evolution.
- Chapter 10 (What about the Different "Races" of People?): We would expect to find one "race" of humans clearly trace back to Adam and Eve only thousands of years ago and human variability that is within the constraints God placed within humankind.
- Chapter 11 (Are Humans and Chimps 98% Similar?): We would expect to find that the Divine Creator of all living things used similar DNA coding to build similar-looking creatures, but with major differences that set humans aside as beings with eternal souls, a conscience, and the dominant physical and mental traits necessary to take dominion over the Earth.
- Chapter 12 (How Modern Genetics Supports a Recent Creation): We would expect to find clear markers that

go back to Adam and Eve only thousands of years ago and a massive dispersion of human variety that occurred immediately following the Flood and Babel event.
- Chapter 13 (Vestigial Structures in Humans and Animals): We would expect to find that virtually every square inch of the human body is necessary and shouts "grand design" from the beginning of Creation. We would also expect to find that certain parts of the body that evolutionists previously claimed "prove evolution" to be debunked by subsequent scientific discovery.

In this book we have tried to refute what students informed us were the most convincing arguments for evolution from their high school biology and earth science textbooks. We hope you noticed that we squarely faced the best that evolutionary-based science offers, and demonstrated how textbooks sometimes use wrong history and inaccurate science.

In many instances, Christians *should* trust science textbooks and the scientific method. Indeed, science has advanced medicine, space exploration, and technology beyond what we could have even imagined one hundred years ago. Thus, science applied in the present can advance so many fields into the future.

But what about the past? How accurately can scientific methods take us into the past? Certainly, in fields like crime scene investigation, scientists have developed very reliable methods for determining when certain events happened, what elements were involved, and other factors. But what about hundreds or even thousands of years ago, when present scientists did not exist? Can we reliably use scientific tools for knowing, for certain, when major events occurred, such as the dinosaurs going extinct some 65 million years ago as evolutionist claim? That's certainly a long time ago to make such a projection—especially by using the supposed age of the rocks to date the fossils.

Put simply, textbooks are often wrong. The largest errors occur where textbook authors and the scientific works that they cite make historical statements. You can easily recognize these by their use of past tense verbs. Whenever you see a past-tense assertion like "The Earth formed 4.6 billion years ago," just ask, "How do they know?"

Often, they have no idea—they just trust that whoever told them does know. In truth, the teller was probably thinking the same thing. When we see past tenses, we can also ask, "Were they there to witness the events they portray?" or, "Is that even a scientific (experiment-based) claim?" If not, then we have strong reasons to suspect that their assertions masquerade as science when in fact they stem from miracle-ignoring histories.

Textbook authors religiously confine their statements to a secularized history that by definition excludes the Bible—regardless of the evidence. This is exactly the attitude that Peter, carried along by the Holy Spirit as he penned the words, foretold would occur. In 2 Peter 3, he wrote, "For this they willfully forget: that by the word of God the heavens were of old, and the Earth standing out of water and in the water, by which the world that then existed perished, being flooded with water." Peter strongly warned his readers—you and I inside the church—"that scoffers will come in the last days" and would deliberately forget the two great historical miracles: creation and the Flood judgment.

He was concerned that their false teachings would derail untrained Christians. That is exactly our concern, too. So, we wrote this book to help train you how to think biblically and scientifically about origins. If secular textbook authors are some of Peter's foretold scoffers who force God and Genesis out of their minds so they can pretend they will escape the judgment of God, then they merely fulfil this very Scripture. In the end, the Bible is right. We can trust its every word. As Jesus said to our Father, "Your word is truth." (John 17: 17)

Helpful Resources

The following websites are recommended for further research:

- Answers in Genesis: *www.answersingenesis.com*
- Answers in Genesis (High School Biology): *www.evolutionexposed.com*
- Creation Ministries International: *www.cmi.org*
- Institute for Creation Research: *www.icr.org*
- Creation Today: *www.creationtoday.org*
- Creation Wiki: *www.creationwiki.org*
- Evolution: The Grand Experiment with by Dr. Carl Werner: *www.thegrandexperiment.com*

Endnotes

[1] Ken Ham, "Culture and Church in Crisis," AnswersinGenesis.com: *http://www.answersingenesis.org/articles/am/v2/n1/culture-church-crisis* (January 1, 2014) and survey data: *http://www.answersingenesis.org/articles/am/v2/n1/aig-poll (data)* (January 1, 2014).

[2] Results for this USA Today/Gallup poll are based on telephone interviews conducted May 10–13, 2012, with a random sample of 1,012 adults, aged 18 and older, living in all 50 U.S. states and the District of Columbia.

[3] Frank Newport, "In U.S., 46% Hold Creationist View of Human Origins: Highly Religious Americans most likely to believe in Creationism," Gallop.com: *http://www.gallup.com/poll/155003/hold-creationist-view-human-origins.aspx* (June 1, 2012).

[4] Kenneth R. Miller & Joseph S. Levine, *Biology* (Boston, Mass: Pearson, 2010): 466.

[5] Introduction and Table from: "The Bible and Science Agree," Creationism.org: *http://www.creationism.org/articles/BibleSci.htm* (January 1, 2014).

[6] Ken Ham and Britt Beemer. Already Gone: Why your Kids will Quit Church and What you can do to Stop it Green Forest: Master Books, 2009.

[7] Several questions were drawn from: Dr. Jason Lisle and Mike Riddle, Chapter 30: What Are Some Good Questions to Ask an Evolutionist? (December 2, 2014): https://answersingenesis.org/evidence-against-evolution/probability/what-are-some-good-questions-to-ask-an-evolutionist/ (January 28, 2016).

[8] Source: Colin Patterson, personal letter to Luther Sutherland, 10 April 1979, quoted in Luther D Sutherland, Darwin's Enigma, 4th ed. (Santee, CA. Master Books, 1988), 89.

[9] Steven M. Stanley, Macroevolution: Pattern and Process, (San Francisco: W.M. Freeman and Co.) p. 39.

[10] Source: Evolution: The Grand Experiment. Volume 1, The Quest for An Answer, by Dr. Carl Werner (see more at: *http://www.thegrandexperiment.com/#sthash.RjBL4QWB.dpuf*).

[11] Mike Riddle, Four Power Questions to ask an Evolutionist, Answers in Genesis (2010). Our summary based on this video is taken from: https://answersingenesis.org/evidence-against-evolution/probability/what-are-some-good-questions-to-ask-an-evolutionist/ (January 28, 2016).

[12] Bradley Thaxton, *The Mystery of Life's Origin*, p. 80.

[13] F. Hoyle and C. Wickramasinghe, *Evolution from Space* (New York: Simon and Schuster, 1984), p. 176.

[14] Colin Patterson, personal letter to Luther Sutherland, 10 April 1979, quoted in Luther D Sutherland, *Darwin's Enigma*, 4th ed. (Santee, CA. Master Books, 1988), 89.

[15] David Norman, *Illustrated Encyclopedia of Dinosaurs*, (Gramercy Publishing (1985).

[16] Tim Gardom & Angela C. Milner, *The Natural History Museum Book of Dinosaurs* (Carlton Books Ltd, 1998, p. 12).

[17] Nicholas Bakalarfeb (February 7, 2011). On Evolution, Biology Teachers Stray from Lesson Plan. Available: *http://www.nytimes.com/2011/02/08/science/08creationism.html?_r=0* (March 26, 2015).

[18] Ken Ham & T. Hillard, *Already Gone: Why your Kids will Quit Church and what you can do stop it* (Green Forest, AR: Master Books, 2009).

[19] S. Michael Houdmann, "How and when was the Canon of the Bible put together?" Got Questions Online: *http://www.gotquestions.org/canon-Bible.html* (November 7, 2013).

[20] The reader is encouraged to review these additional resources: Henry Halley, *Halley's Bible Handbook* (Grand Rapids: Zondervan Publishing House, 1927, 1965); Arthur Maxwell, *Your Bible and You* (Washington D.C.: Review and Herald Publishing Association, 1959); Merrill Unger, *Unger's Bible Handbook* (Chicago: Moody Press, 1967).

[21] For example, in 1946 the Dead Sea Scrolls were discovered, which included over 900 manuscripts dating from 408 B.C. to A.D. 318. These manuscripts were written mostly on parchment (made of animal hide) but with some written on papyrus. Because these materials are fragile, they have to be kept behind special glass in climate controlled areas.

[22] Josh McDowell, *The New Evidence that Demands a Verdict* (Nashville: Thomas Nelson Publishers).

[23] McDowell, *The New Evidence that Demands a Verdict*, p. 38.

[24] McDowell, *The New Evidence that Demands a Verdict*, p. 38.

[25] Most of the 11 verses come from 3 John. See: Norman Geisler & William Nix. *A General Introduction to the Bible* (Chicago: Moody Press, 1986), 430.

[26] Geisler & Nix, *A General Introduction to the Bible,* p. 430.

[27] Theophilus ben Ananus was the High Priest in Jerusalem from A.D. 37 to 41 and was one of the wealthiest and most influential Jewish families in Iudaea Province during the 1st century. He was also the brother-in-law of Joseph Caiaphas, the High Priest before whom Jesus appeared. See Wikipedia and B. Cooper, *The Authenticity of the Book of Genesis* (Portsmouth, UK: Creation Science Movement, 2012).

[28] B. Cooper, *Authenticity of the New Testament, Vol. 1: The Gospels*. Electronic book (2013).

[29] The Digital Dead Sea Scrolls Online, Directory of Qumran Dead Sea

Scroll: *http://dss.collections.imj.org.il/isaiah* (December 10, 2013).
[30] Source for DSS: Fred Mille, "Qumran Great Isaiah Scroll," Great Isaiah Scroll: *http://www.moellerhaus.com/qumdir.htm*; Source for Aleppo Codes JPS: "Mechon Mamre" (Hebrew for Mamre Institute): *http://www.mechon-mamre.org/p/pt/pt1053.htm* (December 10, 2013).
[31] Norman & Nix. *A General Introduction to the Bible.*
[32] Samuel Davidson, *Hebrew Text of the Old Testament,* 2d ed. (London: Samuel Bagster & Sons, 1859), 89.
[33] Mary Fairchild, "44 Prophecies of the Messiah Fulfilled in Jesus Christ," About.com: *http://christianity.about.com/od/biblefactsandlists/a/Prophecies-Jesus.htm* (December 18, 2013).
[34] See: Genesis 7:19 ("all the high hills under the whole heaven were covered"); Genesis 7:21–22 ("all flesh died that moved upon the earth…all that was in the dry land"); Matthew 24:39 ("The flood came, and took them all away"); and 2 Peter 3:6 ("By these waters also the world of that time was deluged and destroyed."). God also promised in Genesis 9:11 that there would be no more floods like the one of Noah's day.
[35] Ken Ham, "They Can't Allow 'It'!" AnswersinGenesis.com: *http://www.answersingenesis.org/articles/au/cant-allow-it* (January 1, 2014).
[36] Eva Vergara & Ian James, "Whale Fossil Bonanza in Desert Poses Mystery," Science on msnbc.com: *http://www.msnbc.msn.com/id/45367885/ns/technology_and_science-science/* (November 20, 2013).
[37] D.A. Eberth, D.B. Brinkman, & V. Barkas, "A Centrosaurine Mega-bonebed from the Upper Cretaceous of Southern Alberta: Implications for Behaviour and Death Events" in *New Perspectives on Horned Dinosaurs: The Ceratopsian Symposium at the Royal Tyrrell Museum* (September 2007).
[38] Michael Reilly, "Dinosaurs' Last Stand Found in China?" Discovery.com: *http://news.discovery.com/earth/dinosaurs-last-stand-found-in-china.htm* (January 1, 2014).
[39] Michael J. Oard, "The Extinction of the Dinosaurs," *Journal of Creation* 11(2) (1997): 137–154.
[40] J.R. Horner & J. Gorman, *Digging Dinosaurs* (New York: Workman Publishing, 1988), 122–123.
[41] John Woodmorappe, "The Karoo Vertebrate Non-Problem: 800 Billion Fossils or Not," *CEN Technical Journal* 14, no.2 (2000): 47.
[42] R. Broom, *The Mammal-like Reptiles of South Africa* (London: H.F.G., 1932), 309.
[43] Steven Austin, "Nautiloid Mass Kill and Burial Event, Redwall Limestone (Lower Mississippian) Grand Canyon Region, Arizona and Nevada," in Ivey Jr. (Ed.). *Proceedings of the Fifth International Conference on Creationism* (Pittsburg, Pennsylvania: Creation Science Fellowship): 55–99.
[44] Andrew Snelling, *Earth's Catastrophic Past: Geology, Creation & the*

Flood, Vol. 2 (Dallas, TX: Institute for Creation Research, 2009), 537.
[45] Snelling, *Earth's Catastrophic Past: Geology, Creation & the Flood*, p. 537.
[46] David Cloud, *An Unshakeable Faith: A Christian Apologetics Course* (Port Huron, MI: Way of Life Literature, 2011).
[47] Snelling, *Earth's Catastrophic Past: Geology, Creation & the Flood*, p. 538.
[48] Snelling, *Earth's Catastrophic Past: Geology, Creation & the Flood*, p. 539.
[49] Andrew Snelling, "The World's a Graveyard Flood Evidence Number Two," AnswersinGenesis: *http://www.answersingenesis.org/articles/am/v3/n2/world-graveyard* (January 1, 2014).
[50] Cloud, *An Unshakeable Faith: A Christian Apologetics Course*.
[51] Cloud, *An Unshakeable Faith: A Christian Apologetics Course*.
[52] N. O. Newell, "Adequacy of the Fossil Record," *Journal of Paleontology*, 33 (1959): 496.
[53] Darwin, *The Origin of Species*, p. 298.
[54] Luther Sunderland, *Darwin's Enigma* (Arkansas: Master Books, 1998), 129.
[55] Cloud, *An Unshakeable Faith: A Christian Apologetics Course*.
[56] Photo by Ian Juby. Reproduced with permission. Tas Walker, "Polystrate Fossils: Evidence for a Young Earth," Creation.com: *http://creation.com/polystrate-fossils-evidence-for-a-young-earth* (January 3, 2014).
[57] John D. Morris, "What Are Polystrate Fossils?" *Acts & Facts*, 24 (9) (1995).
[58] Tas Walker & Carl Wieland, "Kamikaze ichthyosaur? Long-age Thinking Dealt a Lethal Body Blow," *Creation Magazine*, 27 (4) (September 2005). See: Creation.com: *http://creation.com/kamikaze-ichthyosaur* (December 31, 2013).
[59] Walker & Wieland, 2005 (figure reproduced with permission: Creation.com).
[60] Carl Wieland, *Stones and Bones* (Green Forest, AR: Master Books, 1984).
[61] Andrew Snelling, "Transcontinental Rock Layers: Flood Evidence Number Three," Answers Magazine.com: *http://www.answersingenesis.org/articles/am/v3/n3/transcontinental-rock-layers* (December 17, 2013).
[62] David Catchpoole, "Giant Oysters on the Mountain," *Creation*, 24 (2) (March 2002): 54–55.
[63] Richard F. Flint. *Glacial Geology and the Pleistocene Epoch* (New York: Wiley, 1947), 514–515.
[64] Humans lived much longer before the Flood due to both changes in human

DNA (from sin entering the world through the fall of Adam) and climate changes in the post-flood world. See D. Menton & G. Purdom, "Did People Like Adam and Noah Really Live Over 900 Years of Age?" in Ken Ham. *The New Answers Book 2* (Green Forest: AR Master Books), 164; David Menton & Georgia Purdom, "Chapter 16: Did People Like Adam and Noah Really Live Over 900 Years of Age?" (May 27, 2010). AnswersinGenesis.com: *http://www.answersingenesis.org/articles/nab2/adam-and-noah-live* (January 1, 2014).

[65] There is no conflict regarding the estimated age of these trees and the estimated time of Noah's Flood. See: Mark Matthews, "Evidence for multiple ring growth per year in Bristlecone Pines," *Journal of Creation,* 20 (3) (2006): 95–103.

[66] D.E Kreiss, "Can the Redwoods Date the Flood?" *Institute for Creation Research Impact* (Article #134, 1984).

[67] Michael Oard, "The Remarkable African Planation Surface," *Journal of Creation* 25 (1) (2011): 111–122.

[68] Dr. Hong earned his Ph.D. degree in applied mechanics from the University of Michigan, Ann Arbor.

[69] S.W. Hong, S.S. Na, B.S. Hyun, S.Y. Hong, D.S. Gong, K.J. Kang, S.H. Suh, K.H. Lee, and Y.G. Je, "Safety investigation of Noah's Ark in a seaway," Creation.com: *http://creation.com/safety-investigation-of-noahs-ark-in-a-seaway* (January 1, 2014).

[70] John Whitcomb, *The World that Perished* (Grand Rapids, Michigan: Baker Book House, 1988), 24.

[71] See John Woodmorappe, *Noah's Ark: A Feasibility Study* (Dallas, TX: Institute for Creation Research, 2009).

[72] Woodmorappe, *Noah's Ark: A Feasibility Study,* 2009.

[73] Readers are encouraged to study where the water went after the Flood at the AnswersinGenesis.com website.

[74] Humans lived much longer before the Flood due to both changes in human DNA (from sin entering the world through the fall of Adam) and climate changes in the post-flood world. See D. Menton & G. Purdom, "Did People Like Adam and Noah Really Live Over 900 Years of Age?" in Ken Ham. *The New Answers Book 2* (Green Forest: AR Master Books), 164; David Menton & Georgia Purdom, "Chapter 16: Did People Like Adam and Noah Really Live Over 900 Years of Age?" (May 27, 2010). AnswersinGenesis.com: *http://www.answersingenesis.org/articles/nab2/adam-and-noah-live* (January 1, 2014).

[75] There are several resources for this topic of study. See, for example: "Michael Oard, "Chapter 7: The Genesis Flood Caused the Ice Age," (October 1, 2004), AnswersinGenesis.com:

http://www.answersingenesis.org/articles/fit/flood-caused-ice-age (January 6, 2014).

[76] Ken Ham, "What Really Happened to the Dinosaurs?" (October 25, 2007), AnswersinGenesis.com: http://www.answersingenesis.org/articles/nab/what-happened-to-the-dinosaurs (January 6, 2014).

[77] Miller & Levine, *Biology,* p. 466.

[78] Gunter Faure, *Principles of Isotope Geology,* 2nd ed. (John Wiley & Sons, 1986), 41, 119, 288.

[79] A.O. Woodford, *Historical Geology* (W.H. Freeman and Company, 1965), 191–220.

[80] Judah Etinger, *Foolish Faith* (Green Forest, AR: Master Books, 2003), Chapter 3.

[81] Larry Vardiman, "The Age of the Earth's Atmosphere, a Study of the Helium Flux through the Atmosphere," *Institute for Creation Research,* 1990.

[82] C.S. Noble & J.J Naughton, *Science,* 162 (1968): 265–266.

[83] Data compiled and modified after Snelling (1998): Andrew Snelling, "The Cause of Anomalous Potassium-Argon "ages" for Recent Andesite Flows at Mt. Ngauruhoe, New Zealand, and the Implications for Potassium-argon Dating," in Robert E. Walsh (ed.), *Proceedings of the Fourth International Conference on Creationism* (1998), 503–525.

[84] J. Hebert, "Rethinking Carbon-14 Dating: What Does It Really Tell Us about the Age of the Earth?" *Acts & Facts* 42 (4) (2013): 12–14.

[85] Modified from: J. Baumgardner, "Carbon-14 Evidence for a Recent Global Flood and a Young Earth." In *Radioisotopes and the Age of the Earth: Results of a Young-Earth Creationist Research Initiative.* Vardiman, L., A. A. Snelling, and E. F. Chaffin, eds. (San Diego, CA: Institute for Creation Research and Chino Valley, AZ: Creation Research Society), 605 (Table 2).

[86] M.J. Walter, S.C. Kohn, D. Araugo, G.P. Bulanova, C.B. Smith, E. Gaillou, J. Wang, A. Steele, S. B., Shirey, "Deep Mantle Cycling of Oceanic Crust: Evidence from Diamonds and Their Mineral Inclusions," *Science,* 334 no. 6052 (September 15, 2011): 54–57.

[87] Walter et al., 2011.

[88] Modified from Baumgardner, 2005, Table 6, p. 614.

[89] Baumgardner, 2005.

[90] Brian Thomas, *"The Incredible, Edible '190 Million-Year-Old Egg,'"* Institute for Creation Research Online: *http://www.icr.org/article/7415/*) (December 8, 2013).

[91] M.H. Schweitzer, L. Chiappe, A. C. Garrido, J.M. Lowenstein, & S.H. Pincus, "Molecular Preservation in Late Cretaceous Sauropod Dinosaur Eggshells," *Proceedings of the Royal Society B: Biological Sciences,*

Volume 272 (1565) (2005): 775–784.

[92] Brian Thomas, "Published Reports of Original Soft Tissue Fossils" Institute for Creation Research Online: *http://www.icr.org/soft-tissue-list/* (December 20, 2013).

[93] Brian Thomas, "A Review of Original Tissue Fossils and Their Age Implications," in M. Horstemeyer (ed.), *Proceedings of the Seventh International Conference on Creationism* (2013).

[94] Data compiled and simplified from Tables 1 and 2 in Austin and Humphries (1990): Stephen Austin & D. Humphreys, Russell, "The Sea's Missing Salt: A Dilemma for Evolutionists," in R. E. Walsh & C. L. Brooks (eds.), *Proceedings of the Fourth International Conference on Creationism* (1990), 17–33.

[95] Snelling, *Earth's Catastrophic Past*.

[96] Snelling, *Earth's Catastrophic Past*.

[97] Don DeYoung, *Thousands…Not Billions* (Green Forest, AR: Master Books, 2005).

[98] Jonathan Wells, *Icons of Evolution: Science or Myth?—Why Much of What We Teach About Evolution Is Wrong* (Washington, D.C.: Regnery Publishing, Inc., 2000), 35, 37.

[99] The coelacanth is supposedly an ancestor to amphibians that dates back 300 million years; however, the coelacanth appears "suddenly" in the fossil record, and modern coelacanths "were also found to give birth to live young (like some sharks), unlike their supposed descendants, the amphibians." See: K.S. Thomson, *Living Fossil* (New York, NY: W.W. Norton & Company, 1991), 137–144.

[100] Creationwiki.com: *http://creationwiki.org/Archaeopteryx* (January 3, 2014).

[101] Percival Davis, Dean H. Kenyon, & Charles B. Thaxton (ed). *Of Pandas and People: The Central Question of Biological Origins,* 2d ed. (Dallas, TX: Haughton Publishing Company, 1989), 22–23.

[102] John D. Morris, *The Young Earth: The Real History of the Earth, Past, Present, and Future* (Colorado Springs, CO: Master Books, 1994).

[103] Jerry Adler & John Carey, "Is Man a Subtle Accident?" *Newsweek*, 8, no. 95 (Nov. 3, 1980), 96.

[104] Stephen J. Gould & Niles Eldredge, "Punctuated Equilibria: The Tempo and Mode of Evolution Reconsidered," *Paleobiology*, 3, no. 2 (April 1977), 115–151.

[105] Brian Thomas, "150 Years Later, Fossils Still Don't Help Darwin," Institute for Creation Research Online: *http://www.icr.org/article/4546/* (December 20, 2013).

[106] Carl Werner, "Evolution the Grand Experiment," The Grand Experiment: *http://www.thegrandexperiment.com/index.html* (January 1, 2014).

[107] Carl Werner, *Living Fossils. Evolution: The Grand Experiment* (Vol. 2)

(Green Forest, AR: New Leaf Press, 2008), 242.

[108] Carl Werner, *Evolution: The Grand Experiment* (Green Forest, AR: New Leaf Press, 2007), 86.

[109] Chart adapted from: Michael Denton, *Evolution: A Theory in Crisis* (Bethesda: Adler & Adler, 1985).

[110] Charles Darwin, *The Origin of Species by Means of Natural Selection* (New York: The Modern Library, 1859), 124-125.

[111] Wells, *Icons of Evolution: Science or Myth?—Why Much of What We Teach About Evolution Is Wrong*, pp. 41–42.

[112] Robert F. DeHaan & John L. Wiester, "The Cambrian Explosion: The Fossil Record & Intelligent Design," *Touchstone* (July/August 1999), 65–69.

[113] Wells, *Icons of Evolution: Science or Myth?—Why Much of What We Teach About Evolution Is Wrong*, 42.

[114] DeHaan & Wiester, 1999, p. 68.

[115] Richard Dawkins, *River out of Eden* (Basic Books, 1995), 98.

[116] John D. Morris, "Does 'The Beak of the Finch' Prove Darwin Was Right?" ICR.org: *http://www.icr.org/article/1135/* (January 1, 2014).

[117] This orchard model was developed by Dr. Kurt Wise and has been refined by many creation scientists over the years.

[118] Miller & Levine, *Biology,* pp. 466-467.

[119] Other translations, such as the NIV, translate this section as "great creatures of the sea." The Hebrew phrase used for "great sea creatures" is hattannînim haggədōlîm (הגדלים התנינם). The lemma gadôl (גדול) certainly means big or great great. Tannîn (תנין) is often translated "sea monsters" or "dragons." Thus while the KJV translates this as "great whales," the term is broader. It would also include living large sea creatures like the great white shark and the whale shark. Surprising as it is to those used to faulty "millions of years" claims, the term would also include many famous extinct sea creatures. These include ichthyosaurs (from the Greek for "fish lizard"), somewhat like reptilian versions of dolphins; some grew huge, such as the 21-m (69-foot)–long Shastasaurus sikanniensis. Other creatures included in the term tannîn would be the short-necked long-headed pliosaurs, such as Liopleurodon, 6.4 (21 feet) long, although the 1999 BBC series Walking With Dinosaurs portrayed it as 25 m (82 ft.) long, far larger than any known specimen. There were also the long-necked plesiosaurs such as Elasmosaurus, 14 m (46 feet) long, half of it the neck. Other tannin created on Day 5 were mosasaurus, like marine versions of monitor lizards, the largest of which was Hainosaurus, at 17.5 meters (57 ft.) long.

[120] Werner, *Evolution: The Grand Experiment*, p. 40.

[121] N.D. Pyenson, et al., "Discovery of a Sensory Organ that Coordinates Lunge Feeding in Rorqual Whales," *Nature* 485 (7399) 2012: 498–501. J. Sarfati, "Baleen Whales have Unique Sensory Organ," *Creation* 35 (4)

(2013): 38–40.

[122] Charles Darwin, *The Origin of Species* 1st ed. (1865): Chapter 6, p. 184.

[123] Francis Darwin, *More Letters of Charles Darwin* (London: J. Murray, 1903): 162.

[124] Leigh Van Valen, "Deltatheridia, a New Order of Mammals," *Bulletin of the American Museum of Natural History* 132 (1966): 92.

[125] Philip D. Gingerich & D. E. Russell, "Pakicetus inachus, a new archaeocete (Mammalia, Cetacea) from the early-middle Eocene Kuldana Formation of Kohat (Pakistan)," *University of Michigan Museum of Paleontology*, 25 (1981): 235–246.

[126] University Of Michigan, "New Fossils Suggest Whales And Hippos Are Close Kin," *Science Daily* (September 20, 2001); University Of California, Berkeley, "UC Berkeley, French Scientists Find Missing Link Between The Whale And Its Closest Relative, The Hippo," *Science Daily* (February 7, 2005); Patricia Reaney, "Fossil Finds Show Whales Related to Early Pigs," Greenspun: http://www.greenspun.com/bboard/q-and-a-fetch-msg.tcl?msg_id=006QvI.

[127] Werner, Evolution: The Grand Experiment, p. 40.

[128] Casey Luskin, "Nice Try! A Review of Alan Rogers's The Evidence for Evolution," (October 18, 2011), Evolution News: http://www.evolutionnews.org/2012/04/a_review_of_ala058641.html (December 25, 2013).

[129] "Debate on Origins of Life," Discovery Institute: http://www.discovery.org/v/1711, (December 25, 2013).

[130] Luskin, 2011.

[131] Miller & Levine, *Biology*, p. 466.

[132] Philip D. Gingerich, NA. Wells, Donald Russell, S.M. Shaw, "Origin of Whales in Epicontinental Remnant Seas: New Evidence from the Early Eocene of Pakistan," *Science* 220 (4595) (April 22, 1983): 403–406.

[133] Phillip Gingerich, "The Whales of Tethys," *Natural History*, (April 1994): 86.

[134] P.D. Gingerich, "Evidence for Evolution from the Vertebrate Fossil Record," *Journal for Geological Education*, 31 (1983): 140-144.

[135] Christian de Muizon, "Walking with Whales," *Nature* 413, (September 20, 2001): 259–260.

[136] G.M. Thewissen, E.M. Williams, L.J. Roe, & S.T. Hussain, "Skeletons of Terrestrial Cetaceans and the Relationship of Whales to Artiodactyls," *Nature* 413 (September, 2001): 277-281.

[137] David Quammen, "Was Darwin Wrong?" *National Geographic*, 206 (5) (November, 2004): 2–35.

[138] Fossilworks Paleobiology Database: http://fossilworks.org (December 25, 2013).

[139] Miller & Levine, *Biology*, p. 466.

[140] Michael Denton, *Evolution: A Theory in Crisis*, (Bethesda: Adler & Adler, 1985), 210-211.
[141] Werner, *Evolution: The Grand Experiment*, pp. 137–138.
[142] Fossilworks Paleobiology Database: *http://fossilworks.org* (December 25, 2013).
[143] J. G. M. Thewissen & E. M. Williams, "The Early Radiations of Cetacea (Mammalia): Evolutionary Pattern and Developmental Correlations," *Annual Review of Ecological Systems*, 33 (2002): 73–90.
[144] Miller & Levine, *Biology*, p. 466.
[145] Working Group on Teaching Evolution, "National Academy of Sciences Teaching about Evolution and the Nature of Science, (Washington, D.C.: National Academy Press, 1998): 18.
[146] Carl Werner, *Evolution: The Grand Experiment* (DVD) (Based on interview conducted on August 28, 2001), (Green Forest, AR: New Leaf Publishing Group/Audio Visual Consultants Inc.).
[147] "Basilosaurus," Celebrating 100 Years: Explore Our Collections, Smithsonian National Museum of Natural History: *http://www.mnh.si.edu* (February 10, 2012).
[148] Phillip Gingerich, *The Press-Enterprise*, (July 1, 1990): A-15.
[149] Philip Gingerich, B. Holly Smith, & Elwyn L. Simons, "Hind limbs of Eocene Basilosaurus: Evidence of Feet in Whales," Science, Vol. 249, (July 13, 1990): 156.
[150] "Whales with 'non–feet,'" Creation.com: *http://creation.com/focus-142#nonfeet* (December 26, 2013).
[151] Jonathan Sarfati, "Science, Creation and Evolutionism: Response to the Latest Anticreationist Agitprop from the US National Academy of Sciences (NAS)," Creation.com: *http://creation.com/science-creation-and-evolutionism-refutation-of-nas* (December 26, 2013).
[152] D.T. Gish, *Evolution: The Fossils still say no!* (El Cajon, CA: Institute for Creation Research, 1985): 206–208.
[153] Marvin Lubenow, "Recovery of Neanderthal mtDNA: An Evaluation," *Creation Ex Nihilo Technical Journal* 12, 1 (1998): 89.
[154] Erik Trinkaus, "Hard Times Among the Neandertals," *Natural History*, 87, 10 (December 1978: 58-63.
[155] In a similar book (*In Man and the Lower Animals*, 1861), Huxley argued that humans, chimpanzees, and gorillas were more closely related to each other than any of them were to orangutans or gibbons.
[156] Charles Darwin, *The Descent of Man and Selection in Relation to Sex* 2d ed. (London: John Murray, 1874): 178.
[157] See: Jerry Bergman, "Darwinism and the Nazi Race Holocaust," (November 1, 1999), Answers in Genesis: *https://answersingenesis.org/charles-darwin/racism/darwinism-and-the-nazi-race-holocaust/* (September 2, 2015); David Klinghoffer, "Don't Doubt

It: An important historic sidebar on Hitler and Darwin," (April 18, 2008). *National Review Online: www.discovery.org/a/4679* (see also bibliography list).

[158] R.A. Hellman, "Evolution in American School Biology Books from the Late Nineteenth Century until the 1930s," *The American Biology Teacher* 27 (1968): 778-780.

[159] Ernst Haeckel, *Anthropogenie, oder Entwicklungsgeschichte des Menschen* (Leipzig: Verlag von Wilhelm Engelmann, 1891).

[160] Credit: *http://longstreet.typepad.com/thesciencebookstore/industrial_technological_art/page/7/*.

[161] Carl C. Swisher III, Garniss H. Curtis, Roger Lewin, *Java Man: How Two Geologists Changed Our Understanding of Human Evolution* (Chicago: University of Chicago Press, 2000).

[162] *The Living Age*, Volume 209 (Boston, MA: E. Littell & Company, 1896).

[163] B. Theunissien, *Eugene Dubois and the Ape-Man from Java* (Norwell, MA: Kluwer Academic Publishers, 1989): 39.

[164] Garniss Curtis, Carl Swisher, and Roger Lewin, *Java Man* (Abacus, London, 2000): 87.

[165] James Perloff, *Tornado in a Junkyard: The Relentless Myth of Darwinism* (Burlington, MA: Refuge Books, 1999): 85.

[166] Eugene DuBois, "On the Fossil Human Skulls Recently Discovered in Java and Pithecanthropus Erectus," *Man* 37 (January 1937): 4.

[167] Credit: *http://jattwood.blogspot.com/2014/10/blog-3-java-man.html*

[168] Credit: *http://kotawisataindonesia.com/museum-purbakala-sangiran-sragen/welcome-to-sangiran/*

[169] Howard E. Wilson, "The Java Man (Pithecanthropus Erectus)" *Truth Magazine: www.truthmagazine.com/archives/volume2/TM002021.htm* (September 2, 2015).

[170] *Science*, New Series, Vol. 57, June 15, 1923, Supplement 8.

[171] *Science*, New Series, Vol. 58, Aug. 17, 1923, Supplement 8.

[172] Marvin Lubenow, *Bones of Contention* (Grand Rapids, MI: Baker Books, 1992): 95.

[173] *Science*, New Series, Volume 75, Supplement 11 (June 10, 1932) ("In the Smithsonian collection there are 32 American Indian skulls of small statured but otherwise apparently normal individuals ranging in capacity from 910 to 1,020 cc"). See also *1925 Science Supplement: Truth Magazine* (II:3, pp. 8-10, December 1957): *www.truthmagazine.com/archives/volume2/TM002021.htm* (September 2, 2015).

[174] *1925 Science Supplement: Truth Magazine* (II:3, pp. 8-10, December 1957): *www.truthmagazine.com/archives/volume2/TM002021.htm* (September 2, 2015).

[175] O.W. Richards, "The Present Content of Biology in the Secondary Schools," *School Science and Mathematics*, 23 (5) (1923): 409-414.

[176] Pat Shipman, "On the Trail of the Piltdown Fraudsters," *New Scientist*, 128 (October 6, 1990): 52.

[177] Credit: http://up.botstudent.net/piltdown-man-new-york-times.jpg

[178] Lubenow, 1992, 42–43.

[179] Arthur Keith, *The Antiquity of Man* (London: Williams & Norgate, 1915).

[180] Arthur Keith, *The Antiquity of Man* (Philadelphia: J. B. Lippincott Company, 1928).

[181] National Science Foundation, *Evolution of Evolution: Flash Special Report Timeline:* www.nsf.gov/news/special_reports/darwin/textonly/timeline.jsp (September 2, 2015).

[182] Keith, 1915, 305.

[183] Credit: http://www.oakauctions.com/clarence-darrow-signed-%E2%80%9Cthe-antiquity-of-man%E2%80%9D-lot1674.aspx.

[184] *Nature* Volume 274, #4419 (July 10, 1954): 61-62.

[185] Stephen Jay Gould, "Piltdown Revisited," *The Panda's Thumb* (New York: W.W. Norton and Company, 1982).

[186] Credit: Science (May 20, 1927, p. 486) http://bevets.com/piltdowng.htm

[187] Credit: Popular Science (October, 1931, p. 23) http://bevets.com/piltdowng.htm

[188] William K. Gregory, "Hesperopithecus Apparently Not an Ape nor a Man," *Science*, 66 (1720) (December 16, 1927): 579-581.

[189] Ralph M. Wetzel, et al., "Catagonus, An 'Extinct' Peccary, Alive in Paraguay," *Science*, 189 (4200) (Aug. 1, 1975): 379.

[190] Duane T. Gish, *Evolution: The Fossils Still Say NO!* (El Cajon, CA: Institute for Creation Research, 1995): 328.

[191] Piltdown Man and Nebraska Man were mentioned in affidavits by "expert witnesses" Fay-Cooper Cole and Horatio Newman (professors at the University of Chicago), and Judge Raulston allowed their reports to be read into the court record on July 20, 1925.

[192] Paul J. Wendel. *A History of Teaching Evolution in U. S. Schools: Insights from Teacher Surveys and Textbook Reviews* (Columbus, Ohio: Paper presented at the Mid-Western Educational Research Association, October 11-14, 2006).

[193] J. I. Cretzinger, "An Analysis of Principles or Generalities Appearing in Biological Textbooks used in the Secondary Schools of the United States from 1800 to 1933," *Science Education* 25 (6) (1941): 310-313.

[194] Gerald Skoog, "Topic of Evolution in Secondary School Biology Textbooks: 1900-1977," *Science Education* 63 (1979): 622.

[195] The Topic of Evolution in Secondary Schools Revisited, Last updated

February 15, 2010. *Textbook History: www.textbookhistory.com/the-topic-of-evolution-in-secondary-schools-revisited/* (September 2, 2015).
[196] Credit: *http://www.textbookhistory.com/the-topic-of-evolution-in-secondary-schools-revisited/*
[197] Gerald Skoog, "Topic of Evolution in Secondary School Biology Textbooks: 1900-1977," *Science Education* 63 (1979): 622. See also: Paul J. Wendel. *A History of Teaching Evolution in U. S. Schools: Insights from Teacher Surveys and Textbook Review*s (Columbus, Ohio: Paper presented at the Mid-Western Educational Research Association, October 11-14, 2006).
[198] Credit: Life (May 21, 1951, p. 116) (*http://bevets.com/piltdowng.htm*)
[199] Answers in Genesis, "Myth-making: The Power of the Image," (September 1, 1999): *https://answersingenesis.org/creationism/myth-making-the-power-of-the-image/* (September 2, 2015).
[200] Clark F. Howell, *Early Man* (New York: Time Life Books, 1965): 41-45.
[201] John Gurche (Sculptor), *National Geographic* 189 (3) (March 1996): 96-117.
[202] Matthew Thomas (Podiatrist). Podiatry Arena (Blog): *www.podiatry-arena.com/podiatry-forum/showthread.php?t=68691&page=2* (September 2, 2015).
[203] Chris Kirk, "Science the state of the Universe. Map: Publicly Funded Schools That Are Allowed to Teach Creationism," (January 26, 2014). Slate: *www.slate.com/articles/health_and_science/science/2014/01/creationism_in_public_schools_mapped_where_tax_money_supports_alternatives.html* (March 23, 2015).
[204] America's Changing Religious Landscape, (May 12, 2015), *Pew Research Center: www.pewforum.org/2015/05/12/americas-changing-religious-landscape/* (September 2, 2015).
[205] Lubenow, *Recovery of Neandertal mtDNA: An Evaluation*, 89.
[206] Frank Newport, "In U.S., 46% Hold Creationist View of Human Origins: Highly Religious Americans most likely to believe in Creationism," (June 1, 2012), *Gallup: www.gallup.com/poll/155003/hold-creationist-view-human-origins.aspx* (March 23, 2015).
[207] David Catchpoole and Tas Walker, "Charles Lyell's Hidden Agenda—to Free Science "from Moses" (August 19, 2009). *Creation.com: http://creation.com/charles-lyell-free-science-from-moses#endRef3* (March 23, 2015).
[208] "Who are we?" (October 26, 2002), *New Scientist: www.newscientist.com/article/mg17623665-300-who-are-we/* (September 2, 2015).
[209] "Return to the Planet of the Apes," *Nature*, Volume 412 (July 12, 2001): 131.
[210] "The water people," *Science Digest*, Volume 90 (May 1982): 44.
[211] Rinehart, Winston, & Holt, *Social Studies World History: Ancient*

Civilizations (2006): 24-35.
[212] PBS Evolution, "Finding Lucy": *www.pbs.org/wgbh/evolution/library/07/1/l_071_01.html* (September 2, 2015); National Geographic, "What was 'Lucy'? Fast Facts on an Early Human Ancestor" (September 20, 2006). *National Geographic News: http://news.nationalgeographic.com/news/2006/09/060920-lucy.html* (September 2, 2015).
[213] Donald Johanson & Edgar Blake. *From Lucy to Language* (New York: Simon & Schuster, 1996).
[214] NOVA, *In Search of Human Origins (Part I)* (Airdate: June 3, 1997): *http://www.pbs.org/wgbh/nova/transcripts/2106hum1.html* (September 2, 2015).
[215] Time magazine reported in 1977 that Lucy had a tiny skull, a head like an ape, a braincase size the same as that of a chimp—450 cc. and "was surprisingly short legged" (*Time*, November 7, 1979, 68-69). See also: Smithsonian National Museum of Natural History, "Australopithecus afarensis": *http://humanorigins.si.edu/evidence/human-fossils/species/australopithecus-afarensis* (September 2, 2015).
[216] Solly Zuckerman, *Beyond the Ivory Tower* (London: Taplinger Publishing Company, 1970): 78.
[217] Solly Zuckerman and Charles Oxnard used mathematical studies of australopithecine fossils that revealed they did not have upright gait like humans. (Charles E. Oxnard, "The Place of the Australopithecines in Human Evolution: Grounds for Doubt?" *Nature* Volume 258 (December 4, 1975): 389–395; Solly Zuckerman, "Myth and Method in Anatomy," *Journal of the Royal College of Surgeons of Edinburgh*, Volume 11 (2) (1966): 87-114. Solly Zuckerman, *Beyond the Ivory Tower* (New York: Taplinger Publishing Company, 1971): 76-94; P. Shipman, "Those Ears Were Made For Walking, "*New Scientist* 143 (1994): 26–29; R. L. Susman & J.T. Susman, "The Locomotor Anatomy of *Australopithecus* Afarensis," *American Journal of Physical Anthropology* 60 (3) (1983): 279–317; and T. Eardsley, "These Feet Were Made for Walking – and?" *Scientific American* 273 (6) (1995): 19–20.
[218] Charles Oxnard, *The Order of Man: A Biomathematical Anatomy of the Primates* (Yale University Press and Hong Kong University Press, 1984): 3.
[219] Jack Stern & Randall L. Susman, "The Locomotor Anatomy of Australopithecus afarensis," *Journal of Physical Anthropology* 60 (1983): 280.
[220] See Richmond & Strait, *Evidence That Humans Evolved From a Knuckle-Walking Ancestor*, 382-385.
[221] Maggie Fox, "Man's Early Ancestors Were Knuckle Walkers," *San Diego Union Tribune* (Quest Section, March 29, 2000).
[222] Richmond & Strait, *Evidence That Humans Evolved From a Knuckle-*

Walking Ancestor, 382-385.
[223] Donald Johanson & Maitland A. Edey, *Lucy: The Beginnings of Humankind* (London: Penguin, 1981): 358.
[224] Ibid.
[225] Richard Leakey & Roger Lewin, *Origins Reconsidered: In Search of What Makes us Human* (New York: Doubleday, 1992): 193-194.
[226] Peter Schmid as quoted in Leakey and Lewin, *Origins Reconsidered*, 1992, 193-194.
[227] Fred Spoor, Bernard Wood, Frans Zonneveld, "Implications of Early Hominid Labyrinthine Morphology for Evolution of Human Bipedal Locomotion," *Nature* 369 (June 23, 1994): 645-648.
[228] M. Häusler & P. Schmid, "Comparison of the Pelves of Sts 14 and AL 288-1: Implications for Birth and Sexual Dimorphism in Australopithecines." *Journal of Human Evolution* 29 (1995): 363-383.
[229] Alan Boyle, "Lucy or Brucey? It Can Be Tricky to Tell the Sex of Fossil Ancestors," *Science* (April 29, 2015).
[230] Stern & Sussman, *The Locomotor Anatomy of Australopithecus afarensis*, 279-317.
[231] Oxnard, *The Order of Man: A Biomathematical Anatomy of the Primates*, 3.
[232] Roger Lewin, *Bones of Contention* (Chicago: University of Chicago Press, 1987): 164).
[233] Wray Herbert, "Lucy's Uncommon Forbear," *Science News* 123 (February 5, 1983): 89.
[234] Albert W. Mehlert, "Lucy—Evolution's Solitary Claim for an Ape/Man: Her Position is Slipping Away," *Creation Research Society Quarterly*, 22 (3) (December, 1985): 145.
[235] Lubenow, *Bones of Contention*, 179.
[236] DeWitt Steele & Gregory Parker, *Science of the Physical Creation*, 2d ed. (Pensacola, FL: A Beka Book, 1996), 299.
[237] "Before humans left Babel, it appears that apes had already spread over much of the Old World and had diversified into a large array of species... Paleontologists are still discovering species of post-Flood apes. If we are correct about post-Flood rocks, apes were at their highest point of diversity and were buried in local catastrophes just before humans spread out from Babel." Kurt Wise, "Lucy Was Buried First Babel Helps Explain the Sequence of Ape and Human Fossils," (August 20, 2008), *Answers in Genesis: https://answersingenesis.org/human-evolution/lucy/lucy-was-buried-first/* (September 2, 2015).
[238] The 'First Family' location Dr. Johanson refers to is within one mile of where Lucy was found (Donald Johanson as quoted in "Letters to Mr. Jim Lippard," *Institute of Human Origins* (August 8, 1989; May 30, 1990).
[239] Not *A. aferensus*, but *Australopithecines* in general.

[240] Donald Johanson, M. Taieb & Y. Coppens, "Pliocene Hominids from the Hadar Formation, Ethiopia (1973–1977): Stratigraphic, Chronologic and Paleoenvironmental Contexts, with Notes on Hominid Morphology and Systematics," *American Journal of Physical Anthropology* 57 (1982): 501–544.
[241] Global Biodiversity Information Facility (GBIF), "What is GBIF": *http://www.gbif.org/whatisgbif* (September 2, 2015).
[242] Anna K. Behrensmeyer, "Paleoenvironmental Context of the Pliocene A.L. 333 'First Family' Hominin Locality" (Hadar Formation, Ethiopia," *GSA Special Papers* (Volume 446, 2008): 203-214; Jay Quade and Jonathan G. Wynn, "The Geology of Early Humans in the Horn of Africa," (GSA Special Papers 446, 2008).
[243] Donald Johanson, "Lucy, Thirty Years Later: An Expanded View of Australopithecus afarensis," *Journal of Anthropological Research* 60 (4) (Winter, 2004): 471-472.
[244] Lauren E. Bohn, "Q&A: 'Lucy' Discoverer Donald C. Johanson," (March 4, 2009), Time: *http://content.time.com/time/health/article/0,8599,1882969,00.html* (September 2, 2015).
[245] Darwin, *Origin of Species* (1859).
[246] Darwin, *Origin of Species* (1872).
[247] Credit: *http://humanorigins.si.edu/evidence/human-family-tree*
[248] Smithsonian National Museum of Natural History, "*Homo habilis*": *http://humanorigins.si.edu/evidence/human-fossils/species/homo-habilis* (September 2, 2015).
[249] Richard Leakey and Roger Lewin, *Origins Reconsidered* (New York: Doubleday, 1992): p 112. See also: Bernard Wood, "The age of australopithecines," *Nature* 372 (November 3, 1994): 31-32.
[250] Lubenow, *Bones of Contention*, 300.
[251] Richard Leakey and Roger Lewin, *Origins Reconsidered* (New York: Doubleday 1992): 112.
[252] Fred Spoor, Bernard Wood, Frans Zonneveld, "Implications of Early Hominid Labyrinthine Morphology for Evolution of Human Bipedal Locomotion," *Nature* 369 (June 23, 1994): 645.
[253] Ibid., 648.
[254] Credit: *http://thefactofcreation.blogspot.com/2012/08/homo-habilis.html?m=1*
[255] Bernard Wood, "The age of australopithecines," *Nature* 372 (November 3, 1994): 31-32.
[256] Bernard Wood, "Human Evolution: Fifty years after *Homo habilis*," *Nature* 508 (April 2014): 31-33.
[257] Holt, *Ancient Civilizations*, 30.
[258] Bill Mehlert, "Homo Erectus to Modern Man: Evolution or Human

Variability," (April 1, 1994): *Answers in Genesis:* *https://answersingenesis.org/human-evolution/ape-man/homo-erectus-to-modern-man-evolution-or-human-variability/* (September 2, 2015).

[259] Lubenow, *Bones of Contention: A Creationist Assessment of Human Fossils*, 115.

[260] Ibid., 27-128.

[261] Ibid., 115.

[262] John Woodmorappe, "How Different Is the Cranial-vault Thickness of Homo Erectus from Modern Man?" *Creation.com: http://creation.com/how-different-is-the-cranial-vault-thickness-of-homo-erectus-from-modern-man* (September 2, 2015).

[263] Ibid.

[264] Lubenow, *Bones of Contention: A Creationist Assessment of Human Fossils*, 348-51.

[265] Ibid.

[266] Lubenow, *Bones of Contention: A Creationist Assessment of Human Fossils*, 130.

[267] J. J. Hublin, "The Origin of Neandertals," *Proceedings of the National Academy of Sciences* 106 (38) (2009): 16022–7; K. Harvati, S.R. Frost, K.P. McNulty (2004), "Neanderthal Taxonomy Reconsidered: Implications of 3D Primate Models of Intra- and Interspecific Differences," Proceedings of the National Academy of Sciences, USA 101: 1147-1152.

[268] David Menton & John UpChurch, "Who Were Cavemen? Finding a Home for Cavemen," (April 1, 2012), *Answers in Genesis:* *https://answersingenesis.org/human-evolution/cavemen/who-were-cavemen/* (September 2, 2015).

[269] We are grateful to David V. Bassett, M.S. for his contributions to this section that were carried over from the first edition of this book.

[270] Marvin L. Lubenow, "Recovery of Neandertal mDNA: An Evaluation," *CEN Technical Journal*, 12 (1) (1998): 89.

[271] Jack Cuozzo, *Buried Alive: The Truth about Neanderthal Man, Truths That Transform Action Sheet* (Radio Program, aired on March 14–15, 2000).

[272] Lubenow, *Bones of Contention* (1992), 63.

[273] Steele & Parker, *Science of the Physical Creation*, 301.

[274] Lubenow, *Recovery of Neandertal mDNA: An Evaluation*, 89–90.

[275] Jack Cuozzo, *Buried Alive: The Startling Truth About Neanderthal Man* (Green Forest, AZ: Master Books, 1998): 162, 163, 203.

[276] Ibid.

[277] Green, R. E. et al. A Draft Sequence of the Neandertal Genome. *Science* 328 (2010): 710–722.

[278] Steele & Parker, *Science of the Physical Creation*, pp. 301–302.

[279] Vance Ferrell, *The Evolution Cruncher* (Altamont, TN: Evolution Facts, Inc., 2001): 529.

[280] Lubenow, 1992, p. 235.
[281] Ian Taylor, "Fossil Man" Creation Moments Online: *http://www.creationmoments.com/content/fossil-man* (January 1, 2014).
[282] Vance Ferrell, *The Evolution Cruncher* (Altamont, TN: Evolution Facts, Inc., 2001): 529.
[283] Gerhard Meisenberg & William Simmons, *Principles of Medical Biochemistry* (New York: Mosby, 2006).
[284] Susan Chavez Cameron and Susan Macias Wycoff, "The Destructive Nature of the Term 'Race': Growing Beyond a False Paradigm," *Journal of Counseling & Development*, Volume 76, no. 3 (Summer 1998): 277–285. The article cites information from L. Luca Cavalli-Sforza, Paolo Menozzi, and Alberto Piazza, *The History and Geography of Human Genes* (Princeton, NJ: Princeton University Press, 1994): 279.
[285] Darwin, *Descent of Man, and Selection in Relation to Sex*.
[286] Darwin, *Descent of Man, and Selection in Relation to Sex*, Volume 1, 201.
[287] Stephen Jay Gould, *Ontogeny and Phylogeny* (Cambridge, MA: Harvard University Press, 1977): 127.
[288] Darwin, *Descent of Man, and Selection in Relation to Sex*, Volume 2, 327.
[289] Darwin, *Descent of Man, and Selection in Relation to Sex*, Volume 2, 328.
[290] Taylor, 2009, 19.
[291] Jonathan Silvertown (ed), *99% Ape: How Evolution Adds Up* (University of Chicago Press, 2009): 4.
[292] Bagemihl, Bruce. 1999. *Biological Exuberance: Animal Homosexuality and Natural Diversity*. St. Martins Press. New York.
[293] Many attempts have been made and all have failed. See Rossiianov, Kirill. 2002. "Beyond Species: Ii'ya Ivanov and His Experiments on Cross-Breeding Humans with Anthropoid Apes." *Science in Context*. 15(2):277-316.
[294] See the U.S. Department of Health and Human Services (*https://optn.transplant.hrsa.gov/*) (February 1, 2016).
[295] Various sources will show minor differences in these comparisons. These are for example only.
[296] http://useast.ensembl.org/Homo_sapiens/Info/Annotation
[297] Kakuo, S., Asaoka, K. and Ide, T. 1999. 'Human is a unique species among primates in terms of telomere length.' *Biochemistry Biophysics Research Communication*. 263:308-314
[298] Archidiacono, N., Storlazzi, C.T., Spalluto, C., Ricco, A.S., Marzella, R., Rocchi, M. 1998. 'Evolution of chromosome Y in primates.' *Chromosoma* 107:241-246

[299] "What about the Similarity Between Human and Chimp DNA?" *AnswersinGenesis.com:* http://www.answersingenesis.org/articles/nab3/human- and-chimp-dna (January 14, 2014).
[300] R.J. Rummel, "Statistics of Democide: Genocide and Mass Murder Since 1900," *School of Law, University of Virginia* (1997).
[301] Jerry Bergman. 2012. *Hitler and the Nazis Darwinian Worldview: How the Nazis Eugenic Crusade for a Superior Race Caused the Greatest Holocaust in World History.* Kitchener, Ontario, Canada: Joshua Press
[302] J. Bergman & J. Tomkins, "Is the Human Genome Nearly Identical to Chimpanzee? A Reassessment of the Literature" *Journal of Creation* 26 (2012): 54–60.
[303] Ibid.
[304] J. Tomkins, "How Genomes are Sequenced and why it Matters: Implications for Studies in Comparative Genomics of Humans and Chimpanzees," *Answers Research Journal* 4 (2011): 81–88.
[305] I. Ebersberger, D. Metzler, C. Schwarz, & S. Pääbo, "Genomewide Comparison of DNA Sequences between Humans and Chimpanzees," *American Journal of Human Genetics* 70 (2002): 1490–1497.
[306] http://www.icr.org/article/6197/
[307] Chimpanzee Sequencing and Analysis Consortium, "Initial Sequence of the Chimpanzee Genome and Comparison with the Human Genome," *Nature* 437 (2005): 69–87.
[308] J. Tomkins, "Genome-Wide DNA Alignment Similarity (Identity) for 40,000 Chimpanzee DNA Sequences Queried against the Human Genome is 86–89%," *Answers Research Journal* 4 (2011): 233–241.
[309] J. Prado-Martinez, et al. "Great Ape Genetic Diversity and Population History," *Nature* 499 (2013), 471–475.
[310] J. Tomkins, & J. Bergman. "Genomic Monkey Business—Estimates of Nearly Identical Human-Chimp DNA Similarity Re-evaluated using Omitted Data," *Journal of Creation* 26 (2012), 94–100; J. Tomkins, "Comprehensive Analysis of Chimpanzee and Human Chromosomes Reveals Average DNA Similarity of 70%," *Answers Research Journal* 6 (2013): 63–69.
[311] Nathaniel T. Jeanson, "Purpose, Progress, and Promise, Part 4*,"* *Institute for Creation Research: http://www.icr.org/article/purpose-progress-promise-part-4* (September 2, 2015).
[312] Tomkins & Bergman, 63-69.
[313] Tomkins, 2011.
[314] Tomkins & Bergman, 63-69.
[315] Subsequent analyses revealed an anomaly in the BLASTN algorithm used for determining the 70% figure and the revised estimate (88%) has been included in this chapter. See: Jeffrey P. Tomkins, "Documented Anomaly in Recent Versions of the BLASTN Algorithm and a Complete Reanalysis of

Chimpanzee and Human Genome-Wide DNA Similarity Using Nucmer and LASTZ," (October 7, 2015), Answers in Genesis: https://answersingenesis.org/genetics/dna-similarities/blastn-algorithm-anomaly/

[316] Tomkins, 2011.

[317] E. Wijaya, M.C. Frith, P. Horton & K. Asai, "Finding Protein-coding Genes through Human Polymorphisms," *PloS one* 8 (2013).

[318] New Genome Comparison Finds Chimps, Humans Very Similar at the DNA Level, 2005, national human genome research institute http://www.genome.gov/15515096

[319] Christine Elsik. et al. The Genome Sequence of Taurine Cattle: A Window to Ruminant Biology and Evolution. *Science.* 324:522-528.

[320] http://www.eupedia.com/forum/threads/25335-Percentage-of-genetic-similarity-between-humans-and-animals. Source is Pontius, Joan. Et. al. 2007. Initial Sequence and Comparative Analysis of the Cat Genome. *Genome Research.* 17:1675-1689.

[321] http://www.genome.gov/10005835.

[322] NIH/National Human Genome Research Institute. "Researchers Compare Chicken, Human Genomes: Analysis Of First Avian Genome Uncovers Differences Between Birds And Mammals." ScienceDaily. 10 December 2004.

[323] M. J. Hangauer, I.W. Vaughn & M. T. McManus, "Pervasive Transcription of the Human Genome Produces Thousands of Previously Unidentified Long Intergenic Noncoding RNAs," *PLoS genetics* 9 (2013).

[324] S. Djebali, et al. "Landscape of Transcription in Human Cells," *Nature* 489 (2012): 101–108.

[325] M. D. Paraskevopoulou, et al. "DIANA-LncBase: Experimentally Verified and Computationally Predicted MicroRNA Targets on Long Non-coding RNAs," *Nucleic Acids Research* 41 (2013): 239–245.

[326] J. J Yunis & O. Prakash, "The Origin of Man: A Chromosomal Pictorial Legacy," *Science* 215 (1982): 1525–1530.

[327] J. W. Ijdo, A. Baldini, D.C. Ward, S. T. Reeders & R. A. Wells, "Origin of Human Chromosome 2: An Ancestral Telomere-telomere Fusion," *Proceedings of the National Academy of Sciences of the United States of America* 88 (1991): 9051–9055.

[328] J. Bergman & J. Tomkins, "The Chromosome 2 Fusion Model of Human Evolution—Part 1: Re-evaluating the Evidence," *Journal of Creation* 25 (2011): 110–114.

[329] J. Tomkins, "Alleged Human Chromosome 2 'Fusion Site' Encodes an Active DNA Binding Domain Inside a Complex and Highly Expressed Gene—Negating Fusion," *Answers Research Journal* 6 (2013): 367–375.

[330] Y. Fan, E. Linardopoulou, C. Friedman, E. Williams & B.J. Trask, "Genomic Structure and Evolution of the Ancestral Chromosome Fusion

Site in 2q13-2q14.1 and Paralogous Regions on other Human Chromosomes," *Genome Research* 12 (2002): 1651–1662; Y. Fan, T. Newman, E. Linardopoulou, & B.J. Trask, "Gene Content and Function of the Ancestral Chromosome Fusion Site in Human Chromosome 2q13-2q14.1 and Paralogous Regions," *Genome Research* 12 (2002): 1663–1672.

[331] Y.Z. Wen, L. L. Zheng, L.H. Qu, F. J. Ayala & Z.R. Lun, Z. R, "Pseudogenes are not Pseudo Any More," *RNA Biology* 9 (2012): 27–32.

[332] J. Tomkins, "The Human Beta-Globin Pseudogene Is Non-Variable and Functional," *Answers Research Journal* 6 (2013): 293–301.

[333] M. Y. Lachapelle, & G. Drouin, "Inactivation Dates of the Human and Guinea Pig Vitamin C Genes," *Genetica* 139 (2011): 199–207.

[334] J. Sanford, *Genetic Entropy and the Mystery of the Genome*, 3rd ed (FMS Publications, 2010).

[335] J. Tomkins & J. Bergman, "Incomplete Lineage Sorting and Other 'Rogue' Data Fell the Tree of Life," *Journal of Creation* 27 (2013): 63–71.

[336] Dan Biddle, *Creation V. Evolution: What They Won't Tell You in Biology Class* (Maitland, FL: Xulon Press); H. Morris, et al., *Creation Basics & Beyond: An In-Depth Look at Science, Origins, and Evolution* (Dallas, TX: Institute for Creation Research, 2013).

[337] J. C. Sanford, *Genetic Entropy and the Mystery of the Genome*, 3rd ed. (Waterloo, NY: FMS Publications, 2008).

[338] Ibid.

[339] J. A. Tennessen, et al., "Evolution and Functional Impact of Rare Coding Variation from Deep Sequencing of Human Exomes," *Science* 337 (6090) (2012): 64-69; W. Fu, et al., "Analysis of 6,515 Exomes Reveals the Recent Origin of Most Human Protein-coding Variants," *Nature* 493 (7431) (2013): 216-220.

[340] Tennessen, *Evolution and Functional Impact of Rare Coding Variation from Deep Sequencing of Human Exomes*, 64-69.

[341] J. Sanford, J. Pamplin, & C. Rupe, "Genetic Entropy Recorded in the Bible?" (FMS Foundation. Posted on kolbecenter.org July 2014, accessed July 25, 2014).

[342] N. T. Jeanson, "Recent, Functionally Diverse Origin for Mitochondrial Genes from ~2700 Metazoan Species," *Answers Research Journal* 6 (2013): 467-501.

[343] T.J. Parsons, et al., "A High Observed Substitution Rate in the Human Mitochondrial DNA Control Region," *Nature Genetics* 15 (1997): 363-368.

[344] A. Gibbons, "Calibrating the Mitochondrial Clock," *Science* 279 (1998): 28-29.

[345] P. Senter, "Vestigial Skeletal Structures in Dinosaurs," *Journal of Zoology*, 280 (1) (January 2010): 60–71.

[346] Thomas Heinze, *Creation vs. Evolution Handbook* (Grand Rapids, MI: Baker, 1973).

[347] Isaac Asimov, *1959 Words of Science* (New York: Signet Reference Books, 1959), 30.
[348] J. Bergman, "Are Wisdom Teeth (third molars) Vestiges of Human Evolution?" *CEN Tech Journal*. 12 (3) (1998): 297–304.
[349] Charles Darwin, *The Descent of Man and Selection in Relation to Sex* (London: John Murray, 1871), 21.
[350] Charles Darwin, *The Origin of Species* (New York: Modern Library, 1859), 346–350.
[351] S. R. Scadding, "Do Vestigial Organs Provide Evidence for Evolution?" *Evolutionary Theory* 5 (1981): 173–176.
[352] Robert Wiedersheim, *The Structure of Man: An Index to his Past History* (London: Macmillan, 1895, Translated by H. and M. Bernard).
[353] David Starr Jordan & Vernon Lyman Kellogg, *Evolution and Animal Life* (New York: Appleton, 1908), 175.
[354] Wiedersheim, 1895, p. 3.
[355] Darwin, 1871, p. 29.
[356] Cora A. Reno, *Evolution on Trial* (Chicago: Moody Press, 1970), 81.
[357] Diane Newman, *The Urinary Incontinence Sourcebook* (Los Angeles, CA.: Lowell House, 1997), 13.
[358] Warren Walker, *Functional Anatomy of the Vertebrates: An Evolutionary Perspective* (Philadelphia, PA: Saunders, 1987), 253.
[359] Catherine Parker Anthony, *Textbook of Anatomy and Physiology*, 6th ed. (St. Louis, MO: Mosby, 1963), 411.
[360] Anthony Smith, *The Body* (New York: Viking Penguin, 1986), 134.
[361] Henry Gray, *Gray's Anatomy* (Philadelphia: Lea Febiger, 1966), 130.
[362] Dorothy Allford, *Instant Creation—Not Evolution* (New York: Stein and Day, 1978), 42; Saul Weischnitzer, *Outline of Human Anatomy* (Baltimore, MD: University Park Press, 1978), 285.
[363] J. D. Ratcliff, *Your Body and How it Works* (New York: Delacorte Press, 1975), 137.
[364] Lawrence Galton, "All those Tonsil Operations: Useless? Dangerous?" *Parade* (May 2, 1976): 26.
[365] Martin L. Gross, *The Doctors* (New York: Random House, 1966).
[366] Jacob Stanley, Clarice Francone, & Walter Lossow, *Structure and Function in Man,* 5th ed. (Philadelphia: Saunders, 1982).
[367] Alvin Eden, "When Should Tonsils and Adenoids be Removed?" *Family Weekly* (September 25, 1977): 24.
[368] Syzmanowski as quoted in Dolores Katz, "Tonsillectomy: Boom or Boondoggle?" *The Detroit Free Press* (April 13, 1966).
[369] Katz, 1972, p. 1-C.
[370] N. J. Vianna, Petter Greenwald & U. N. Davies, "Tonsillectomy" In: *Medical World News* (September 10, 1973).
[371] Katz, 1972.

[372] Darwin, 1871, pp. 27–28.
[373] Peter Raven & George Johnson, *Understanding Biology* (St. Louis: Times Mirror Mosby, 1988), 322.
[374] Rebecca E. Fisher, "The Primate Appendix: A Reassessment," *The Anatomical Record*, 261 (2000): 228–236.
[375] R. Randal Bollinger, Andrew S. Barbas, Errol L. Bush, Shu S. Lin and William Parker, "Biofilms in the Large Bowel Suggest an Apparent Function of the Human Vermiform Appendix," *Journal of Theoretical Biology*, 249 (4) (2007): 826–831; Thomas Morrison (ed.). *Human Physiology* (New York: Holt, Rinehart, and Winston, 1967).
[376] Loren Martin, "What is the Function of the Human Appendix?" *Scientific American Online* (1999).
[377] Thomas Judge & Gary R. Lichtenstein, "Is the Appendix a Vestigial Organ? Its Role in Ulcerative Colitis," *Gastroenterology*, 121 (3) (2001): 730–732.
[378] Rod R. Seeley, Trent D. Stephens, & Philip Tate, *Anatomy and Physiology* (Boston: McGraw-Hill, 2003).
[379] Ernst Haeckel, *The Evolution of Man: A Popular Exposition of the Principal Points of Human Ontogeny and Phylogeny* (New York: D. Appleton, 1879), 438.
[380] Wiedersheim, 1895, p. 163.
[381] O. Levy, G. Dai, C. Riedel, C.S. Ginter, E.M. Paul, A. N. Lebowitz & N. Carrasco, "Characterization of the thyroid Na+/I- symporter with an anti-COOH terminus antibody," *Proceedings from the National Academy of Science*, 94 (1997): 5568–5573.
[382] Albert Maisel, "The useless glands that guard our health." *Reader's Digest* (November, 1966): 229–235.
[383] John Clayton, "Vestigial Organs Continue to Diminish," *Focus on Truth*, 6 (6) (1983): 6–7.
[384] Seeley, Stephens, & Tate, *Anatomy and Physiology* (McGraw-Hill Education, 2003), 778.
[385] Maisel, 1966, p. 229.
[386] Arthur Guyton, *Textbook of Medical Physiology* (Philadelphia: W. B. Saunders, 1966): 139.
[387] Helen G. Durkin & Byron H. Waksman. "Thymus and Tolerance. Is Regulation the Major Function of the Thymus?" *Immunological Reviews*, 182 (2001): 33–57.
[388] Durkin & Waksman, 2001, p. 49.
[389] Benedict Seddon & Don Mason, "The Third Function of the Thymus," *Immunology Today*, 21 (2) (2000): 95–99.
[390] Maisel, 1966.
[391] Joel R. L. Ehrenkranz, "A Gland for all Seasons," *Natural History*, 92 (6) (1983): 18.

[392] Stanley Yolles, "The Pineal Gland," *Today's Health*, 44 (3) (1966): 76–79.
[393] David Blask, "Potential Role of the Pineal Gland in the Human Menstrual Cycle," Chapter 9 in *Changing Perspectives on Menopause,* Edited by A. M. Voda (Austin: University of Texas Press, 1982), 124.
[394] A. C. Greiner & S. C. Chan, "Melatonin Content of the Human Pineal Gland," *Science*, 199 (1978): 83–84.
[395] Esther Greisheimer & Mary Wideman, *Physiology and Anatomy*, 9th ed. (Philadelphia: Lippincott, 1972).
[396] Rosa M. Sainz, Juan C. Mayo, R.J. Reiter, D.X. Tan, and C. Rodriguez, "Apoptosis in Primary Lymphoid Organs with Aging," *Microscopy Research and Technique*, 62 (2003): 524–539.
[397] Sharon Begley & William Cook, "The SAD Days of Winter," *Newsweek*, 155 (2) (January 14, 1985): 64.
[398] Sainz, et al., 2003.
[399] G.J. Maestroni, A. Conti, & P. Lisson, "Colony-stimulating activity and hematopoietic rescue from cancer chemotherapy compounds are induced by melatonin via endogenous interleukin," *Cancer Research*, 54 (1994): 4740-4743.
[400] B.D. Jankovic, K. Isakovic, S. Petrovic, "Effect of Pinealectomy on Immune Reactions in the Rat," *Immunology*, 18 (1) (1970): 1–6.
[401] Lennert Wetterberg, Edward Geller, & Arthur Yuwiler, "Harderian Gland: An Extraretinal Photoreceptor Influencing the Pineal Gland in Neonatal Rats?" *Science*, 167 (1970): 884–885.
[402] Ehrenkranz, 1983, p. 18.
[403] Philip Stibbe, "A Comparative Study of the Nictitating Membrane of Birds and Mammals," *Journal of Anatomy,* 163 (1928): 159–176.
[404] Darwin, 1871, p. 23.
[405] Henry Drummond, *The Ascent of Man* (New York: James Potts and Co., 1903).
[406] Richard Snell & Michael Lemp, *Clinical Anatomy of the Eye* (Boston: Blackwell Scientific Pub, 1997), 93.
[407] Eugene Wolff (Revised by Robert Warwick), *Anatomy of the Eye and Orbit* 7th ed. (Philadelphia: W B. Saunders, 1976), 221.
[408] John King, Personal communication, Dr. King is a professor of ophthalmology at The Ohio State School of Medicine and an authority on the eye (October 18, 1979).
[409] E. P. Stibbe, "A Comparative Study of the Nictitating Membrane of Birds and Mammals," *Journal of Anatomy* 62 (1928): 159–176.
[410] Wiedersheim, 1895.
[411] D. Peck, "A Proposed Mechanoreceptor Role for the Small Redundant Muscles which Act in Parallel with Large Prime movers" in P. Hinick, T. Soukup, R. Vejsada, & J. Zelena's (eds.) *Mechanoreceptors: Development,*

Structure and Function (New York: Plenum Press, 1988), 377–382.
[412] David N. Menton, "The Plantaris and the Question of Vestigial Muscles in Man," *CEN Technical Journal*, 14 (2) (2000): 50–53.
[413] Herbert DeVries, *Physiology of Exercise for Physical Education and Athletics* (Dubuque, IA: William C. Brown, 1980), 16–18.

CPSIA information can be obtained
at www.ICGtesting.com
Printed in the USA
LVHW022224161218
600692LV00013BA/1234/P